GASPAR DE PORTOLÁ

EXPLORER OF CALIFORNIA

J. CARNER-RIBALTA

Tecolote Publications

English version published in 1990 by Tecolote Publications, San Diego, California, in cooperation with the Friends of Gaspar de Portolá and the government of Catalonia.

Cover design by Jodi Baca, Huntington Beach, California

Typesetting by True Grid Graphics, La Mesa, California

ISBN 0-938711-07-5

Library of Congress Cataloging Number 90-70278

Printed in the United States of America

Gaspar de Portolá

The name of Gaspar de Portolá, explorer and first governor of Baja and Alta California, occupies an important place in the early history of the state of California. His biographer, Carner-Ribalta, presents us not only the historical profile of the explorer, but in a very profoundly human manner, Gaspar de Portolá as a person. The present volume is a narration of the heroic deeds of one of the last explorers of America, and also of his private life, as a man of the world, with his romantic adventures, and of his own singular philosophy as a *bon vivant,* enamored of life. Carner-Ribalta has investigated the details of Portolá's private life since his early youth in Balaguer, and he has followed him to the School of Education for Nobility, in Madrid, Spain, to the war campaigns in Italy and Portugal, to the Viceroy Court, in Mexico City, during Spain colonial times, as well as to the elegant society of the city of Barcelona in the 18th century.

J. Carner-Ribalta

Josep Carner-Ribalta was born in Balaguer, Catalonia, Spain, in 1898, the same city where Gaspar de Portolá was born, many years earlier. Being still a student, Carner-Ribalta left Barcelona and went to England and France where he continued his studies and spent part of his youth. In Paris he published his first book of poems, product of his early literary initiation in Catalonia. In time he became well-known as a poet in his own country with his books of poems, written in Catalan, "Songs of Love," "The Blessings of this Earth," and "The Happy Traveler." Towards the end of the Spanish Civil War Carner-Ribalta emigrated to the United States as a political refugee. After a few years in New York, Washington, D.C., and North Carolina, he moved to California, where he spent the latter years of his life until his death in 1988. He left two sons, one working for the federal government in Washington, D.C., and the other a businessman in California. His widow, Ester, a Catalonian herself, lives in their former residence in Simi Valley.

In addition to being a poet, Carner-Ribalta excelled in the writing of novels and dramas. He also had a special ability for writing interesting biographies as the ones about Gaspar de Portolá, the first overland explorer of California, and Francesc Macia, the beloved President of Catalonia during the early 1930s, to whom he had been secretary. Carner-Ribalta is also well known for his translations into Catalan of classic works of literature as those of Joseph Conrad, Oscar Wilde, William B. Yeats, Tagore, Ronsard, Mallarme, and the poetic works of Paul Valery.

Foreword

An earlier version of this book, written in Catalan by Carner-Ribalta, was published some time ago by Editorial Selecta in Barcelona, Spain. It was the reading of this book, while I was a member of the Catalonian Parliament in the early 1980's, that inspired me to create the Association of Friends of Gaspar de Portolá, in Catalonia. This was done together with Mr. Josep Borrás and other parliamentary colleagues and friends, in order to strengthen the historical and cultural relations between California and Catalonia, which had been initiated more than two centuries ago by Gaspar de Portolá with the discoveries of San Francisco and Monterey bays and by Father Junipero Serra and other Franciscan fathers with the founding of the California missions. In a parallel manner, and more recently, at the initiative of Senator Henry J. Mello, the California Legislature has passed a Resolution establishing the California sister-state relationship with the region of Catalonia, Spain, for the purpose of developing further the historical and cultural bonds of friendship as well as the social and economic relations between the people of these two lands.

I have to say that I enjoyed so much reading the Catalan version of this biographical novel on Gaspar de Portolá, that I suggested to Carner-Ribalta to write a new English version of this book, primarily for the Californians and other English-speaking people interested in knowing some of the adventures, exploits and personalities of the first overland explorers of California. I am very pleased and grateful to the writer for having so effectively responded to my suggestion, thus fulfilling the wishes of so many friends of Portolá. I believe this book will make many new friends not only for Gaspar de Portolá, but also for Carner-Ribalta as well. For those who wish a detailed historical account of the exploration of California, a more complete and documented biography of Portolá, with the itinerary of the expeditions, has been published recently in English by Dr. Ferran Boneu, with the help of the Provincial Government of Lleida, the sister city of Monterey, in Catalonia where Portolá saw his last years and died in October 10, 1784. Other books about some of the notable Catalonian volunteers accompanying Portolá in his California expeditions are being planned by our Association. I would like to acknowledge the Association of Friends of Gaspar de Portolá and the President of the Government of Catalonia, Mr. Jordi Pujol for their help in sponsoring the publication of this book, as well as Mr. Sebastia Borras of Editorial Selecta, for allowing us to use the drawing on the cover of the Catalonian version of his book, and to Carol Bowers, of Tecolote Publications, for the excellent printing of this new English version by Carner-Ribalta.

Joan Oró
President
Association of Friends of Gaspar de Portolá

Illustrations

Chapter One

Through the arched baroque windows of the memorial residence came the chirping of birds and the perfume of the mild Mediterranean climate. It was a bright sunny morning in the spring of 1764. Beyond the windows peaceful, tidy Barcelona spread its urban grace as it inclined from the verdant hills to the translucent sea. The stately living room of the residence of Don Gaspar de Portolá, lieutenant of dragoons, Regiment of Numancia, showed the elegant disorder characteristic of the quarters of an inveterate bachelor scion of an old family of the nobility.

Vincent, the loyal orderly and meticulous *valet de chambre,* stopped momentarily in his menial chores to stare, as disconcerted as always, at the ancient coat of arms of the Portolá family which was displayed prominently on the main wall of the living room. As he had done hundreds of times before, he read silently the rather astonishing motto which was carved at the foot of the escutcheon: "King or Nothing." Still incapable of understanding this strange motto, he shook his head dejectedly and resumed his duties.

In the next room, beyond the library, Don Gaspar de Portolá was practicing fencing and performing his daily ritual of physical exercises. Through the open doors of the gymnasium he could be seen, bare from the waist up, displaying a shapely, muscular body. At the moment he was making a dashing attack on an imaginary opponent after having dodged several masterly blows of his invisible adversary.

After taking a cold shower, Don Gaspar once again felt vigorous and exultant. He donned a casual, loose, off-white silk blouse and semi-formal black satin breeches, his usual house "uniform."

From the street, through the wide arched window came the catchy sentimental music of an organ grinder. Don Gaspar looked at the clock; as usual, it was nine o'clock. The organ grinder was as punctual as he was every morning. From the vague, dreamy smile on his face, it was apparent that Don Gaspar was an easy prey to music and romance. He walked to the sunny window, enjoying the music of the organ.

The organ grinder was a blind man accompanied by a charming, typically Spanish young daughter who was wearing a red carnation in her black hair. She seemed to expect the daily appearance of Don Gaspar at the same window. The elegant officer looked fondly at the young girl and listened with pleasure to the music. At the conclusion of the short serenade Don Gaspar rewarded the blind artist by tossing him a coin which the young girl swiftly gathered from the ground while compensating her gallant customer with a kiss which she blew to him gracefully from the tips of her fingers.

Vincent had stopped working, and once more he stood still staring at the escutcheon bearing the Portolá family coat of arms. He was not admiring the perfect arrangement of the heraldic symbols on the rich polychromed piece of carved granite; rather, as usual, he was upset and almost scandalized by the preposterous motto.

"KING OR — " Frankly the intended meaning of the last part of the motto was beyond his comprehension! Although he was fully aware of, and constantly regretted the lack of true ambition of his master in spite of the exceptional qualities with which he was endowed, he could not comprehend the premeditated conditional renunciation. Of course, Vincent knew perfectly well the difficult situation and the meager possibilities of promotion with which young officers, like his own master, were confronted on entering the army as their inescapable duty as members of the nobility.

These young men enlisted when they were mere adolescents and served twelve to fifteen years before being promoted to lieutenant — provided, that is, that they had previously gained war merits — and then were left to rot in some nameless garrison, with no other benefits than the privilege of bearing a sword and of wearing a sumptuous dress coat. Their salaries scarcely covered the bare essentials of living so that young noblemen ended by consuming their entire patrimony to maintain themselves in accordance with their noble rank.

As Don Gaspar entered the living room, he was amused to see Vincent laboriously trying to move a heavy suit of armor which was standing near the coat of arms carved on the wall.

"What are you up to now, Vincent?" asked Don Gaspar good humoredly.

The loyal orderly, caught in the act, tried to disguise his motive. He was visibly embarrassed.

"Never mind, Vincent. Don't let it worry you," the lieutenant of dragoons recommended kindly, knowing the conscientious concern of his orderly. He added, "I have already told you so hundreds of times."

Vincent explained needlessly that by moving the suit of armor only about twenty inches, he could make the objectionable last part of the motto less visible.

Don Gaspar smiled. Condescendingly, patiently, he tried once more to formulate a justification. "Vincent," he said. "Most of the time it is more comfortable to be nothing than to be a king."

"But — " Vincent objected, "My master could be king in every way — if he only wished."

"If he wished!" quoted Don Gaspar. "That's exactly the point. Thus when I choose to be nothing, I am still faithful to my motto."

Vincent considered it useless to argue further.

"Any messages this morning?" asked Don Gaspar, dropping the subject.

"Yes, my master," answered Vincent, without enthusiasm. "A letter."

Vincent picked up the silver tray containing the letter and presented it to his master. "It was delivered by hand," he explained.

As he picked up the letter from the tray, Don Gaspar detected a strange expression on Vincent's face.

"It's perfumed!" stated the elderly, almost offended, before Don Gaspar could question his attitude.

Don Gaspar brought the envelope to his nostrils, and then opened it. There was no letter; the envelope contained only a lady's garter. The only reading matter consisted of a small decoration in the shape of a heart with the word "Lucia" which was tucked among the ribbons.

"Add it to the collection, Vincent!" exclaimed the lieutenant, flippantly, while tossing the garter onto his writing desk.

That same morning, two hours later, Lucia, the owner of the elaborate garter was laughing without restraint as she promenaded by the side of Ensign Ruiz Mendez, her current suitor, along flower-lined pathways of the park. It was the hour of the customary morning promenade, and the elegant people of Barcelona, especially the young men and women, were strolling about. Lucia was laughing with obvious mockery.

"Lucia, please don't laugh at me. I am serious. I love you!" protested Ensign Mendez.

Once again laughter from the frivolous Lucia burst like bubbles of crystal popping in the morning light. Furious, the young ensign insinuated that at the bottom of her refusal lay the actions of the detested Lieutenant Gaspar de Portolá. His fear was apparently so justified that Lucia laughed not only loudly, but most wickedly at this time.

A group of young ladies, also taking part in the morning promenade, passed by in an open carriage.

"There's Lucia!" observed one of the girls.

"And Ensign Mendez," added another, commenting further, "Poor fellow! He is wasting his time — Lucia now is longing only for Don Gaspar de Portolá."

"Who isn't?" concluded a third girl amid the general laughter as the carriage drove on.

Ruiz Mendez broke into a long tirade against Portolá: "He is a man incapable of taking any serious interest in anything, be it in his own career or the love of a woman. He could be the most prominent nobleman in Spain, but is content only with a placid sterile vegetating. He is just a *bon vivant*, a loafer — a detestable character. He could marry any woman of the highest rank, but he spends his life in banal adventure and dubious liaisons."

Mendez was only partially correct. The facts were somewhat different. At the age of forty-six, Don Gaspar de Portolá, had returned to Barcelona from service in the war campaigns of Italy and Portugal, and accepted with pleasure his permanent assignment in the suburbs of the big city. There he devoted himself to bringing to perfection the art of living in accordance with his philosophy of a *dolce far niente*, "a sweet doing nothing" which was very fashionable at that time. In fact, even public affairs were by then in a dormant state.

The short reign of Ferdinand VI, 1746-1759, had characterized itself by the absence of almost any event, political or otherwise. It was truly a period of "peace" if "stagnation" can be considered to be synonymous. Ferdinand VI, deficient in many respects, scarcely participated in the affairs of the state, and often showed a tendency to melancholy and even to dementia. Even so, he maintained his firm conviction that what Spain needed was harmony. The disturbed peninsula had had to wait long years to learn this indisputable truth from a semidemented ruler!

The apathetic attitude of the crown had the virtue of benefitting the moral regeneration and the economic consolidation of the country. In fact, for the first time, after several centuries, the people could forget that in Madrid there was a monarchy apparently intent on taking poor Spain constantly from one calamitous adventure to a still more catastrophic one. The Catalonians, principally, could live without the obsession that the current Bourbon ruler, persistent in making them feel their condition of national enslavement day after day, actually existed. If fact, they took advantage of this period of calm to strengthen, if not their spirit, at least their material lives by recovering from the destruction and ruin of the war and revolt years.

A curious thing to note: Ferdinand's attitude in allowing the Catalonians to live in peace, and in practically forgetting this people who were so bent on idolizing their sovereigns and in fighting all usurpers, engendered a glacial feeling in the souls of the Catalonians. The second Bourbon ruler, although he did not make enemies among the Catalonians, did not gain friends either. If he did not arouse any hatred, he did not kindle any flame that could turn old resentments into the beginnings of affection, or at least of reconciliation.

The warm heart of the Catalonian is not different from any other human heart; covered embers are always a potential flame. The same is true for apparently extinct volcanoes as for human entrails. There had to come a second Bourbon ruler for the Catalonians to discover this axiom and to derive from it certain advantages. This had happened in the year 1759; the enlightened monarch was Charles III; the place, Barcelona, the capitol of Catalonia.

On a memorable day, in this Catalonian capital, under many layers of gelid appearance, a smoldering fire revived. In many a heart a breath of hope flickered. This was due to a mere gesture, a hint from a single man — to a mere token of willingness to understand coming from this new monarch. Human nature lives not only by food, but also by light flattery and kind caresses from fellow creatures, and if these cajoleries and tokens of affection come from persons who have been indifferent to us, or even from those who have belonged to a segment of hated people, they are doubly effective.

Of course, not all the Catalonians of that period were in absolute accord with this line of reasoning. Many lively spirits could not forget the past, nor the typical Bourbon despotism which still remained instituted in Catalonia. Many would exclaim, "After all, Charles III is but another Bourbon, the son of Philip V, the annihilator of the Catalonian liberties!"

"However," someone else would argue, "the new ruler who under the name of Charles III has inherited the Spanish crown, had at least the courtesy to stop at Barcelona on his way back to Madrid, and this is a partial rectification of the many years of utter abandon and scorn from the Castilian kings for the capital of Catalonia and for its people."

The greater number of Barcelonans, however, in their eagerness for hope, reasoned that Charles III was dynasty-raised and educated mainly abroad, not in the Castilian atmosphere, in the arid and cruel lands of deep Spain from which historically had arisen all the winds of despotism and oppression that had devastated the liberties of the once-free nations of the Iberian Peninsula. Charles III came from lands where, in the past — from 1443 to 1713 — Catalonian kings had ruled and had implanted the spirit of justice and democracy. In Naples from which Charles III came, he probably had not learned to dislike the Catalonians systematically as the Castilians were usually taught to do. On the other hand — at least this was what was said of him — the new monarch was a man of the present, a learned prince, educated under the modern ideas which the French Encyclopedists were beginning to spread, and which contained the seed of the future great charter of the Rights of Man.

Hungry for freedom, and with hearts full of hope, the Catalonians celebrated the proclamation of the new king with extraordinary festivities which took place in Barcelona on September 29, 1759. Later, October 17 of the same year, when Charles III landed in Barcelona, the Catalonians welcomed him with the same pomp and joy with which they had welcomed the Catalonian kings in the past on their return from naval campaigns.

"Who can say whether or not this royal visit might be the beginning of a policy favoring our aspirations for a free Catalonia!" Don Gaspar de Portolá commented as he watched the passage of the king's carriage from the balcony of the palace of the Dukes of Medinaceli, indicating by this politically-minded remark that he was not as indifferent to essential things concerning his country as Ensign Luis Mendez let it be supposed.

"It's about time that such fundamental problems were tackled in Spain under the light of reason and justice in line with the current practice of modern states!" exclaimed the illustrious dean of the University of Cervera, Don Ramon Llátzer de Dou, member of the aristocratic Dou family of Barcelona, who was standing next to Don Gaspar.

Don Josep Finestres, prominent historian and patriot, added, "Let the visit of the new monarch to Barcelona be the beginning of the reparation of so many grievances of the past!"

Along the broad avenue, the royal cavalcade received the same evidences of popular affection which Charles had met with at the Portal de la Muralla immediately after landing. Of svelte silhouette, bright-eyed, and, for the first time in an individual of his lineage, with Bourbon facial features brightened by intelligence more than by sensuality, the new monarch rode by smiling with evident kindness in answer to the spontaneous cheers of the populace. He smilingly acknowledged the graceful gestures of young ladies who were offering bouquets of flowers from windows and balconies along his passage.

Seated next to the king, Queen Maria Amelia of Saxony watched contentedly as homage was paid by both the privileged class and the man of the street — the nobles and the artisans. Rather overwhelmed, but grateful, she watched the excited multitude express its feelings in a language unknown to her and with a vehemence quite foreign to those of her northern race.

The parade was truly dazzling. Opening the way, a squad of lancers brandished their halberds bearing colored plumes, their white belts and bandoleers shining against their bright yellow coats, their impeccable white breeches and black patent leather boots gleaming, as they rode their spirited Andalusian horses. Next followed the representatives of the guilds and trades, the delegates of the military forces and the church dignitaries, the municipal councilmen wearing their long purple velvet robes, and a long procession of noblemen and court officers with white wigs and three-cornered hats. At last came the carriage of the king and queen and their entourage. All this extravagance of color and luxury reverberated under the bright Mediterranean sun, under the flags and banners hanging on the facades all along the street in the dazzling brilliance of a clear Barcelonan autumn day.

"The best of the celebration is yet to come!" whispered an artisan belonging to a guild who was in on the secret of the apotheosic finale which was in preparation to climax the festivities.

In effect, on the evening of the next day, the grand finale took place in the form of the "Royal Allegoric Revelry" which the guilds, the academic colleges, the Commerce and Maritime Committee, the Medical School, the Academy of Arts and Letters, and other cultural institutions were offering to the monarch. From the palace window Charles III, surrounded by beautiful ladies, noblemen and high officials — the cream of Barcelonan society — watched the sparkling nocturnal cavalcade.

The magnificent parade advanced by the light of hundreds of torches. The procession presented a mythological allegory, divided into three parts which symbolized, respectively, the Earth, the Sea, and the Heavens. Taking part were about one thousand subjects, afoot or on horseback.

Fifteen floats, artistically decorated, represented ideal gardens, forests, ships and temples where silks, laces, silver brocades, and damask fabrics combined into a fantasy of color. One of the most remarkable floats represented the river god Alpheius, seated at a scenic fluvial spot where, for six hours consecutively, an abundant waterfall of real water flowed from the top of a simulated mountain. Another float, equally celebrated, bore the name of Argus and represented in faithful reproduction the fabulous ship of Odysseus in his adventurous wanderings.

The float, however, which touched the hearts of the industrious, laboring Catalonians was the one which had been built and designed by the Guild of Metal Workers, representing Vulcan at his forge. During the course of the parade through the streets of Barcelona, a steel escutcheon bearing the royal coat of arms was being wrought, to be offered later as a gift to the honored king, Charles III, from the Catalonians.

The flattered monarch could see in the sparkling spectacle not only an obvious proof of affection from the Barcelonan citizenry, but also a demonstration that the resources and skills of industry and art continued to be assets of the capital of Catalonia.

The activities of homage to the liberal and progressive new monarch were to continue until the moment of the last farewell consisting of a massive popular acclamation in every village and town of the principality as far as the border of the Catalonian territory.

The new Spanish king was touched and felt very grateful for such

manifestations of affection. So, as some farsighted Catalonians had predicted, very soon, on October 21, before his departure for Madrid, Charles
III reinstated partially the old privileges of the principality, cancelling
many repressive and punitive decrees issued by his own father Philip V.
As a general provision, reflecting his royal munificence, the king made
the following declaration: "The King reserves the right to dispense to the
worthy Principality, after thorough study of its necessities, further attention and favors from the Crown."

It was in this placid and hopeful Barcelona that Don Gaspar de Portolá felt in his element. Well-thought-of and appreciated in the high levels
of the military command; assigned to a garrison that required few
obligations; well-loved by his colleagues — excepting the occasional
rivals in matters of love — he led an easy, free existence, and the most
perfect epicurean could not wish for a more voluptuous one.

Because of his physical presence, his elegant bearing, his gift of
speech and his impeccable style of dress, Don Gaspar was practically a
permanent idol to the feminine world of Barcelona. In fact, in the Barcelona of that period there was no mildly romantic or adventurous
feminine heart that did not sigh for his attention, be it only a passing
"requiebro," a gallant word, from the attractive lieutenant of dragoons.
This consistently general admiration was easy to explain — not because
Don Gaspar might have discovered a magic fountain of eternal youth, but
because, due to his special nature, he never carried any of his enterprises,
gallant or otherwise, to a climax, to the ultimate consequences. He was
wise enough to stop always, even in the worst cases, not when the matter
had become a failure or a hopeless issue, but while it could still present a
possibility of hope in the future.

These extraordinary gifts had made him occasional enemies, and he
often became the target for angry envy. He was, however, admirably tactful in his ability not to appear offended, and so to disarm his opponent
without need of combat. Altercations or quarrels around him lasted only
as a summer tempest does which dissolves with the appearance of a blue
sky, resulting in benevolent smiles and pleasantries.

The secret of the success, professional or personal, of Don Gaspar de
Portolá rested on the fact that he was not always an actual positive reality,
but an exceptional potential. From the captain general down to the least
officer of the Barcelonan Garrison, everyone knew, for example, that
when the proper moment came, they would find in Gaspar de Portolá an
extraordinary commander, capable of the most decided victories and the
highest glories. Even his possible enemies were to know that, after the
inevitable reconciliation, they would find him the best of friends. The
ladies of Barcelonan society, both the virtuous and the frail, suspected

that under the most trivial or wicked gallantries of Don Gaspar existed the earnest affection of a perfect lover or of the most ideal and desirable husband.

Portolá himself was conscious of his perpetual superficiality and realized that the banality of his daily life could become, overnight, a transcendental commitment if circumstances so demanded. With sly benevolence, the analytical lieutenant of dragoons smiled when his superiors, his eager and sincere friends, or the ambitious high society ladies showed impatience for the brilliant career for which Don Gaspar seemed predestined. Like the loyal orderly Vincent, many were dismayed by Don Gaspar's almost exclusive dedication to the second part of the motto in his family's coat of arms. The aristocrat from Balaguer knew very well, however, that his apparent choice to remain "nothing" was only a temporary, a simulated indolence, while he waited for the unique moment in which he could be "all." "KING OR NOTHING" read his motto. With apparent pride he now boasted of being "nothing." One day would come — perhaps — in which, with similar pride he would be able to boast of being, in some aspects, or in all, a real "king."

The Iberian Peninsula during the fifteenth century. Later in the century, during the reign of Ferdinand and Isabella, all the kingdoms and provinces, with the exception of Portugal, were consolidated into the kingdom of Spain. Catalonia, the birthplace and homeland of Gaspar de Portolá, has retained its unique language and culture throughout the centuries.

Chapter Two

I t would be proper to mention here that a combination of tradition, family environment, and historical and political circumstances had made Don Gaspar de Portolá, to a large extent, the kind of man he was or was forced to become. He had come from an ancient aristocratic lineage, the origin of which was lost in the centuries. The original House of Portolá, like many other medieval castles, stood in the high ranges of the Pyrenees, in Vall d'Aran. Subsequently, in an era of less heroic strain with daily existence less plagued by war and struggle, the Portolás, like many other families of nobility, descended to the plain, to less rugged surroundings, and established their main residence in Balaguer, in western Catalonia, a medieval city by the Segre River.

Don Gaspar de Portolá i Pont, grandfather of the present Don Gaspar, on the day of his death, March 10, 1687, held many noble and territorial titles: Baron of Castellnou de Montsec; Seigneur of Beniure, of Estorm and of Saint Esteve de la Sarga; honorary Justice of Gotlar; Jurisdictional Seigneur for the castles of Claramunt and Montlleó in the Ager Valley; Seigneur of the districts of Pradell and Margalef, in the jurisdictional lands of Lleids. He also had been granted seigniory of the castle of Abella and the lands of Querans and the Aspres of Ager. Later, under the Spanish rule, sundry noble titles and honors were conferred on the Portolás.

The present Don Gaspar had inherited his share of these distinctions and patrimony in addition to the family traditional, political, moral, and philosophical points of view. He received a prince-like education, mainly through an extraordinary resident preceptor, Don Claudi de Montclús, who for many years was like a fixture in the Portolá mansion.

Don Claudi took exceptional interest in the education and development of the last scion of the whole family. When Gaspar was only a teenager, the conscientious teacher often exclaimed, "Very soon we shall have a perfect gentleman!" referring to Gaspar. "However," Don Claudi added immediately, "it will be necessary that he increase his efforts and attention."

These comments were usually made at the table where Don Fransesc, Gaspar's father, presided with a stern countenance while Gaspar's mother, Doña Teresa, smiling sweetly and benevolently, acted as an ever-present conciliator.

At the noon meal one day Don Claudi had persisted, "I would like to make Gaspar a real gentleman as befits his noble lineage; however," he continued, being a little daring because of the encouragement he saw in Don Francesc's expression, "at times Gaspar gets interested in things which are completely out of tune. Too often he has a tendency to enjoy practical and plebeian things."

"As the times go," Doña Teresa interposed, "maybe he is not altogether wrong. The future of the nobility is rather uncertain. Besides — "

"Uncertain or not," interrupted Don Francesc with his usual severity, "Gaspar's destiny is the career of arms even if it may mean certain material sacrifice for him and for us all."

Don Claudi was on the brink of expanding into a lengthy dissertation on Don Francesc's ideas, but he met with a disapproving look from Doña Teresa, so restrained himself. He kept silent also because he did not want to provoke another incident like that which had occurred a few days before at that very table. That day, Don Claudi de Montclús had hinted that street influences were interfering dangerously with the studies and the education of the young Portolá. He referred specifically to the occasional escapades of Gaspar when he escaped to play and roam the streets with some "good for nothing" town children.

Don Francesc had thundered, "This must not be tolerated! No Portolá, even in these difficult times, at least while I am here, is to become a ragamuffin."

"Let's not exaggerate," protested Gaspar's mother. "Bear in mind that, even if we belong to the nobility, we live in a small town, not in the capital with its large aristocratic society. Gaspar has to have some friends of his own age, and the only boys here are from the common people. We cannot keep him at home like a bird in a cage."

"So," exploded Don Francesc, "we don't need any Don Claudi with his vast knowledge to waste efforts on him!"

"It will not do him any harm to know life other than through books!" insisted his mother, heatedly. And with definite intent, she requested Don Claudi's opinion.

Caught unaware, Don Claudi spoke sincerely, "With all due respect, madame, I cannot agree with your — mmm — let's say, democratic ideas. Besides, too direct experience is usually more harmful than good."

"And a life based on pure theory usually leads to failure, as many we have seen!"

Don Claudi caught the implication, her almost direct allusion to his own case. He kept quiet. Nothing more was said on the subject during the rest of the meal. Don Claudi could not avoid turning his thoughts toward the circumstances of his own life to which Doña Teresa had alluded.

He pondered: truly was he himself not a victim of theory brought to the extreme? Was not his passion for reading and intellectual theory and speculation the cause of his failure and ruin? It was undeniable that in the spiritual, mental or intellectual domain he could sometimes feel like a giant. But he should also recognize that in the practical things of life, in the daily routine, in material things, he was helpless, a cripple, a nonentity.

Don Claudi de Montclús was a typical case of a small-town bookworm. He was the only son of a fairly important landowner who had spent his life and his entire inheritance in intellectual folly and study. He cultivated his brains like a luxurious garden, but allowed his family lands and crops to dry out and rot. With his feverish reading he had become, as the town's people said, "a well of science." However, not being a genius, he did not succeed in shining among the famous scholars of the time, and when economic strain caught up with him he had to take refuge in becoming a preceptor, a teacher.

On being entrusted with the education of young Portolá, Don Claudi felt happy and proud to a certain extent. He would instill all his learning and ideas into a noble young man who had a great future in the high levels of the society of which he himself had dreamed. His vast store of reading would not become a wasted pile of knowledge, not even on such peculiar subjects as novels of chivalry and heraldry, treatises of astrology and necromancy, genealogy, numismatics, fencing, the art of poetry, courtly manners and etiquette, and many other subjects which could be of much use to an aristocratic young man who would shine in the important fashionable world.

Actually Don Claudi conducted Gaspar's education as though he were teaching a prince. When Gaspar reached seventeen years of age, the conscientious mentor considered all the required subjects exhausted, and proclaimed Don Gaspar de Portolá i Revira an accomplished gentleman and a perfect courtesan. He had taught him all that books could teach; charm, gallantry, winning manners, elegance and the rest were natural gifts inherent in Gaspar. Now he was on his own; his future depended on him, on him and on luck — his own luck and that of the course of the history of Spain.

The moment had come to make a final decision as to how best to plan a military career for Gaspar since this was the only apparent choice the circumstances allowed. Gaspar de Portolá, at the early age of seventeen years, was by derivative family right holder of a noble title, with equestrian privileges and right to use arms and to display the family heraldic shield. This empowered him to attain the highest military rank — provided his ambition did not fall.

Don Francesc, Gaspar's father, although he might keep quiet about the matter, saw certain handicaps other than eventual lack of ambition in his son's possible career. Having spent many sleepless nights pondering the best line of conduct for the entire family, particularly through adverse periods, he had come to very definite conclusions. He knew that Catalonian nobility in the last fifty years had entered a definite period of decadence in a way which paralleled the political decadence of Catalonia itself. Furthermore, through this retrospective analysis, the cautious Don Francesc had observed that there was a gap, a quiet period almost of stagnation, in the progress of the House of Portolá which could easily be equated with the turn of fortune of Catalonia as a nation.

In fact, at the death of Marti l'Humà in 1410, with the lack of a male descendant and without an appointed successor, the long line of the Catalonian royal dynasty had come to an end. With the extinction of the Catalonian House, the Aragón-Catalonian crown was disposed of, not by the Certes, but by a commission assembled at Caspe who decided in favor of Ferdinand of Antequera, the Castilian candidate, and against his chief rival, the Catalonian Count of Urgell, whose ancestral house was located at Balaguer.

With this adverse turn of events the destiny of the House of Portolá was doomed for all future progress. The hopeless destiny of the entire Catalonian nobility was sealed. It was evident that from that time on the Catalonian nobles would be considered third-rate *hidalgoes,* while the ancient Catalonian nation would be outshone by the grandees of central Spain whose influence radiated from the Court of Madrid. This was even more certain for those Catalonian nobles, including the members of the House of Portolá, who had always been faithful to the traditional liberties of Catalonia. These nobles had sided with the Catalonian candidate, Count Jaume d'Urgell, in 1410, and had fought with his armies in the bloody war he had unleashed against Ferdinand, considered by the Count and the majority of the Catalonians as an illegitimate successor and an usurper of the throne.

Young Gaspar knew almost by heart every word of this page of Catalonian history since his mentor, Don Claudi, had recited it to him repeatedly. The rebellion of Jaume d'Urgell against the decision at Caspe, aside from its inherent dramatism, had even more importance in the mind of the young student because the center of the action in the rancorous struggle was his own home town, Balaguer, where the castle of Urgell stood high on a hill overlooking the Segre River on whose banks the House of Portolá was located.

Young Gaspar admired the courage of Count Jaume in refusing to accept the verdict reached at Caspe. A great injustice had been committed there. Jaume was the closest kin and a descendant of King Marti, and even as a candidate had claimed the office of *primegenit* or Lieutenant of Catalonia, customarily held by the heir to the throne. Jaume, in fact, besides being a grandson of King Marti, was a great-grandchild of Alfens III of Aragon and Alfens II of Catalonia. In addition, Marti himself had stated that after the death of his only son, Marti the young, King of Sicily, who died in 1409, Jaume d'Urgell was his next of kin. Count Jaume d'Urgell, his fellow-citizen from Balaguer, rightly had to be nominated king, he would exclaim.

With an angry, firm conviction young Gaspar thought about all the incidents of the Catalonian-Castillian wars and mainly about the heroic defense of his home-town Balaguer whose siege by the army of Ferdinand of Antegquera was a crucial turning point in the national history of Catalonia. On August 5, 1413, Ferdinand's army had reached the banks of the Segre after having forced the retreat of Jaume's partisans, much inferior in numbers, and had besieged Balaguer. Balaguer was fortified behind strong, ancient walls, dating, according to many, from the time of the Moors. Equally fortified was the lofty palace-castle where Count Jaume's family resided. The Balaguerians resisted to the last.

The siege lasted almost three months, until all provisions were exhausted. Famine and every manner of horror and calamity prevailed. The Count and his followers had agreed not to surrender until death. The Countess-mother, Margarita d'Urgell, from the walls of the palace of Almatà, on the hill overlooking the Segre, kept haranguing her son and his faithful warriors, "My son, King or nothing! — King or nothing. —King or nothing!"

Nevertheless, Count Jaume, wishing to spare lives and to stop the horror by not prolonging the useless fight, ordered the white flag raised. On October 31, 1413, Balaguer capitulated. The troops of Ferdinand the Castilian burst into the town through the reluctantly-opened doors of the still-intact thick walls. The terms of the usurper were horribly cruel. Taken prisoner, Count Jaume was brought before a tribunal headed by Ferdinand himself in Lleida, and on November 29 the Count was condemned to life in captivity. He was brought, ignominiously, under irons to the Castle of Xativa, where, after a few years, he died very mysteriously.

Perhaps much of the pessimism about the future of the House of Portolá was not necessary. Even Don Francesc did not fail to recognize that the Castilian rulers had not been as resentful as might be imagined. After the fall of the Catalonian dynasty the Catalonian nobility had been favored with occasional rights and privileges. Philip IV of the House of Austria, for example, on March 26, 1665, had clearly conferred upon the elder Portolá and on all his male descendants the right to wear the military band and to use an heraldic escutcheon consisting, in the upper half, of two mountains with three stars on one side and sky and land on the other; in the lower half, a river and a bridge. Later, on November 4, 1682, Charles II, also of the House of Austria, granted to the elder Don Gaspar de Portolá i Pont, and to all his male descendents, the high rank of grandee.

Of course, these new noble titles, granted by the Castilian kings to the Catalonian noblemen, were generally considered in Catalonia to be of dubious and temporary value. It was well known that those granted later by Phillip IV to families who, during the critical hours of disturbance in June, 1640, had supported the peasant rebellion of Corpus Christy, did not represent any merits acquired or high services rendered, but were intended only as appeasements — a political gesture — to mitigate the determined spirit of independence and the desire for national rights. One could not compare the doubtful validity of these belated titles with the sound, legitimate value of the ancient Catalonian distinction each family had actually earned and had not received as mere gifts or bribes.

One of the barons of the Portolá family came to understand the precariousness of these Spanish-granted titles. Under Phillip V, the first Bourbon ruler, on the occasion of the War of Succession (1704-1714) in which Catalonia sided with Archduke Charles of Austria, the Catalonian nobility were deprived of their grandeeships by a simple decree of the central government, issued with the same simplicity and haste as they had been granted earlier.

All these matters and eventualities were taken into consideration at the time of the decision that young Gaspar was to follow a military career and be sent to Madrid to enter the Royal Seminary for the Education of Noblemen. This decision was based on two incontrovertible arguments: first, tradition, history and family position made it almost mandatory that young Gaspar de Portolá become an officer in the royal armies; secondly, in considering a choice between participation and non-participation in public affairs, the latter course might well result in disaster.

In discussing whether or not Gaspar should participate in public affairs as a member of the royal armies, even if it were under a Castilian king, Don Claudi advised young Gaspar that he was not to renounce any of his Catalonian characteristics or attributes. He should continue to be proud of being a Catalonian nobleman with a long glorious family tradition. He must always remember that times change very swiftly, and so do matters of state and the course of history.

Young Gaspar was very conscious of his special place in the modern affairs of the House of Portolá and shared in the spirit of tradition — the retention of the old ideals and aspirations. He approved the tendency of the Portolás in recent years to return to the authentic origins of his nobility — the true and pure source of their lineage. He had always approved the decision of one of his recent ancestors to discard the escutcheon of nobility adopted after the diploma granted by Phillip IV in 1665, and the reinstitution of the traditional one, or royal Catalonian origin, consisting of the following heraldic quarters: field one and four, red with a golden eagle; fields two and three, blue with a silver wing *(ala)*; the whole under a small blue escutcheon with a golden door *(porta) (porta-ala)*.

Gaspar felt well-equipped, both morally and physically, to be a worthy successor to the family tradition. He had never forgotten the bits of advice given by his grandfather on his death bed: "Always aim high — never belittle things, enhance them! Be an idealist, but be also on the watch for the opportune moment. Be ambitious, but for big things. Get away from mediocrity and average degrees; if an enterprise is not really big, it is not worth the undertaking. Aspire to the maximum always; less than the maximum is worthless — All or nothing!"

In preparation for the journey to Madrid, Dos Gaspar de Portolá requested letters of introduction from the most prominent members of Barcelonan nobility to be presented to the most influential people at Phillip V's Court in Madrid.

The day of departure arrived. Travelling to Madrid around the year 1735 was an arduous enterprise. For the Balaguer township, the prospect of such a journey was an exciting event. The departure of young Portolá raised many differing emotions and a general curiosity.

Balaguer was not a large town. Its fame was merely historic. Surrounded by heavy walls and dominated by the citadel overlooking the Segre River, it had been a stronghold in all armed struggles. As a bridgehead, it had been of great strategic value in all wars. For those approaching from the west, the Spanish side, it was actually the door to Catalonia. The town had changed little physically from the time of the Middle Ages; it could still be described as a group of houses in four rows around a public square. But, it must be said, the Balaguer square was really imposing — in fact, it was one of the most spacious and well-designed public squares in the country.

The wealthy people, the *señores,* lived around this *plaza.* The poor, the common people, the plebeians, the peasants lived in crooked streets adjacent to the square, compressed between the hills and the river, enclosed within the thick fortifications.

The Portolá mansion was located on the southern side of the big square, almost at a corner. Its architecture was like the rest of the buildings. Like the rest, it had porticos in front so that they formed, with those of the neighboring houses, an arched passageway all around the plaza — a reminder of the dread the ancient peoples of Spain had felt for the sun. These porticos were made of solid ashlar stones, gracefully arched and with little or no decoration. The central portico of the Portolá mansion, however, had carved on the keystone the family escutcheon with the heraldic *Portal* and the *Ala* which distinguished it from the rest of the houses.

The stage coach for Lleida, which that day was to take away the illustrious son of the town, stopped not far from the Portolá mansion in the plaza. All the populace not busily engaged otherwise came to the plaza to watch. There was a feeling of sadness in the hearts of these good citizens. To send a son to Madrid, for a Catalonian, was like sowing in barren soil; far from the homeland, seeds do not yield any crop.

Don Francesc and other members of the household, including the servants and Tomás, the old stableman who had taken care of the equestrian training of the young master, were their to say their final good-byes to the traveler. Don Claudi de Montclús who would accompany Gaspar to Madrid looked proud and content. Young Gaspar had mixed emotions — regret and expectation.

When the long whip of the stage-coach driver cracked a couple of feet above the ears of the spirited horses, a few white handkerchiefs were waved in farewell. Young Gaspar looked once more at the top of the hill beyond the plaza, to the monumental church of Saint Mary with its lofty bell tower, golden in the sun like the adjacent rampart walls built of stone from the same quarry. Gaspar wanted to carry with him the deeply impressed memory of the characteristic silhouette of this, his home town. Like the features of a former sweetheart, he always would remember it with tenderness and emotion, no matter where he might be.

Chapter Three

Even for seventeen-year-old Gaspar, eager and curious, the journey from the banks of the Segre River to the high Castilian plateau was monotonous and tiresome. Once the stage coach had left the green fields of Catalonia, it started to climb the dry desert characteristic of central Spain. The days within that uncomfortable shake box of a carriage were interminable. Gaspar, sensitive to the influence of the landscape, felt rather depressed. He was leaving behind the familiar verdant banks of the Segre to enter this dry desolate unknown land called Spain. To judge by the appearance of his surroundings one would seem to have regressed to an area and time in backward civilization.

Oversimplifying matters, in the course of his silent meditation, Gaspar put some puzzling questions to himself: "How can the Castilians be so proud and haughty when they come from a land like this? How can they install themselves as dominators of the rest of the peoples of the peninsula?" With the simplicity born of inexperience and the intemperance of youth he asked himself, "Why should my old father be concerned about the ominous shadow of Spain over Catalonia?" He concluded, "The solution is simple — let the Catalonians take over the steering of the ship of state and replace the dominance of the Castilians!"

On arriving in Madrid, Don Claudi, Gaspar's conscientious mentor, engaged in numerous activities. A few days elapsed, and after much exertion and many visits to very important persons, following absolute protocol, Don Claudi de Montclús finally left his distinguished pupil at the admission hall of the Royal Seminary for the Education of Noblemen, the institution where the young noble from Balaguer was to refine his education and experience the surprises which exist between theory and actual practice.

Gaspar went through the red tape of the inscription at the seminary without the least apprehension, rather with the peevish air of a student who enrolls in a required course in an unavoidable subject. Soon, however, he found himself submerged in the routine and practices of the curriculum, and the novelty itself brought him a certain enthusiasm.

At first, Gaspar suffered disillusionment with Madrid, the capital; he felt it had been overpraised. He found the courtesans' manners rather stilted. The daily use of the Castilian language, so different from his own Catalan — although he spoke it fluently and elegantly — gave him an impression of artificiality. He had to get accustomed to pretending a personality not his own. But, thanks to his handsome appearance, his affable nature, and his gentility, he soon made new friends. It did not take long for him to shine among the young men about town.

The novelty of brilliant receptions, stately balls, gay parties, and the continuous social activities kept him excited and pleased. He was invited and sought out, particularly by the ladies, and he was astonished to receive such distinction from even the highest ranks of the aristocracy since he was so new to the court. Good humoredly he concluded that his attraction was probably like that of an exotic plant which had been transplanted to Madrid.

Occasionally Gaspar longed for the quiet life and simplicity of his ancestral home in peaceful Balaguer and for the sober manners of his fellow country-men like the cordial affection of Don Claudi. He missed the familiarities he was able to take with old Tomás, the loyal servant who was so plain and so humane, and who treated and talked to his horses as though they were people. Gaspar missed family life.

To a certain extent Gaspar had been hungry for maternal affection a great part of his life. After the sudden death of Doña Teresa in 1730 when he was an adolescent, he had taken refuge in the paternal affection of Don Francesc, his father, whom he loved with a timid and deep tenderness even though he never could understand him well because of his stern character. Now he found that the artificial life of the court was in great contrast to these simple, elementary values. Fortunately enough, Gaspar had an accommodating nature, and was used to making the best of any unfavorable situation. He soon accepted the new moral climate with his usual attitude of indifference to all events of slight transcendental value.

A curious, rather mysterious circumstance, however, contributed after a while to keeping Gaspar's mind occupied. This circumstance concerned his status within the seminary. When he first entered he had produced a good impression on both his fellow students and the members of the faculty. Several times instructors had singled out Gaspar in class as an example because of his demeanor and his thorough preparedness. Somewhat embarrassed, Gaspar quickly assured his colleagues that he certainly would not boast of virtues these instructors appeared to find in him. This helped to make him accepted as a regular fellow and not as a teacher's pet.

This state of affairs did not last long, however. Suddenly, without any apparent reason, Gaspar started to notice a certain vacuum around him. He had the impression that he was being isolated. This unexplainable attitude worried him for some time, and he devoted many hours to trying to solve the mystery. Finally he adopted his natural attitude of shrugging his shoulders as the correct one to adopt when thing occurred without plausible reason.

There was a reason, however, and a very definite one — a reason he would not even come to know during his lifetime, and one which would constitute a secret to his entire public career; something that appeared surrepticiously in his record of services as a bad mark, completely independent of his merits and regardless of the commendability of his achievements.

As the noticeable isolation continued, Gaspar began to feel undeclared hostility and lack of cordiality as intolerable. He attempted to investigate, but he learned nothing. Each time that he thought he had uncovered a clue that might bring some light, greater obscurity and confusion were sure to follow.

One day Gaspar was called, ceremoniously, before the director of the seminary, and for a moment he thought that he had come to the end of his doubts and suspicions. The first cautious words of the director, however, convinced him that any effort on his part would be to no avail toward discovering any conspiracy against him, if indeed such a conspiracy existed.

The meticulous director tried to give Gaspar the impression that the meeting was one of the many regular formalities of the seminary, but, without preamble, the director began to submit Gaspar to a series of questions as though trying to pry into his innermost personal ideas and his most intimate principles.

Gaspar de Portolá, instinctively on guard, confined his answers to mere generalizations that could have no bearing one way or another. When the director made indirect reference to the reigning monarch and his royal prerogatives, Gaspar expressed his loyalty as the most devout of subjects. Concerning his philosophic points of view, with sincerity and openness, he declared that for the military career he was planning to pursue, the only indispensable baggage was the greatest possible knowledge of military science. Any intellectual or philosophic preoccupation was a useless impediment. When, finally, the director mentioned the church and the power of the Holy Inquisition, the cautious seminarist excused himself from making any statement by saying that it was the function of the statesmen and the king himself to dictate to the citizenry the just and patriotic position regarding these and all religious matters.

The way the meeting progressed and the obvious results rather quieted and reassured the young cadet. He reached the conclusion that the supposed conspiracy of which he was the target was probably due to some political intrigue, one of the many ever brewing in the court environment. He decided to forget the whole matter entirely, and lost interest in pursuing any further investigation about what might have happened.

Actually what had happened was very simple. Simultaneous with the entrance of young Gaspar into the Royal Seminary for the Education of Nobility, following the routine background investigation of all new cadets, the registrar had ordered the customary search into the records and archives of the nobility as well as into the genealogical tree of the family, seeking any illegitimacy or irregularity. This search was mandatory for all accepted pupils. On analyzing the transcript of the search of Gaspar de Portolá's background, the registrar was appalled and disconcerted to discover among the data a mysterious sign, of ominous appearance, although utterly enigmatic, in spite of its having been carried from generation to generation through the centuries. On the transcript, next to the genealogical ascendancy, appeared the list of noble titles and privileges conferred on the Portolá family; this was normal information. But on the top left corner of the search form, prominently reproduced, was a strange symbol consisting of a capital H with an inverted small cross in the middle hyphen: ♯

Puzzled by this unusual and seemingly malignant sign, the conscientious registrar became alarmed. In spite of all his vast heraldic and genealogical knowledge, he declared himself incapable of diciphering the enigma. He decided to submit the product of his search to higher authority.

The findings created a commotion. The trustees of the seminary met in secret session. The nature of the unprecedented symbol caused long investigation, discussion, and argument. The representative of the church was the most concerned and mystified. Used to handling the most esoteric texts of the Holy Office, the stern prelate had never encountered in any document, no matter how old, such an enigmatic mark as the one which appeared in the Portolá genealogy. That H with the inverted cross was a mystery that defied the most thorough scholarship.

After long consideration and after having consulted the highest ecclesiastical hierarchism, the church trustee read his report: That exceptional mark, even if it did not agree with any of the traditionally secret indictions used by the Tribunal and the Archivist of the Holy Inquisition (such as the Sanbenite Symbol) was a clear indication that there must have been, nobody knew when, some declared heretic or some concealed enemy of the church in the Portolá ancestry. The heresy or dissension must have been of such special nature that extraordinary or extenuating circumstances required a designation of the mark as secret and symbolic. No matter how, the church trustee asserted, the H in the nobility record of the Portolá family accused the aristocratic family of disguised heresy, a stigma that no one could ever remove form the record, and consequently all the descendants were to suffer from it inescapably.

This secret, but final report was the direct reason for the mysterious conspiracy of isolation which resulted in the seminary around the young nobleman from Balaguer who was later subjected to interrogation before the seminary's director.

By sheer luck and because of the tact and wise evasiveness of the interrogated, no immediate sanction was applied and none was foreseeable in the near future. In any other case, where the stigma projected no shadow of doubt, the penalty would have been immediate expulsion from the seminary. On the other hand, the investigating director could detect no indication of rebellion or of non-conformist temperament in Gaspar which would have allowed his being included in the list of suspicious or dangerous elements against the holy aims of the Sacred Mother Church of the Catholic religion. Furthermore the times were not propitious for condemnation or reprisals in defense of the Catholic interests.

The accession to the throne of Spain of Philip of Anjou, the first Bourbon ruler, the nephew of Louis XIV of France, had brought into Spain from the neighboring court a wide tolerance in religious ideas and a relaxation in social conventions. At that precise moment, the state, the sovereign himself, his Majesty the King Philip V, was in open struggle with the Holy See and its hierarchies, and even the Holy Inquisition structure was somewhat threatened.

The board of trustees of the Royal Seminary for the Education of Noblemen, therefore, decided to maintain secrecy and, with the mystery, the stigma suspended like the sword of Damocles over the House of Portolá and its members present, past, and future, was to continue.

That Gaspar was never to know about the secret stigma spared him from need to be concerned about it. He was not spared, however, from less severe, indirect punishment which was to result in several periods of his life and long career, falling as though from an invisible hand high above.

At the moment, Gaspar had found a good way to forget the discrimination and obvious isolation of which he was made object at the seminary. His smooth actions and elegant manners had allowed him to gain many friends in the aristocratic circles of Madrid, chiefly among the feminine ranks of society, and even among high ranking officials. If government leaders saw a definite promise in Gaspar's obvious intelligence and agility of mind, the ladies of the court saw a present reality in his manly appearance. Gaspar had become a great friend of the famous Countess of Lemos in particular. She was the most influential lady of the epoch and was endowed with great beauty and superior intelligence. In the course of a few months this friendship had become very intimate and all of Madrid was talking about the supposed, but not very legitimate, liaison between the handsome cadet and the influential countess.

Aside from these social activities, Gaspar, nonchalant by nature, led an aloof, free and easy life which made him quite different from the rest of the young men of the court. Contrary to the apparent lack of cultural accomplishments of the majority of the illustrious youngsters, Gaspar de Portolá had shown a keen interest in the arts and in letters. Perhaps his interest in these intellectual pursuits was enhanced by the social-aristocratic aspects inherent in them, but it is a well-known fact that he kept up friendships with and held a decided admiration for the most fashionable writers and for the foreign artists brought to Spain under the sponsorship of the court. Jean Ranc, L.M. Vanlee and Rafael Mengs, introducers of neoclassic painting, had a special esteem for Gaspar de Portolá. Gaspar was an indefatigable activist in the literary revival that the French influence had brought into Spanish letters, and which had given birth to the national academies which were to promote culture so widely. Still in the period of full baroque dominance, Madrid's intellectual life was an extravagant jumble of vulgar pedantry and affection brought to a climax.

Gaspar had the good taste to declare himself in favor of a middle point tending toward eclecticism, an attitude which gave him a very personal distinction. Besides, he was probably the only young man of the native nobility who assiduously attended the gatherings in the literary salons, particularly the exclusive one patronized by his lively friend the Countess of Lemos, founder of the most reputable Academy of Good Taste, in which, beside discussions on the most lofty subjects, were debates on all the controversial topics of the day: the theatre, poetry, bullfighting, and, of course, love and romance.

About the time when his romantic entanglements were on the point of becoming dangerous, young Gaspar graduated from the Seminary for the Education of Noblemen to enter, in accordance with the planned schedule, the Royal Military Academy of Guadalajara, located in the illustrious old Castilian town.

During the first months of his stay in the military academy Gaspar tred softly, cautious lest the terrain might prove as brittle as that of the seminary. He watched for any look, gesture, or word that might reveal any prejudice or discrimination against him, but very soon, to his profound satisfaction, he decided that none of these obstacles existed. It was evident that the Royal Military Academy of Guadalajara was a strictly military institution, free from the influences and political vicissitudes of life in Madrid.

Thus, completely reassured, Gaspar de Portolá began to give full expression to his real personality so that after a short while people of importance began to notice the cadet of svelte stature who revealed the stamina of a future leader. Consequently Gaspar found a friendly welcome among the future captains of the Spanish Army. He began to feel at ease among them, and he discovered there a more congenial, sincere, and virile environment than that of the court of the Bourbon monarch.

In Guadalajara Gaspar experienced an even more decided worldly success than in Madrid. All social life there was centered in a single noble family, the Dukes of Infantade who seemed the only reason for the existence of the notorious Castilian town. Gaspar, naturally, became an essential part of the activities of this small, provincial, opulent world. He became so indispensable that a popular saying actually grew up asserting that no reception or ball at the Palance of the Dukes of Infantade was truly brilliant if the figure of the gallant cadet, Gaspar de Portolá, was absent.

But, of course he was never absent. He was present during all his long youth and celibacy at all festivities or worldly gatherings where people talked, laughed, drank, danced, and made love. At the age of twenty-one, Gaspar exulted in exhibiting the gold and purple insignia of military merit, the highest distinction for any young nobleman of that time. He cut a striking figure in his bright uniform of a cadet of the Royal Military Academy of Guadalajara with the coveted rank of ensign.

Catalonia: showing Balaguer, the birthplace of Portolá, as well as Barcelona, where the popular captain of dragoons spent many of his adult years.

Chapter Four

The reign of Philip V, 1700-1746, was notable chiefly for the French influence on the manners, habits, customs, and even on the destiny of Spain. Because of the important role played by Louis XIV of Franch in the accession of his grandson Philip to the Spanish throne, these influences were only natural. On the young monarch himself, however, feminine influences weighed more heavily than those of the old royal grandfather more than once.

These feminine influences were embodied alternately in the two wives of the feeble, irresolute Bourbon. Aware of the weakness of his grandchild, the shrewd Louis XIV planned to rule Spain through him, and, as a security measure, had made him promise that he would never forget that he was a Frenchman. Moreover, the old man had crowded the Spanish court with auxiliary royal personnel, advisors, generals, ambassadors, and attachés of all kinds, charged with the task of watching constantly, each one from his own strategic high post, for the interests of France. Among these many valuable envoys was the famous Princess of Ursins, who, as lady of honor for Queen Maria Louise of Savoy, the wife of Philip V, enjoyed the queen's trust and confidence, and through the wife was able to dominate the husband on more than one occasion.

The intrigues of the princess came to be so thickly woven and dominating that even Philip himself rebelled against his grandfather's pressure in favor of the princess, and extraordinary events ensued which culminated in the expulsion from Spain of the active lady of honor. Immediately after the death of Philip's first wife early in 1714, the princess set about looking for a worthy successor for the king's nuptial bed. At the time an Italian abbot, Alberoni, was frequenting the court at Madrid and suggested Isabel of Farnesio, the young heiress to the duchies of Parma and Pleasance, to Princess of the Ursins as a fitting candidate. According to Alberoni's description, Isabel would make a most appropriate wife for King Philip. Besides, her natural gentle character would allow the princess to maintain her power in the court. What the abbot did not say, however, was that his plan was to use Isabel's sweetness of character for his personal purposes.

Abbot Alberoni undertook the necessary preparations and in December of that year the royal wedding took place. At the first meeting between the new queen and Princess of the Ursins, the princess was released as lady of honor, and it did not take long for Isabel to have the princess expelled from Spain, and from then on it was the queen who exerted all the influence on her husband, even against the wishes of Louis XIV of France.

Isabel of Farnesio proved to be a woman of extraordinary energy and will power. This combined with her beauty made her irresistible to the weak Philip. The latter, a man of violent whims and caprices fell madly in love with Isabel, and, on occasions, carried away by jealousy, he whipped her brutally. Isabel endured every ill treatment as long as she could dominate the king completely. She had a purpose. She had limitless ambition on behalf of her sons who had been left in Italy, but whom she planned to favor through Spanish power.

Early in 1715 Isabel succeeded in having Abbot Alberoni promoted to a position in the court which was soon to make him a Cardinal, and eventually Minister of Foreign Affairs. This turn of events was to serve Isabel's motherly designs perfectly. The main points of the political plan were to cut short the close Spanish relations with France gradually; then, by expelling the House of Austria from Italian territory, to recover for Spain its old possessions in Italy which would then be converted into principalities for Isabel of Farnesio's sons.

The opportunity for the success of this great plan came about in 1740 with the death of the Austrian emperor and the resultant conflict created by the succession. Urged by Isabel, and advised by Alberoni, Philip V renewed Spanish demands for the return of the Italian territories then in the hands of the Austrians. This brought about the war between Austria and Spain.

It was in this European war that Gaspar de Portolá, the young ensign from the Military School of Guadalajara, saw action for the first time. In the battlefields of Italy, fighting against the Austrians, he had the opportunity to prove that he was not only brave and daring, but that he also possessed remarkable stoic capacity, practical sense, and presence of mind — all commendable virtues which were to accompany him all through his life.

In January 13, 1742 the young aristocrat officer from Balaguer boarded the *San Pedro*, a unit of the King's Fleet, with the port of La Spezzia, Italia, as its destination. He was ensign of the Regiment of Dragoons of Numancia which was part of an army comprising ten thousand prime infantry men who were carried by seventeen war vessels, or by the entire Spanish Armada for the Italian campaign.

Gaspar de Portolá walked on board with his already proverbial non-chalant smile. Coolly and skeptically, he analysed the chances for military success in the war in which he was to take part. He could not expect much personal glory — he coveted none. As for practical national results, he considered them doubtful and slim. This war would be, he thought, another futile adventure of the innumerable ones in which Spain had embarked within the course of the current European intrigues.

With this calculating nature, Gaspar was thinking of the exalted legions of youth, crowded on board and piled together with all their military impediments, and he doubted the fighting efficiency in spite of their bubbling ambition. He himself was not sure of his own bravery. His military service record very clearly stated: "Valor: He is supposed to possess it. ... However ..."

Digging into his memory, the young ensign tried to find some incident that might confirm or justify that "supposed" valor of his. He had to trace back to his childhood to a remote incident during his early days in Balaguer which could be so construed.

On Thursdays during his school years under the tutorship of Don Claudi de Montclús, Gaspar used to indulge in juvenile escapades with boys "from the street" which the severe preceptor opposed and Doña Teresa, Gaspar's mother, usually condoned. On such days, free from school discipline, Gaspar's conduct did not fall under the jurisdiction of Don Claudi, and he could engage in lively activities, even plebian ones, like any boy from the street. Far from the richly carpeted halls of his family mansion, he could walk barefoot through the sandy banks and by the chaparral along the Segre River, a true barefoot prince from some child's story book.

Customarily, immediately after lunch on these special days, a few of his ragged friends would be waiting for him at the livery back door.

"Let's go!" Gaspar, as ringleader, would order. Gaspar walked at the head of the group with Quim and Genis on each side as lieutenants. One particular day, however, they were not going along the river for a swim or through the meandering pathways along the orchards to snatch an apple here or a bunch of grapes beyond. This day, they were marching toward a great and special event.

Since the beginning of summer there had been a standing challenge from the boys of the nearby village of Gerp. The disagreement was over the right to pick the small ripe fruit of some hackberry trees located precisely on the boundary line between the townships of Gerp and Balaguer on the hill above the dirt road between the town and the small village. The peasant boys of Gerp felt that the city lads of Balaguer could not claim any rights in this countryside matter. The group headed by Gaspar de Portolá understood that it was a matter of law — if the location of the trees' position was uncertain, at least the Balaguerians had equal rights with the peasant boys from Gerp. And this was the right they were about to defend, since a few days before, even before the berries were ripe, two boys from Balaguer had been chased away from the trees by a shower of stones from the peasant youngsters.

Now the boys from Balaguer were coming armed also, with long slings made of strong hemp rope to be able to throw stones for long distances. There was going to be a real stone-throwing battle. The Gerpolians had gathered the boys from all the farms around. The small Portolá group was to be strengthened by gangs of youngsters from the various districts of the town, including the peasant quarter. The concentration point had been pre-established; Gaspar de Portolá would be Commander-in-Chief.

A state of war existed between the two factions. On the past Thursdays there had been slight skirmishes by impatient partisans of both sides, but today the decisive battle was going to take place.

Gaspar's group was marching eagerly along the dirt road toward Gerp.

"Look!" said Gaspar to his lieutenants, showing them the new sling he had tied around his waist. "It's made of cotton wick, more flexible than hemp!"

Quim and Genis wore all admiring eyes.

"Our stableman braided it for me," added Gaspar, proudly.

"And it is brand new!" exclaimed one of the lieutenants.

"You'll see how it cracks!" said the ringleader, picking up a rock and setting it into the strap. He got ready to shoot the stone.

"Be careful, Gaspar," warned Genis. "See that you don't hit across the river. It may give us away to the peasants."

Gaspar stepped back two paces, swung the sling full length over his head, and with vigor and skill shot the powerful missile. The small tuft of loose wick left at one end of the sling string cracked like a whip. The impact of the powerful missile caused it to imbed itself in a sandy patch far upstream.

After this performance no other boy dared show his hemp sling which he kept in his pocket or tied around his waist like a belt.

The Brickyard Gully, halfway to the village of Gerp, was the designated place of concentration. All the teenage boy-gangs of Balaguer were to be there. The town was left without any young lads that afternoon. Gaspar and his group arrived all dusty and sweaty under the hot sun of early afternoon. At the swimming hole they were joined by the rest of the general staff. The "troops" by groups bivouacked under the few shady patches of trees clumped around the swimming hole.

"Nothing unusual, sir," reported a young "officer" to Gaspar.

"How is the morale of the men?" inquired the Commander-in-Chief.

"All are ready to fight!" was the answer.

"Today is the decisive battle," observed Portolá, as a warning. "Either we settle our right definitely, or goodbye hackberries!" he concluded.

The staff began to discuss strategy.

Simultaneously, up on the hill by the hackberry trees the sons of the peasants from Gerp, fortified by parapets, smiled scornfully.

"We'll cut them to bits. As soon as they get in range of our slings, we'll pulverize them like clods of soil!" they boasted.

"They won't even dare appear! What can you expect from such city nits!" exclaimed one of the defenders.

"I heard that some peasant boys from the Balaguer rural district will be here too," commented a non-com.

"Peasants?" retorted the commander, "Mere orchard rats!"

The Gerpolian troops waited, lying low among the furze bushes, barefooted and with torn and mud-smeared clothes, half camouflaged in the red clay. There were quite a great number. They had come from the fields all around, those fields where now their parents were wondering about the general disappearance of their young helpers.

The peasant boys were waiting for the fight without emotion; they did not even feel hatred. For them a boy from Balaguer was something despicable. School boys! Pampered sons of rich families. "And such sissies want to fight with sturdy country guys like us. They will be chased from the hackberry trees like a flock of frightened sparrows."

Gaspar had just briefed the Balaguerian "army." He had warned them all that they were going to face a tough adversary, not easily beaten. They were going to fight a real battle. It was true war action. It was not like the usual local fights between two city gangs over a trifling matter — those struggles by comparison should be considered as mere military maneuvers. Now it was a fight between two different towns, Balaguer against Gerp. The slings should crack like whips and each stone flung should be a bull's eye. Each should be on the alert for the battle's appointed time, and then, in accordance with pre-established tactics, should advance in order and with discipline. No personal initiative! Just follow the superior's commands. It had to be a coordinated action, and the joint staff knew how to move every unit at a given time.

As time passed, the Gerpolians were beginning to doubt the appearance of the enemy. It was already late afternoon, and the sun was low, but the Balaguerians had not appeared. Of course, they knew that to reach the hackberry trees took a forty-five minute walk from Balaguer.

Then, also, the city boys had to be back home before dusk if they wanted to avoid a thrashing from their parents. So they had probably "turned chicken" and given up the fight.

This upsetting of the logical schedule, however, was part of the Portolá strategy. This time, in this decisive battle, Portolá's hosts were not going to commit the former error; this time they would not march under the scorching noon sun to arrive at the site of the battle already worn out and exhausted. They would wait until the sun was low, and then, from the sunny side instead of the shady side of the hill from where they were expected, they would fall on the enemy by surprise. They would not give him time to turn around for the change of front.

The Gerpolian forces were confused. They had sent a scout down to the approach of Brickyard Gully, and he had returned to report that no Balaguerians were in sight.

"I told you they wouldn't even show up!" exclaimed one hoe-and-shovel general.

Scarcely had the wind hushed down this exclamation when another member of the staff cried, "Look!"

All turned to look toward the sunny side. At the top of the next hill, on the flank, the Balaguerian hosts had just appeared. Rocks began to fall all around the Gerpolian general staff. Shouts! Whistles! Counter orders. Disbandment. Confusion. Like shepherds trying to corral their flocks under a sudden thunderstorm, the high command of the Gerp forces tried to cope with the situation. They were flabbergasted at the suddenness of the change in their situation, the shifting of their line of fire, and the loss of the strategic position. They had waited for the enemy to arrive through the valley below, and instead it had appeared all of a sudden at the crest of the hill. They reacted immediately. Under the fire of the enemy they corrected their lines, made a change of front, and combat was formally engaged between the two armies.

Portolá had planned to use the momentary confusion of the adversary to take over the position, but the distance from the tops of the hill and the quick reaction of the Gerpolians forced him to stop short of the reach of the enemy's fire and fortify the men behind the rocks.

What was to have been a storm assault became a stationary, protracted battle. The young *gerrilleros* fought well, but they began to get bored. Someone prudently suggested a withdrawal. Portolá refused to listen to any such suggestion. For a minute he stood in meditation. The next minute, however, he reached a decision. He would put into execution one of the coups for which he was to become well known.

During this minute of hesitation the enemy seemed to become extraordinarily bold, and the fight became almost untenable, to the point that some of the Balaguerians felt that they were being defeated already. At this point, however, Portolá jumped ahead out of the parapets and leading the battle personally, commanded, "Out! All into the open!"

His men were disoriented, but they obeyed him blindly, with discipline.

Under the increasing shower of stones from the Gerpolians' slings, Gaspar gave another order, "Throw your slings away — obviously!"

The Gerpolians could not believe their eyes. The enemy was there enduring the heavy fire, and besides the men were throwing away their weapons! For a moment, they had the impression the Balaguerians were surrendering. But then, Gaspar commanded, "Forward! To the assault! To the hackberry trees! on the double!"

The Balaguerians threw themselves into the assault, dashing downhill like an avalanche. The first thirty yards progress was made under violently heavy fire from the enemy. A few of the Balaguerians had to advance after receiving direct hits, some with mere bruises, others with bloody head wounds. But if the disciplined assailants were flabbergasted, the defenders of the position were utterly disconcerted by this sudden strange maneuver.

Soon they were to discover its purpose. At first the unexpected action inhibited them and curtailed their agressiveness, but presently they discovered that the reckless rush was a masterly military move. By shortening the distance between the two lines of combatants, the defending line, the Gerpolians, was put in a position of being disarmed — their slings became useless suddenly. At short distance rock throwing was impractical with the slings. The boys were overcome by surprise.

Of course, they too could bombard the enemy by throwing rocks by hand, but by the time this fact dawned on them the enemy was already approaching the outer parapets of the position. They panicked. Someone tried to turn back and to run. A few minutes later the disputed line of hackberry trees was taken and gained forever by the Balaguerian boys!

After the victory, Gaspar's general staff surrounded their genial leader, momentarily taken by silent admiration. Finally, Genis dared to say, "Listen, Gaspar, by having us throw away our slings, had you decided already to go into hand to hand fighting?"

"That was the impression that was to be given the enemy," Gaspar answered. "I knew they would be so confused that they would turn around and run. See them; they are still running!" He concluded, "The best battles are those won without being fought!"

Now, on the deck of the *San Pedro*, reminiscing about this incident, Gaspar smiled tenderly at his first "military victory."

"Remembering happy times?" someone asked discreetly not far from the side rail on which he was leaning.

"Oh, pardon me, Marquis!" exclaimed Gaspar, turning around to greet his friend and superior.

Marquis Francois de Croix was an officer in the Walloon Guards. He was the eldest son of an aristocratic family from Flanders. He enjoyed a higher rank than was usual at his age, and a brilliant military and political career was waiting for him in the service of Spain.

A spontaneous friendship which was to be of long duration came about on board the Spanish battleship between this Flemish officer and the dragoons ensign from Balaguer. The former had been attracted immediately by the frank joviality of Gaspar, and in spite of their difference in rank, the marquis had sought his company since the first day on board. Now the *San Pedro* had been at sea only four days, and the two friends had enjoyed several conversations while strolling along the deck as the ship sailed through the Mediterranean waters toward northern Italy.

Through these conversations Gaspar de Portolá had quickly reached the conclusion that de Croix was a complete idealist, somewhat naive. This prompted him to listen more than to talk lest his own cynical leanings might harm their budding friendship. The marquis interpreted the reserved demeanor of the young ensign as a discreet, respectful attitude toward someone of higher rank, and, erroneously, as a normal shyness on the part of the young officer. Since he was by nature a loquacious man, with a heavy tendency to listen to himself, the marquis welcomed Gaspar's attitude.

Today, de Croix was very excited and burned with patriotic zeal. In a few hours a great event was to take place. The French navy with a total of fourteen large battleships would join the Spanish fleet. The fiery Marquis was already anxious to detect the high masts of the French ships on the horizon.

In the heat of patriotic talk, more than a holding conversation, the marquis was giving a monologue: "Thus escorted, strengthened by the French navy, I should not think Admiral Haddek would dare to cross our path — that is, if the British really intend to molest us!"

To kill time, Portolá inserted trivial questions with an interest which was simulated rather than real. However, he took advantage of the opportunity to learn the destination of the expedition.

"Shall we land at La Spezzia or will we proceed toward the south?" asked Portolá.

"At this time of the year," exclaimed de Croix, "it would be risky to head the armada further down than La Spezzia. Probably we will land there and then proceed by land to Orbitello. That is unless the admiralty decides to tranship the troops at La Spezzia on board tartans or galleys.

Shortly past noon the fourteen units bearing the flag of the King of France appeared in majestic formation to the north. By advancing directly, with a favorable wind, it would not take long for the fleet to come alongside the Spanish expedition. Then, by veering with mathematical precision, there would be soon two parallel lines of ships forming a single armada.

For five days, sailing toward western Mediterranean waters, the imposing France-Spanish fleet continued on calm seas without any sudden appearance of British men-of-war. On a clear sunny morning, the admiral-ship broke into the blue waters of La Spezzia harbor while the rest of the ships remained outside in the wide, protected bay.

The army to which Gaspar de Portolá belonged remained on board awaiting orders. These orders did not come for several hours which, to the expeditionary forces, seemed an eternity.

There was some indecision among the Spanish general staff established at the Tuscan city. The bulk of the Spanish army in Italy was at Orbitello under the command of the Duke of Montemar. The fresh expeditionary forces were to join this army, but the news of the situation in the intermediate duchies between La Spezzia and Orbitello were none too clear. In order to make a final decision, they awaited the arrival of the Duke of Montemar.

Coincidental with the arrival of this high army commander, news reached La Spezzia that the Austro-Sardinians had seized the Modena and Reggie duchies, and this changed the plan for the concentration of new forces. So, it was agreed, the meeting of the two bodies of troops would take place in Bologne instead of Orbitello; therefore, orders to land were issued.

The fifteen thousand infantry men from Orbitello and the ten thousand from the expeditionary fleet among whose officers was Gaspar de Portolá, proceeded toward Bologne by different routes. The meeting took place on May 17, and the ranks were organized immediately to proceed to encounter the enemy which was then encamped by the banks of the Panaro. Portolá was assigned to the forces under the command of the Count of Gages, among which were the Walloon guards in which Marquis de Croix was serving.

On may 27 the Spaniards came to within five miles of the Panaro. The enemy was on the opposite side of the river; it was composed of the troops of the king of Sardinia and those of the queen of Hungary.

The first contact with the enemy, with an almost equal deployment of strength, was extremely violent. Both sides suffered heavy casualties. However, the battle ended indecisively as did many future battles — a situation which was to characterize the Italian campaign as a whole.

Through the long, sterile sequence of battles, Gaspar de Portolá suffered the same vicissitudes as did all the army of which he was a part. He fought, surprising himself many times, with the ferocity of someone defending a cause which he felt intensely and considered his own. During the long campaign, which lasted from 1742 to 1746, Gaspar saw action at Demonte, Ceni, Testona, on the Panare and Tidoni Rivers, and at the bitter battle of Valencia on the Po, in which he was wounded.

Nevertheless, often Portolá thought about the futility of this chimerical war and felt sad about the useless blood-shedding for a Spain already bled and feeble. Once in awhile he felt disgust, as he did at the battle of Espello at the approach to Foligno. A pathetic caprice of destiny arranged the composition of the contending forces in such a way that Portolá had the impression that he was participating in a fratricidal fight, a sort of civil war which nobody had forseen.

The action consisted of attacking the rear guard of General Lobkowitz's army which was assaulting Perugia. The officer in charge of protecting the baggage train of the Austrian troops was the Count of Soro, an Aragonese aristocrat who had resided for many years in Catalonia, and who had commanded troops in the war against Philip V when Catalonia declared itself in favor of Archduke Charles of Austria, pretender to the Spanish throne. When the Archduke's cause failed at the end of the war in 1714, Philip V undertook cruel reprisals against the former partisans of the Archduke. The result was a great number of exiles who naturally went to Vienna, Austria, for refuge and protection. Among these exiles was the Count of Soro who saw the opportunity for his revenge against Philip V in this Austro-Italian war against Spain. The count and many of the exiles enlisted as volunteers in this war against their own countrymen.

Soro's troops for the protection of the baggage train of the Austrian army consisted of these very volunteers who were included in a body of four thousand fusileers. It was these fusileers, among whom were many Catalonians, that Portolá had to attack. He fought with deep sorrow in his heart, realizing that because of this tragic coincidence, the battle was brother against brother.

As a whole the Espello battle went in favor of the Austrian army. However, the Spaniards took over eight hundred prisoners, and Portolá cried in silent, powerless protest on seeing many of his compatriots, the former exiles, executed on the spot in an act of cruel revenge.

On this occasion, for the first time, Gaspar de Portolá felt the kind of humiliation of which his uncle Don Nicolas and his father had spoken — that of having been denied the right to speak out because of the peculiar position in which any member of the Catalonian nobility would find itself while serving the king of Spain. He was to experience this same feeling many times in the course of his career and all through his lifetime.

Finally the war ended to the great relief of Portolá. In 1748 a treaty was signed restoring peace in Italy. His first war experience had been a great disappointment to Portolá, and he carried this disillusionment for a long time in his demeanor. Even some of his military commanders noticed and reproached him for such an attitude. They were unable to identify the cause of his obvious apathy, and they interpreted it as lack of ambition. They lamented audibly that a military man with such qualifications should shun excellent opportunities to advance when others with less merit made off with the glories and awards.

After a short campaign in Provende — where the only personal profit Portolá derived was that of making a valuable friendship with Marquis de Mina — Gaspar de Portolá, now lieutenant of Dragoons and Grenadiers of Numancia, returned to Barcelona where he was to remain for several years.

Chapter Five

By 1762, the Spanish dominions overseas were in serious danger of falling into the hands of the English. During the seventeenth century France had been the great enemy of Spain, but in the eighteenth century, after the enthronement of the House of Bourbon on the peninsula, England became Spain's irreconcilable enemy. As England gradually became more and more the "mistress of the sea," Spain found herself forced to take defensive measures in all matters directly or indirectly related to America. Under the weak monarchs of the Hapsburg House, present conditions would no doubt have caused the loss of some of the Spanish colonies in America, but in the Bourbons England found an aggressive and tenacious contender, not only equal to her in strength, but also capable of standing face to face against her any place in the world. And this she did, daily. Along the Spanish Main and even in the territorial waters of the Spanish colonies themselves, Spanish ships had suffered many humiliations from the British fleet and from the hosts of pirates. Spanish frigates were often stopped and searched and their cargoes confiscated under some ridiculous pretext.

Spain refused to tolerate this any longer. She concerted a joint policy with France against their common enemy — a new modality of action to be added to the already established tactics known as "defensive aggression." For their mutual protection, the two Bourbon crowns, that of France and that of Spain, signed the historically-known "Family Pact" of reciprocal aid in 1761-1762. The first step of the Franco-Spanish union was formal declaration of war against England in 1762. Spain fortified the most important ports in the peninsula and ordered all her ships to sea. In order to deny England any shelter on the Atlantic coast, Charles III ordered the invasion of Portugal, the peninsular kingdom openly allied with Great Britain.

During this time of political agitation, men like Gaspar de Portolá were called again to duty. Hence, Portolá was assigned to a company of the army commanded by Marques de Sarria which was to invade the neighboring kingdom.

The Portuguese campaign was short and resulted in a victory for Spain. The Spanish troops arrived at Ciudad Rodrigo on April 1, 1762, and by the twentieth of the same month they were encamped near Zamora, nine leagues from Miranda de Duero. Marques de Sarria, Lieutenant General and Commander-in-Chief of the Castilian army, completed the plan of attack. Marques de Croix of the Flemish Guards would command an observation army stationed in Galicia to cover the flank and to foil any lateral attack by the British. On April 26 the poorly fortified town of Miranda was to be attacked and it was expected to fall after a short fight. Then the army would advance toward Torre de Moncorvo where bridges would be laid over the Douro in order to be in position for an attack on Almeida, the best fortified town in all Portugal and the key city for the first phase of the campaign. With the conquest of Almeida, Extremadura and Castilla would become totally protected.

On the scheduled date the Spanish army advanced. After the initial skirmishes it became clear that the Portuguese resistance would be more powerful than had been anticipated. Two cavalry regiments, the "Brabante" and the "Ordenes" were sent immediately to reinforce the troops of Marques de Sarria, giving them now the strength of five thousand horsemen.

On June 5 the Spaniards were in possession of Miranda, Braganza, Chaves and Moncorvo in the Province of Tras os Montes. The plan was to take Valencia, Lamego and Porto and thus dominate the Douro River and so be able to count on sea communication with Galicia.

A detachment would attack these towns while the bulk of the army would lay siege to Almeida whose fall would surely involve the capitulation of Portugal and thus end the war.

On June 25, at midnight, the fight started against the well-fortified city. According to intelligence data, the defense of Almeida consisted of a garrison of three thousand men, one thousand of which were regular troops and two thousand militia. There were eighty-two bronze cannon, nine iron cannon, twenty mortars, fifteen grenade throwers, and abundant ammunition and provisions including four hundred and eighty wagons of hay.

The capture of Almeida required a long and fiery fight, but the Portuguese finally capitulated on August 25 at 2:45 in the afternoon with the hoisting of a white flag requesting a truce. The rendition was signed at midnight. The old walls still stood, but the city itself was almost entirely destroyed.

Just as he had done in the campaigns of Italy and Provence, Gaspar de

Portolá distinguished himself at Miranda, Braganza, Moncorvo and on other fields of battle. The cool-headed nobleman fought courageously and with a strict sense of duty, although with just as much aloofness as he had fought in Italy. Gaspar realized during the Portuguese campaign that the scattered Spanish military action in the various European countries was not as disarticulated as he had first thought. He was able to visualize the real political chessboard that Europe was so that he was able to understand that it was necessary sometimes to move a rook or a bishop to a distant position to protect a precariously defended piece. Spain sometimes bled for no apparent purpose in such unlikely places as Lombardy or Piedmont but this bleeding was part of the wide battle for America which was the most important piece they were trying to defend.

Portolá, along with many of his compatriots, could not understand this game for the simple reason that America had been a myth for them for such a long time. Now, at last, America was something real and tangible for Portolá, a little bit his own. For this reason the courageous military man felt a certain pride in accomplishment which he had not felt at the end of the other campaigns.

The lifting of the ban on Catalonian's participation in America, had overtaken some of his compatriots who for the first time had realized the American reality. That very year the Catalonian Miquel Boix had organized with his private means, a company of twelve hundred Catalonian volunteers, later to be known as *Primer Regimiento de Infantería Ligera de Cataluña,* which was to cross the Atlantic to serve in the New World.

A few years later, in 1767, another company of free troops of Catalonia was to sail for Nueva España (Mexico) under the command of Pere Fages. Other important individuals or groups (navigators, engineers, missionaries and military men) would leave the Catalonian Territories, the Principality, Valencia and the Baliaric Islands to contribute to the colonization of America. Among the navigators was the Majorcan Joan Perés who was to become famous for discovering and exploring the island of Nutka in the North Pacific in 1773; and the noted mapmaker and engineer Miguel Costansó, who was to establish the maps for many still unexplored regions, and who would distinguish himself by the construction of the important drains of Lake Texcoco in the Valley of Mexico.

Other Catalonian organizers of joint expeditions like Vicens Oliver, a ship-builder or Tossa de Mar, who fitted out two vessels for sailing to Honduras in 1702, had a more realistic and utilitarian idea of America, certainly more practical than that of the typical Andalusian or Extremenian *conquistadores* who had gone to the New World only for glory and personal adventure. The Catalonians, master in the art of commerce since time immemorial, dreamed of creating in America institutions like those of the famous British and Dutch Indian companies which were to produce such practical result later on other continents. Portolá's countrymen understood that colonization consisted of development of resources, exchange of products and a general creation of material well-being rather than dependence on the predominance of the "sword and the cross."

This practice had been followed for two centuries in the Mediterranean islands and territories (such as Sardina, Sicily, and Naples) where the Catalonian-Aragonian flag had flown temporarily. From long experience, they knew that commerce was also an excellent way to foment the exchange of ideas, laws and customs which is the essence of a liberal and democratic civilization.

As the news of the victory in Portugal reached Madrid, great popular festivities were organized; people celebrated the happy event with real joy. The king signed promotions and personally decorated many of the officers who had taken place in the campaign. Suddenly, however, the general happiness was turned into frustration with the arrival of the news of a catastrophe on the coasts of America. The daring and impudence of the British navy had gone so far as not only to seize Pensacola in Florida, but also to surround the island of Cuba with a number of vessels under the command of Admiral Pocock, who had succeeded in landing in force in Havana.

The daring act of the British was considered disastrous for the Spanish Crown since Cuba constituted the key to all the Spanish possessions in America. The coup stunned all of Spain. The British had secretly been preparing this action and had shrewdly maneuvered the ships, foreseeing the inevitable hostilities with Spain. Distance caused Carlos III's orders to be long delayed in arriving so the lightning attack of the British was an appalling surprise to the island authorities since they had never been warned to take precautions against an eventual attack of such a daring nature.

The British found Havana practically undefended: however, Governor Juan Prado heroically resisted the British onslaught for twenty-five days. Finally he was forced to capitulate. The booty was even more than the British had anticipated — besides the gold in storage awaiting a ship for its transfer to the peninsula, Admiral Pocock seized nine regular ships equipped with sixty cannon, and three smaller frigates anchored in the bay.

The news of the terrible misfortune in the Caribbean was soon topped by the no-less-alarming news that the British had taken the important city of Manila and the port of Cavite in the Phillipines. At the same time it was learned that British ships had seized a galleon on the high seas which had sailed from Acapulco transporting gold and silver ingots worth three million pesos to Spain.

All this alarming news aroused extreme indignation and unleashed violent demonstrations of hatred against the British. The Spanish populace demanded war to the death against Great Britain. Even the most moderate became inflamed with patriotism. Public demands were to take the war to the very doors of the United Kingdom.

Thanks to the decisive intervention of France, no open declaration of war was made. On the contrary, on February 4, 1763 a tripartite peace treaty was signed between France and Spain on one side and England on the other. The treaty was signed in Versailles, and through it France and Britain returned to one another many of the territories they had previously taken. Louis XV returned the Dominion of Canada to the King of England with its capital Quebec and its famous fishery at Cape Breton in Terranova which had been developed to compete with Norway.

Charles III of Spain ceded the Spanish possessions north, south and east of the Mississippi (Florida) to the King of England. In return, England returned the island of Cuba to Spain on condition that the Spanish troops evacuate Portugal and return its territory to it. The treaty was executed immediately.

Chapter Six

We rejoin our hero where we left him in 1764, in placid and beautiful Barcelona, where he was waging far-from-bloody battles with such adversaries as Ensign Ruiz Mendez for positions so little fortified as the heart of Lucia.

When Gaspar de Portolá's rival, Ensign Mendez, hurt by Lucia's contempt, asserted that the handsome lieutenant of dragoons was incapable of loving a woman seriously, he was badly informed. The aristocratic officer from Balaguer had acquired a well-deserved fame as an incurable Don Juan. His love adventures were notorious, and he was surrounded by a legend of innumerable would-be seductions. A short while ago, however, although secretly, a notable change had taken place in his romantic behavior and in his philosophy of love. Finally, he had actually and truly fallen in love, possibly for the first time.

Gaspar himself honestly admitted that now his intentions were truly honorable, and his recent deeds seemed to confirm such commendable purposes. The clear proof of this would seem to be the fact of finding him kneeling before the image of the Holy Virgin which stood in the altar of the little church annexed to the historical Monastery of Pedralbes near Portolá's residence on the outskirts of Barcelona. It was generally known that the young officer had never been prone to religious practice and to acts of devotion. In fact, in religious matters he was known to be entirely indifferent, if not an agnostic.

On that day, however, there he was kneeling before a church altar, head bent in apparent devotion and as though in prayer. But he was not praying at all; through the corner of his eye, through a lateral window of the church, he was watching the main entrance to the monastery. There, by the heavy wooden and metal peg door, stood Vincent, Portolá's valet, ringing the bell for the purpose of carrying out a very delicate errand for his master. Presently a soft, high-pitched voice of a nun behind the door was heard.

"Ave Maria Purisima..."

"Good morning, Sister," Vincent responded piously. And handing over a small package, he added, "For Señorita Elisa de Siscar. Her father sends it."

Gaspar, inside the church, smiled enigmatically, satisfied with the initial success of his scheme.

Inside the convent, which was at the same time a most exclusive boarding school where the girls of the high society of Barcelona received a prudent and cautious education, the nun delivered the package to Elisa, one of these girl boarders. At the moment she was in her room with her room mate, Juanita. She opened the package excitedly.

"Oh!" she exclaimed on opening it and seeing its contents, "Father is always afraid that my feet will get cold in bed."

The nun smiled tenderly and withdrew.

"How strange!" said Elisa while examining the pair of heavy woolen socks. "Father is coming to see me tomorrow, and he could have brought the package himself!"

Juanita, suspicious, put her hand inside one of the heavy socks, and as she had suspected, found a message. Elisa grabbed it. She opened the little piece of paper, and while reading it she almost fainted. It was signed "Gaspar de Portolá."

Juanita took the note, and read it aloud: "Señorita Elisa, since the day I saw you at your father's home last time, I have been thinking of you constantly. I must talk to you urgently — tonight. Please arrange to be at the rear gate grille of the garden at ten o'clock. Your most devoted admirer — Gaspar de Portolá."

Juanita screamed with excitement. Elisa tried to stifle the shriek lest the nun might hear.

"What does all this mean?" asked Elisa, frightened.

"He loves you! Can't you see?" shouted Juanita.

Elisa glanced over the words once more. She felt that her heart was weakening.

"What shall I do?" she asked weakly.

"Go and talk to him, of course!" retorted Juanita immediately.

"Talk to him? Are you crazy?"

Juanita began planning all the details of the great adventure, arranging the tryst between her friend and Gaspar for that night. Elisa spent the day worrying and trembling. How could she sneak out to the rear grating of the convent at night and meet a man? Juanita was truly crazy.

Elisa was the only daughter of Don Oleguer de Siscar, the Chief Justice of the Barcelona Audiencia and head of a family whom Gaspar de Portolá visited regularly. Gaspar had known Elisa since she was a child. Since she had been in the boarding school, the young officer had not seen her for some time, but one day Elisa's monthly visit to her parents coincided with one of Portolá's visits. Astonished, he found himself before a most charming young lady with the bearing of an angel and with golden curls framing an innocent face.

Gaspar could not explain the miracle, but he was deeply impressed. He took special care not to betray his inner feelings, however, although the image of the young beauty could not be obliterated from his mind easily. As he had written in his message, he thought about her constantly.

Elisa remembered Gaspar de Portolá as seen with the dazzled eyes of an infant. Her most permanent image was the magnificence of the dragoon's uniform and the ominous long sword the tall lieutenant was carrying. Through her classmates Elisa had heard of the reputation for gallantry that Gaspar enjoyed, and she had witnessed the admiration for the amorous man which some of the girls who were more precocious than she were displaying. All this had added to the childish image she had of him — an aura of perversity and sin. She remembered, of course, the last time she had seen Portolá at her parent's home, but she had not noticed any difference in his demeanor from other previous visits, hence the great surprise at the note she had received at the convent. Was it like this, like a thunderbolt, that first love strikes?

That night, shortly before ten o'clock, urged on by the excited Juanita, Elisa reluctantly sneaked through the shadows of the rear garden of the convent toward the back grille. Gaspar had just arrived, punctually, at the other side of the gate.

While Juanita was watching for any extemporaneous approach of the nun along the inner corridor, Vincent was holding the two horses and covering the rear guard of his master lest the night watchman pop up to foil the clandestine idyllic activity.

"I love you, Elisa," Gaspar kept saying to the terrified school girl. "Say something, please! Can I hope to gain a little place in your heart?"

Elisa would not answer because she could not. She felt the presence of that famous officer of dragoons before her and could not believe it. Many ladies of high society had been sighing for just such a happening, but she felt only embarrassment and fear. She fumbled with the chain of a small religious medal she was wearing, only wondering how she could escape. Discreetly Portolá took hold of the suspended medal as if to examine it; the clasp broke and the medal fell loose into his hand. Gaspar kissed it and asked, "Can I keep it as a token?"

Elisa could find no words. She could only breathe hastily, "I must go!"

As a final request, with deep emotion, the lieutenant asked uselessly, "Won't you give me some hope, Elisa?" Realizing her youth, and the reason for the lack of an answer, he added, "You do not need to give me an answer tonight. Think it over. As for now, just promise me that you will give me the opportunity to see you soon. Promise me that you'll attend the Spring Ball at the Captaincy General on Easter Eve, in two weeks, with your parents. Then you can answer me. Then we can talk. Will you promise me that?"

Elisa promised nothing; her heart was in turmoil.

At a short distance from the convent Vincent was in some sort of trouble with the night watchman. He tried to get rid of him by alleging that he was walking the two horses on his way from the livery stable to pick up his master. The man continued on his beat, but suspiciously. As agreed, Vincent whistled through his fingers to make known to his master that it was time to go. Elisa and Gaspar parted, she leaving as upset as when she came; he, elated and dreamy.

The Spring Ball at the Captaincy General was the most talked-about event of the year. Many things were expected to occur during the course of that night, especially things related to love and marriage. When the great event came, however, things did not seem to get started. The bright lights of the huge candelabra in the vast salon were lighted, but there was an air of general expectancy. Maybe it was because handsome Lieutenant Gaspar de Portolá had not yet arrived in spite of the fact that even the captain general and all the "brass" were there.

Lucia was dancing with Ensign Ruiz Mendez, but she was obviously more interested in watching the door than in her partner's gallantries. A group of girls were commenting on the absence of Don Gaspar, and the wildest and most scandalous suppositions were being made because of his absence.

When Don Gaspar finally arrived there was genuine commotion. The popular lieutenant was wearing the colorful uniform of the dragoons and attracted everyone's attention. He was immediately surrounded by the ladies. He was polite to everyone but advanced resolutely to pay his respects and to present his excuses to the captain general and his charming wife who reproached him gently for keeping everybody wondering and waiting. Everyone laughed at his witty excuses and adroitness. Even the Captain General, the Marquis de Mina, a friend and protector of the lieutenant since they had become friends during the Provence campaign, smiled amusedly at the tall story Gaspar improvised to excuse his delayed appearance.

Only Gaspar knew the reason for his delay. Even after he was dressed and ready to start for the Ball, the lieutenant continued until the last minute awaiting a messenger from Elisa. If her answer were no, his attending the ball would become a mere formality. For the past two weeks, day after day, both Gaspar, as a man in love, and Vincent as his faithful servant had been expectant about the arrival of the important message. The heavy iron door knocker, however, had remained still and mute. Thwarted by this new kind of personal failure to which he was not accustomed, Gaspar composed himself, donned once more his usual nonchalant air, and appeared at the annual great ball.

After having complimented the captain general and his wife, Portolá walked across the shining parquet with definite destination in mind. The captain general could not help thinking as he did persistently that Portolá was cut out for a brilliant military and political career if he would but express such a desire.

When Gaspar first entered the large hall a quick glance had sufficed for him to locate the loge where Don Oleguer de Siscar's family, without Elisa, was seated. Now he walked directly to the loge. The venerable and stately silhouette of Don Oleguer cut an imposing figure as became a Chief Justice. Next to him was Doña Amalia, Elisa's mother, and her spinster aunt Lucrecia. Casually, he asked about Elisa.

"She is already a beautiful young lady. She should be present at the ball tonight," he commented.

"Elisa does not seem to enjoy these social gatherings; she is shy and withdrawn," explained Doña Amalia. "Besides, she is so pious — she feels so happy at the convent.."

Later, while dancing with Aunt Lucrecia, Don Gaspar learned that Elisa was planning to become a nun. The news was a great blow to him, and he could hardly conceal his feelings. Kindheartedly, Lucrecia, who could not suspect that Don Gaspar was in love with her niece, praised Lucia — such a nice girl!

"Take her out to dance!" Lucrecia insisted, "She is pining for you!"

Gaspar promised. "Why not?" he exclaimed jovially, "even if it means I may risk my life at the hands of jealous Ensign Mendez!" He laughed.

The next dance was the formal "lanceros", a sort of quadrille or square dance — Spanish minuet during which the ladies had an opportunity to maneuver and get close to their preferred partner. Lucia succeeded in getting rid of the persistent Mendez and to secure Gaspar de Portolá for herself. Barely had the "lanceros" ended when Lucia manuevered Gaspar to the terrace. There she put all her flirtatious art to play. She let him guess that she had sent him her garter in advance — just as a hint. Gaspar took her pleading lightly and showed coolness until Lucia began to mix her sweetness with bitterness and, to his great surprise, told him that she knew all about his being in love with Elisa whom she laughingly called a "silly school girl."

In the stag line in the meantine some young officers were making fun of poor Ruiz Mendez who had been so pitifully deserted by Lucia. During this innocent fun an elderly character of indefinite rank approached the young officers and secretly suggested to them the idea of playing a practical joke on Mendez. He had the right item. He invited them to follow him into one of the adjacent rooms. The officers gleefully welcomed the opportunity.

In the secluded room, the joker produced a lady's garter. "It belongs to Lucia," he explained. "Apparently she sent it to Gaspar as a quite eloquent invitation!" Then he lied, "I just picked it up from the ground in the terrace; Portolá must have dropped it!"

Laughing in anticipation, the officers in their eagerness for fun did not waste a moment in going to play the practical joke on irascible Mendez, without measuring the possible implications. The reaction of the young ensign on learning of this latest treason from Lucia and malicious offense from Portolá was so violent that the young officers were frightened. Ruiz Mendez dashed across the ballroom toward Gaspar to demand an explanation or to challenge him to a duel.

On the terrace, however, Mendez found Lucia alone, crying, "He does not love me, the ungrateful one!" She whined, "He has just told me in plain words to my face!"

Without listening, Mendez asked in a menacing voice, "Where is he?"

"I don't know! He left me here alone! He disappeared. He probably went home," she cried.

The fiery ensign dashed to the hall, stopped just long enough to claim his gloves and hat and sped toward the General Captaincy.

Meanwhile the remorseful officers who had played the heavyhanded practical joke stood almost frightened at the dance hall, aware suddenly of the consequences their foolery might bring about. One of them, losing courage or feeling morally concerned, suggested approaching the captain general's adjutant and confessing their reproachful behavior in order to avoid the scandal and the possible duel which could ensue. The rest of the officers, however, less sensitive or incapable of such gallantry lent only a deaf ear and waited the end of the ball to leave and to wait for the next morning's developments.

The next day, toward noon, Gaspar de Portolá was greatly surprised to receive a call from an infantry lieutenant and a captain of grenadiers, both friends of his, who with macabre seriousness announced that they were calling on him in their capacity as seconds for Ensign Ruiz Mendez. They invited him to choose weapons and the place to settle on the field of honor the offense perpetrated by him against their patron.

At first Gaspar took the entire thing as a joke and laughed heartily at the comical farce his friends, he thought, were staging. The seconds, however, stayed completely "dead pan" serious, and as the only explanation, one of them took from his breast-buttoned coat the already famous garter with pink ribbons belonging to Lucia.

Gaspar began to understand, and he found the entire idea even funnier. He was about to burst into still louder laughter when he began to realize that he had nothing to do with that garter. On asking where or how they had gotten the item, one of the seconds accused Gaspar of having lost it the night before at the Spring Ball — hence, the offense.

Not so to excuse himself as to obtain personal satisfaction, Gaspar asked the seconds to wait a moment. He went to his writing table where he should find the garter he had received from Lucia. After a thorough search, to no avail, Gaspar decided that this too must be part of a large-scale farce, and that he had no choice but to follow along with all seriousness, at least in appearance, until he could discover the entire plot, and at the same time derive some amusement along the way.

Thus, with utmost earnestness, Portolá adopted the same funeral countenance of the seconds and stated the terms of the duel:

Nature of the encounter: to the death!

Weapons: fire arms

Time and day: the following Friday, May 13, at dawn.

Place: the summit of the Saint Peter Martyr Mountain.

The seconds, on hearing the harsh terms became terrified, and on learning the place selected were astonished. One of them dared to object, "St. Peter Martyr's peak is almost inaccessible! It must be climbed by foot; no horse can set its hooves on it!"

"Precisely!" specified Portolá, simulating extreme severity, "the honor of a lady is involved and the hardest sacrifice is insignificant! Besides," he added with a touch of genial humor, "the greatest sacrifice will be on my part, since your patron in remaining dead on the field at the top of the mountain, will be spared the hardships of the return trip downhill."

When the seconds left, Portolá had to throw himself on the sofa in a fit of laughter.

On Friday, May 13, at four o'clock in the morning, at the first streak of the new day's light, the scene of the duel was complete with all details and appropriate dramatics. The seconds of both parties and the mandatory doctor had demanded and fulfilled rigoriously all requirements and formalities.

On one side, Ensign Ruiz Mendez, fuming with indignation and because of the long, arduous climb up the mountain, was standing erect and proud twenty paces away from his adversary. Opposite him, Gaspar de Portolá, also heated by the steep ascent, but cool as a cucumber in spirit, was also standing, pistol in hand, enjoying the proceedings of the high-handed tragicomedy.

When one of the seconds, after the required consultation as to whether or not a reconciliation were possible, was making himself ready to proceed with the ordering of the ritual of the duel and the command to fire, shouting in the distance from a newcomer to the scene of the duel stopped the fatal words. An emissary from the palace of the captain general had just appeared at the summit, and bathed in perspiration and out of breath was shouting for them to stop the duel while brandishing an official paper in his hand. The messenger had arrived at the precise moment for which Portolá and his seconds had pre-arranged.

The elder of the seconds snatched the paper from the hand of the messenger and read it aloud. It was a communication from the captain general which read: "By order of his Excellency the captain general for the province, I hereby order the officers of the Barcelona garrison, the Lieutenant of Dragoons of Numancia, Don Gaspar de Portolá i Revira and the Ensign of Infantry of the Royal Regiment, Don Felix Ruiz Mendez, to suspend the illegitimate duel concerted between them and to appear immediately before me at this General Captaincy. Signed — The Adjutant."

In the face of this communication, the duel was *ipso facto* suspended. Portolá had to make great efforts not to laugh at the well carried-out stratagem. Ruiz Mendez persisted in his grotesque attitude of offended man.

For a moment, Portolá felt bound to go directly to his blinded adversary to offer him his hand and explain sincerely. Ruiz Mendez, however, guessed Portolá's intentions and, arrogantly turned his back and walked toward the rock where his coat and other parts of his uniform were lying after being discarded for the duel.

Portolá's first reaction was to let Mendez go, and to forget him as a fool, but compassion moved him to persist in his initial intention. So, accompanied by one of his seconds, he went toward the frowning ensign and offered him his hand sincerely. Ruiz Mendez refused to shake it.

Adopting a position of superiority, Portolá requested his second to explain to Mendez how the misunderstanding had occurred and the playful conspiracy of which both had been victims. The second faithfully related the facts that had motivated the offense and the duel. He explained that Portolá's friends had removed Lucia's garter from a drawer of his writing table, and had used it to stage the despicable joke. Portolá was the first to lament it, and was begging the pardon of Ruiz Mendez.

Mendez remained inflexible to the point where Gaspar felt like giving him a friendly slap. The second continued to insist on the explanation, but did not attain a sign of reconciliation.

Portolá by now was truly offended, momentarily, of course, by the childish stubbornness of his opponent. He was already speculating on some way to lead him into reason, even if it meant playing another trick on him. While the second continued to plead to no avail, Ruiz Mendez continued dressing slowly with deliberate fastidiousness, donning piece by piece the parts of his uniform. Gaspar noticed that on the ground, next to a rock, the gold watch and chain belonging to Mendez were lying. Eureka! thought Portolá, and with a slight, hidden movement of his foot, he pushed the gold watch and chain under the rock where it could not be noted.

All efforts for a cordial reconciliation having failed, once the ensign had finished dressing, the party undertook the return downhill, by foot, along the steep mountain. During the difficult descent, Mendez no doubt had time enough to reconsider the whole matter and to admit that Portolá was not to blame, but, proud by nature, he would not give in and continued in his sullen mood.

When, an hour and a half later, the expedition reached the foot of the hill under the already scorching sun, Portolá approached one of the seconds who was walking next to Ruiz Mendez and asked, "What time is it?"

"I cannot tell you. I have no watch."

Ruiz Mendez, already a little placated by the toil of the long walk, agreed to give the time to his rival. Suddenly, however, feeling the breast pocket of his jacket, he exclaimed, "I've lost my gold watch!"

Everyone stopped. The alarmed officer searched all his pockets, and, of course, did not find the watch.

"I've lost it," he repeated.

"Are you sure you wore it?" asked one of the seconds.

"I am sure. I removed it from my pocket before the duel."

"How was it?" asked Portolá, feigning indifference.

"Made of gold — with its chain!" Mendez replied quickly, before becoming suspicious immediately.

With great aplomb, Portolá asserted calmly, "Yes, you wore it. I saw it lying on the ground by the rock where you were dressing. You must have forgotten it up there."

Ruiz Mendez, accompanied by his reluctant seconds, had to undertake the arduous trek up the hill to the top of Saint Peter Martyr Mountain where the frustrated duel was to have taken place. In the meantime, Portolá and his retinue mounted on well-rested horses which Vincent had waiting at the foot of the hill, laughing at the witty and exemplary punishment inflicted on the stubborn officer by Gaspar, proceeded toward the still-slumbering Barcelona, which was unaware of the picaresque comedy that had just taken place in its suburbs.

Chapter Seven

There was an explanation for Elisa's absence from the Springtime Ball at the Captaincy General. This explanation, however, was neither simple nor concrete since nothing is either simple or concrete in matters of love. A storm in the human heart always results in a complexity of indefinable elements.

On the night of the furtive meeting of Gaspar de Portolá and the timid school girl at the rear grille of the convent garden, Elisa had found herself overwhelmed by a conflagration. Her heart had lost its normal beat and her mind all its coordination.

After that first meeting when Juanita, her roommate, welcomed her with the impatience of a protective accomplice, Elisa barely heard the tumultuous and excited questions of her friend. Stunned, she walked instinctively toward her own room without looking elsewhere. She flung herself onto the bed face downward, hiding her head under her arms, ashamed and in tears.

Juanita, in spite of the irrepressible curiosity that urged her, ceased her questioning and smiled patronizingly at the inexperience of her young roommate. She began to undress. In the morning she would extract all the details from Elisa.

That night Elisa could not close her eyes in sleep. She felt as though she were shipwrecked in a sea of confusion. She tried vainly to set some order in the tumult of emotions that assailed her. She tried many times to analyze how she really felt, but to no avail. Was she flattered to have been able to inspire the love of such a consummate lover as Gaspar? Should she respond to such intense courting? Did she want the love of that gallant man? She simply did not know.

A kind of strange fear that Elisa felt prompted her to answer all the above questions in the negative. Then, after thinking awhile, she asked herself if she truly did not want any part of that love, why was she so terribly disturbed?

In a brief lucid moment, Elisa succeeded in calming her emotions and in letting her mind command. She concluded that, as clear as the light of day, her heart was inclined to accede to Don Gaspar's pleas, if only for the pleasure of delighting in the romantic proposal — after all, she was a girl!

But then, there were moral considerations; even if it were true that she welcomed that romance, was it really correct to accept and encourage it? Prejudice and a sense of fright urged her to answer no. In the first place, there was a great difference of age between them. Secondly, there was Gaspar's reputation as a worldly love-maker — this fact alone was enough to make the elegant lieutenant appear sinful in her eyes.

Finally, toward morning and between consideration of the alternatives of her plight, Elisa fell asleep only to awaken twice because of monstrous nightmares. At dawn, the tormented school girl finally slept out of exhaustion.

When the reveille bell rang, Elisa found it hard to awaken. Juanita watched her carefully. She wanted to catch any of Elisa's reactions, but Elisa avoided her searching look. Cautious and understanding, Juanita respected her friend's attitude and postponed her interrogation for a more opportune time.

For most of the morning Elisa remained silent, although she was obviously unusually nervous. It was Sunday and Juanita decided that there would be time enough to be alone and to talk after mass at the chapel. She would manage some way to make Elisa more communicative.

After mass, however, Elisa did not appear for breakfast. Juanita sat at a table with two other girls, wrapped in thought.

Shortly before lunch, Juanita, who had spent most of the morning anxiously waiting and watching from the window in their room for her friend, finally saw Elisa coming toward the dormitory building. She was approaching slowly with her head bent and with her prayer book and rosary held tightly against her breast.

As Elisa entered, Juanita cried impatiently, "Elisa where have you been? I need so much to talk to you!"

Elisa replied calmly, "I went to confession with Father Alonso."

"Was it really so urgent? Friday is the last day of the month and we'll have general communication and confession. Couldn't you wait until then?" Juanita asked.

"My conscience wasn't at ease, Juanita."

"Because of last night's tryst?"

"I felt myself in mortal sin," muttered Elisa, lowering her eyes.

"Just for talking to Gaspar de Portolá?"

"Yes — secret date with a man — he touched my hand — he almost kissed me."

"Is there anything wrong with that? If he loves you — "

"I wanted to get advice from my confessor."

"I can well imagine what Father Alonso's advice was! Don't you really like Gaspar?"

Elisa took a while to answer. "I don't know. Maybe too much — that's why I wanted some advice."

"You are a dumbbell! I could have given you much better advice. What can you expect a monk to say?"

"He has been very understanding."

"Did you tell him that the man in question is Gaspar de Portolá?"

"Yes."

"Then you really made a mistake! Father Alonso will spoil everything for you. His first move will be to go and tell your parents."

"It doesn't matter. Portolá himself told me that he would speak to my father."

"So — then his intentions are honorable! Ah, hah!"

"He wants me to attend the Spring Ball at the Captaincy General, to announce our betrothal there."

"What in the world are you afraid of then? I envy your luck, Elisa."

After a moment of reticence, the prudent school girl confessed, "I'm going to make use of such luck, if it is luck, I can tell you now. Quite awhile ago I decided to become a nun. I already have told father Alonso."

"You crazy girl! To become a nun! That's a childish malady we all go through when we enter this college. You'll overcome it. Don't rush into any decisions. You're too young yet. The only girls who don't recover from this illness are the ugly ones. Neither you nor I will run that risk. You'll have no trouble finding suitors. Here you have the proof — no less than Don Gaspar de Portolá himself!"

"Don't make me laugh!" cried Elisa, smiling in spite of herself.

"Do you want my advice, Elisa?" asked Juanita with her characteristic vivacity, "Forget all this nunnish silliness and don't speak to Father Alonso any more."

In spite of the "understanding" which the shrewd confessor had appeared to have in advising the troubled Elisa, he did not waste any time in making a serious study of the implications of the marriage proposal made by Gaspar de Portolá. The zealous reverend began the necessary research to make certain that the notorious lieutenant of dragoons was a suitable mate for the only daughter of the honorable family of Don Oleguer de Siscar.

Although the frightened Elisa had assured Father Alonso most sincerely that she did not wish to marry Don Gaspar de Portolá or any other man, the cautious monk had interpreted the denial as clear evidence that she really wanted to marry the gallant military man. Before talking to her family, however, Father Alonso wanted to obtain every bit of evidence possible in order to be able to recommend or discourage the eventual marriage. First, the zealous Dominican monk must carefully check the ascendancy and family line of the notorious nobleman from Belaguer. Then he would state his verdict for the consideration of the firm believer and devout Catholic, Justice Don Oleguer de Siscar, whose confessor and spiritual adviser he was also.

Father Alonso knew that Gaspar de Portolá was not a fervent believer and that in matters of romance, if one were to believe the general opinion, he was not a man to be trusted, and, quite frankly, should probably be considered to be an unscrupulous seducer. However, this was, after all, only hearsay. The matter was important enough, Father Alonso thought, to take the trouble to go by his own standards and to tap the most authentic sources of information.

The religious order to which Elisa's confessor belonged traditionally specialized in this sort of investigation. Since the year 1214 when Saint Domingo de Guzman founded it under the name of the Holy Predication, the Dominican Order had been entrusted almost exclusively with the administration of the Holy Inquisition. Even at that time, the Order was the custodian of the secret historical files of the Holy Office. It was precisely to these files, so stubbornly kept, that Father Alonso resorted in order to investigate Elisa's suitor.

For two full weeks the methodical Dominican eagerly searched through hundreds of pages of ancient documents, dockets of old papers and regularly classified archives, although in the papers of the Holy Tribunal he failed to find any reference to the Portolá family. To be doubly sure, he personally consulted the curator of the Archives of the Bishopric of Barcelona and those of the Bishopric of Urgall, the diocese to which the Portolás belonged, for more recent references. These inquiries were also without result.

Ultimately, the untiring investigator made a search into the historic Annals of the Nobility. Upon arriving at the Portolá heading, Father Alonso was startled to discover the family name enigmatically marked with the strange sign ⍦ . If no other written indication made allusion to the traditional religious belief of the Portolás, this ominous anathema was sufficient to suggest to the rigid Dominican what he had suspected and had wanted to learn all along. From that very moment, with the discovery of the mysterious H with the inverted cross, although he did not know its meaning, he considered his investigation successfully concluded. In his mind, he was definitely resolved that the marriage between the nobleman Don Gaspar de Portolá i Rovira and the only daughter of the Catholic Justive Don Obeguer de Siscar would never be allowed to take place.

Gaspar, of course, was not to learn about these subterranean machinations to make his wedding with this angelic sweetheart impossible — that sweetheart to whose unique beauty and candor he was more and more fevently devoted. He could not obliterate from his mind for a single hour the glittering image of Elisa. If he failed to sense her presence for a moment, the token he had received from her, the small gold medal of the Virgin which he kept always near his heart, was enough to return his thoughts immediately to his love.

Gaspar had left the exciting nocturnal meeting at the convent garden grille almost as deeply moved as Elisa was. The clandestine meeting under the benevolent mantle of night had turned out to be a chaste brief idyll which was to mark the tumultuous shadowy way of his amorous adventure like a shining white stone.

That night, the sensuous lieutenant of dragoons lay awake until dawn on one of the sofas in his studio. The emotion he felt was so alien to him, so intense, so pure and so different from that he had felt with other women that he did not dare fall asleep lest the entire image dissolve into a dream.

Portolá confessed to himself sincerely that truly and in fact this was the first time he had ever really fallen in love. For some strange reason, his memory returned to his early youth when he was still a flighty lad in his native Balaguer, and to the cheerful image of Annette, the youthful daughter of the innkeeper of the "Lilac Grove," the first feminine creature to stir his youthful heart. Of course, Gaspar had never considered his naive sentiment toward the lively Annette as his first love, but, curiously enough, the atmosphere surrounding his childish wooing of Annette had some similarity to the scene of his first meeting with Elisa.

The idyll had flowered, as had the earlier affair, near a historical and almost legendary monastery — later both were to be secularized as though to prevent the eventual romantic adventures of Don Gaspar from seeming a kind of sacrilegious profanation. In both cases the predominant emotion had been the naive candor of all platonic love. Even so, his flirting with the innocent Annette might be considered the authentic forerunner of the impetuous adventures which, as an emulator of d'Artagnan, Gaspar had carried on with so many ladies of rank and so many hostelry maids he had met along the tortuous roads of his life.

But with Elisa it was different. Now, in full maturity as a lover, at the height of his agressive virility, Gaspar was once again feeling the naivete of a boy. Before Elisa he had lost all initiative, as though his learned art of seduction had come to nothing. His heart was stirred by intense and pure emotion!

Since his first evening meeting with Elisa, a complete change had taken place in Gaspar's life. He began to look at his entire scale of values in a new light. Matters which formerly had appeared to him to be fundamental to the secret of good living now seemed almost laughable trivialities. His heart was now concerned about an ideal that was the true essence of life.

Only three days after this admitted transformation, a great doubt assailed the consummate lover. Suddenly he became alarmed. What if Elisa should reject his love? The chasm of silence that kept Elisa far from him was intolerable torture. He decided to send her a new message, again through a stratagem suggested by Vincent.

Once the message was on its way — a message in which Gaspar reiterated his honorable intentions — the fiery lover felt reassured once again. He was confident of winning the battle.

Several days went by in silence. Gaspar persisted in sending other messages which ran the gamut of amorous exaltation. Occasionally he felt lucky at having found a resistance in his beloved. Bored with too many easy conquests, Elisa's resistance excited him tremendously. Now he considered the struggle for Elisa's love the most exciting adventure of his life. Returning to his youthful romantic spirit, he imagined Elisa as the captive princess who was to be rescued. The enterprise was worthy of a gallant cavalier such as he. Maybe the moment had come to make the strong motto of his coat of arms come true. In the heraldic escutcheon there was written, "King or Nothing!"

Gaspar felt certain that he could become king in the heart of Elisa. He was so convinced of gaining this idealistic kingdom that he had stopped thinking about any other woman or romantic adventure. At the same time he had put far back in his mind any idea of ambition or any plan concerning his promising military career. He had come to the conclusion that his true object and his only ambition in life would be to become a happy man at the side of Elisa.

This new philosophy and attitude was obvious in all his behavior. His friends were astonished to notice that for no apparent reason, Gaspar showed complete disinterest in matters that had excited him formerly. In the regular weekly gatherings of friends which took place in the residence of the worldly captain, there now reigned a strange disconcert.

At that time, in the active civic and military centers of Barcelona, America was a predominant topic. The secret or openly confessed idea of going to the New World, in those quiet and monotonous days, was the true aim of almost the entire rank of young officers in the king's army. When one of his colleagues mentioned the name of America with excitement, Gaspar de Portolá scarcely reacted. When the excited officer, also the scion of a local noble family, commented, "Now with the new regulations of King Charles III, the Catalonians will be able to participate in the colonization of America!" Portolá retorted:

"We have participated in it since its discovery!" and with his usual jovial air which left people uncertain as to his seriousness, he added, "I personally am almost convinced that Columbus was a Catalonian!"

"That's a good one!" a young officer laughed heartily.

"No, I am serious." asserted Portolá.

"It's a well-known fact that Columbus was a Genoese!"

"Chicanery!" insisted the nobleman from Balaguer, "there are authentic letters written by his own hand and it is an established historical fact that the great discoverer signed "Colom" in Catalán, and not "Colombo" in Italian, or "Colón" in Spanish. The family name of Colom, which means "dove", is very common throughout the Catalonian speaking lands. It is used frequently in Majorca. I myself know a family with such a name at the delta of the Ebro. I would not be surprised if the great discoverer of America was found to be born in Tortosa or around the Alfacs."

"If it were so, it would then be a greater injustice to have forbidden the Catalonians until now to trade with America," complained the young officer.

Portolá proceeded to round out his thesis: "It is truly ironical that Castile would retain all the glory of this discovery made by a Catalonian. And, truly, without Catalonia maybe the trip itself would never have been accomplished. The funds to finance the expedition were put up by Barcelona. With my own eyes I have seen at the Archives of Saint Jeroni de la Hurtra, an ancient document which literally reads, 'Barcelona furnished to Cristobal Colom the sum of 17 thousand ducats, a loan from Luis de Santangel, accountant for King Ferdinand the Catholic,' the amount which allowed Colom to rig his small fleet to sail to the discovery of America."

"I understand that Queen Isabella sold her jewels to finance the expedition."

"It is another official lie!" asserted Portolá. "When Columbus, disheartened, was on his way back to France to offer his project to King Charles VIII, Lluis de Santangel begged his royal employers not to allow a French monarch to make use of the offer that he understood would bring greatness to the country which undertook it. It was then that Queen Isabella ordered Columbus recalled. But the royal treasury was exhausted at the time because of the extraordinary expenses of the war against the Moorish kingdom of Granada. Columbus declared that he could not defer his trip any longer, and then Isabella offered to sell her jewels, something that Santangel could not allow. He offered to loan the necessary funds; so it was with Catalonian money, found in Barcelona, that on August 3, 1492, Columbus could sail from Palos to the discovery of the New World."

"One thing I don't understand," the young officer said, "is why

Columbus or Colom, would hide his nationality."

"Well," commented Portolá, peevishly, "don't we hide it, you and I, even today, often? From laziness or for convenience, don't you yourself often allow yourself to be taken for a Spaniard, and aren't there other times when you do not dare admit that you are a Catalonian?"

"It is true," the young officer admitted ruefully.

"Well, in the fifteenth century this sad convenience was a necessity. No one has yet found out or imagined what crime or what fears forced Colom to present himself as a Genoese! Keep in mind that those were the times of the Holy Inquisition and fanatic persecutions were the order of the day. If Columbus was really a Genoese, why then didn't he offer his project to his own country, the republic of Genoa, which was then a maritime power while Castile was not?"

Chapter Eight

The duel caused by the celebrated garter of Lucia had resulted in a general scandal. Even though there had been a truce declared between the two contenders, the captain general summoned both Gaspar de Portolá and Ensign Ruiz Mendez to appear before him.

The morning of the appointment, Gaspar met Ruiz Mendez, already leaving, at the entrance to the Captaincy building. "What did the captain general have to say?" he asked, merely to be courteous.

Mendez replied, ill-humoredly, "I don't know what he will want from you, but as for me, I requested to be transferred overseas."

"To America? How interesting!"

"Yes, far from here — and yet it will not be far enough to lose sight of certain people!" Then he continued, sarcastically philosophical, "But life has many ups and downs and I haven't given up the opportunity to settle accounts with you yet."

Gaspar smiled indifferently and disappeared up the wide marble steps.

After Gaspar had been received ceremoniously, the lieutenant of dragoons asked, "Your Excellency desired to talk to me?"

"Yes, Gaspar," said the aging Marquis de Mina, adding, "but I have not called the lieutenant of dragoons of Numancia here, I want to talk to my friend." And rising from behind his shining mahogany, gold-decorated desk, he pointed to one of the sofas, inviting Portolá to sit next to him.

Coming directly to the point without alluding to the duel, the captain general spoke, "I suppose you have read the recent royal regulations referring to America — Have you read them, Gaspar?"

"Yes," Portolá responded, "His majesty proves himself to be very magnanimous toward the Catalonian nobility."

This was exactly what the Marquis de Mina wanted his friend Gaspar to answer; so he charged head-on. "Now it behooves the Catalonian nobles and particularly the military to reply with an equally generous gesture."

Although Portolá had guessed what Mina was aiming at, he kept silent diplomatically. The captain general continued, "America offers enormous possibilities. There is still much to be accomplished, even today, in these virgin territories — particularly for a man like you, Gaspar."

"Why do you talk about me, Excellency. The king has not issued these new regulations especially for me."

"No, of course not, but do you remember, my dear friend, our talks during the campaign in Provence?"

The high military chief paused awaiting in vain a reaction from the captain. All at once, impatient and almost furious, Mina cried, "I can't understand you, Gaspar! At the heat of battle you fight with a bravery no one can surpass. Then, when the time comes for gathering laurels and glory, through neglect or lack of ambition, you allow others less gifted and with fewer merits than you to pick up the rewards! With your exceptional qualities — "

Portolá interrupted, "Please, my dear friend, do not contribute to the legend about my humble person! There is nothing exceptional about me. People are always trying to create heroes!"

"No! People are usually extraordinarily foresighted and always regret watching genuine talent go to waste. It's about time the Barcelona garrison stops being an excellent place to kill time!"

"An hour of tranquility and good living is worth all glories and honors," exclaimed Portolá, relishing every word, but startled by the abruptness and anger with which the captain general got up from the sofa.

Portolá stood and remained standing while the marquis walked back and forth in front of his official desk. Once Mina seemed about to explode verbally, and Portolá prepared to cope with the oncoming tempest, but the next moment the aging marquis composed himself and came close to his old friend.

"Listen, Gaspar, let's talk man to man! It is exactly this *bon vivant* spirit of yours of which I am complaining! It is a charming idea, but sometimes it is suicide, or worse — a cowardice, a treason. There are men who owe themselves more to other men than to themselves, and to the times and the society in which they live. You are one of these. The king needs men with the ability to organize, to lead. Public affairs are not going as they should simply because of the lack of such qualified leaders. Men like you, Gaspar, are the kind our king needs. In the name of His Majesty, I request your cooperation. Think of America, my friend. There is magnificent opportunity for you there. With a little ambition — "

"Ambition for what?" Portolá dared to ask.

"For everything — land, riches, rank."

"My family estate now has lands that a man walking all day long could not cross. My revenues allow me to lead, if not an extravagant life, at least an easy one. As for social position — real or fictitious — I now enjoy as much esteem as any person in the highest public office."

"Do it for Spain. There are still vast territories to colonize, kingdoms to conquer."

"The crown has more kingdoms and colonies than it can handle."

"Do it, then, if nothing else, for personal satisfaction. It's a great feeling to conquer kingdoms if only to present them as a gift to someone."

"Who would thank me?"

"I, your friends, your native land. Do it, if you wish, as a Catalonian."

"A Catalonian conquistador?" laughed Gaspar. "The idea is quite original, but my countrymen despise any conquest made by the sword."

"There are weapons which you can handle much better than any sword — your tact, your *savoir faire*. The era of warriors is passing; we are in a period of diplomacy. sometimes a smile is more powerful than a sword. Ask your lady friends! The Catalonians may not understand your valuable work, and the king may not thank you, but there is something waiting for you personally in America. Go, for personal price, even vanity, if you wish. You can become another Hernan Cortés, another Pizarro — a discoverer of new territories, a great ruler, a viceroy, practically a king, even though it may be without crown or scepter."

During the final part of his speech by the captain general, Portolá could not help feeling flattered, and he didn't stop caressing Elisa's medal which he held between his fingers. The Marquis de Mina's offer was tempting, and if Elisa persisted in her silence, or if she finally refused him —.

The marquis waited for an answer. He watched Gaspar closely, understanding his silence. Portolá would want to think about it.

Gaspar did not want to commit himself. Finally, looking at the medal of the Virgin between his fingers, he replied, "Allow me two weeks to think about it, Excellency."

"Of course, Gaspar. Take all the time you need," exclaimed the captain general cheerfully.

"No. Two weeks only; that's all I'll need. By then I'll give you a yes or no answer."

That same after noon Portolá paid a formal visit to Elisa's father, Justice Don Oleguer de Siscar.

The austere justice was truly surprised to hear the gallant captain declare his love for his daughter and his desire to marry her. The venerable old man indulged in a humorous commentary, "Frankly, Gaspar, I would have never expected such noble intentions from a Don Juan like you!"

Portolá confessed sincerely that this was the first time in his life that he had really fallen in love.

After a brief reflection, Don Oleguer commented, "You know that I am a friend and admirer of yours. Anything else that you might request from me I could not deny; in this matter, however, it is my wife and Elisa herself who must make the decision. I hope you will understand."

Gaspar did understand and did not insist. Don Oleguer invited his daughter's suitor to a family dinner the following Sunday at which time they could discuss the matter more fully in Elisa's presence.

After Portolá had gone, the news of the cause for the visit created great excitement in the placid atmosphere of the Siscar home. Doña Amalia, a soft-hearted mother, was moved to the point of tears. Aunt Lucrecia felt such a joy in her lonely heart that it was as though the proposal had been addressed to her. After the first moment of utter astonishment, she became overexcited. Of course, she considered the marriage as good as accomplished, and began planning all the details of the wedding ceremony, the reception, the nuptial gown, the bouquet — Doña Amalia cut her short. Without hinting at any of the mental reservations she might have, the cautious mother said that it was useless to discuss these things without knowing what Elisa thought of the whole idea.

Lucrecia exploded, "Elisa? How do you expect her to feel; it's like receiving a gift from Heaven!"

We know, however, how the shy college girl felt, and, accordingly, Elisa told her father frankly her reaction to Portolá's proposal.

The following Sunday, when Elisa arrived home to attend the formal dinner to which Don Gaspar de Portolá had been invited, she was quite disturbed. Her good mother welcomed her with special tenderness.

Lucrecia insisted on going up to Elisa's room for an intimate talk. The romantic spinster couldn't wait until they were both alone in Elisa's room to break the news, as though the girl was ignorant of it. With extreme excitement, Lucrecia, in a secretive voice, notified her niece of the marital intentions of Don Gaspar. To her aunt's astonishment, Elisa, burst into tears and rushed to lock herself alone in her room.

Aunt Lucrecia stood perplexed and astonished. Doña Amalia went to her, took her by the arm and said, "Let her cry! My poor daughter! We all have cried at moments like this."

Lucrecia felt that she understood, "Of course, she cries with happiness!" Doña Amalia didn't correct the romantic aunt's wrong interpretation.

Shortly before dinner, Elisa's mother and aunt went to her room to announce that Don Gaspar has just arrived. Aunt Lucrecia was jubilant and presented her niece with the luxuriant bouquet of red roses Portolá had brought for his beloved.

Elisa didn't open the door immediately. She was still crying, and it took a few minutes to compose herself and to dry her eyes.

"Keep calm, dear daughter!" her mother told her as she kissed her cheek. "You know how we all love you, and that we won't force you into marriage. The decision will be entirely up to you. So, come down calmly without making a scene." Her mother left.

As soon as Lucrecia was alone with Elisa she lost no time in expressing her enthusiasm for Don Gaspar's decision. "Look at the beautiful roses! Smell them; they are divine!" She went quickly to pick out a porcelain vase from Elisa's dressing table and began arranging the flowers. While absorbed in the delights of floral artistry, she didn't stop talking, "You're such a lucky girl! In all of Barcelona there isn't a better match than Don Gaspar de Portolá! You'll be the most envied girl in town! How many girls would be crazy to catch such a handsome and distinguished husband! You can consider yourself the luckiest girl in the world!"

During the dinner, the famous lieutenant of dragoons appeared to be anything but a Don Juan; his manner was so shy! Lucrecia was disconcerted; she had expected him to be more flashy and more irresistible than ever. Quite to the contrary, he looked as shy as an adolescent. Always courteous and discreet, Gaspar was behaving with charming simplicity.

The amenities and lightness of the conversation during dinner calmed and reassured Elisa somewhat. She hadn't had to be so dramatic and fearful about matters. Portolá was a civilized man. As she glanced at him furtively from time to time from the corner of her eye, Elisa discovered how naturally attractive, simple and distinguished he was. She could detect no trace of the devilish spirit the legend tried to see in him. She saw him now, not as a gallant of a vulgar love story, but, on the contrary, as a refined and even spiritual kind of man.

Elisa was almost on the edge of deciding that she would like to talk to Gaspar in another intimate moment, but immediately she was seized by that strange and trembling she had felt since the moment she first received Portolá's message declaring his love.

When dinner was over, with her parent's consent, Gaspar invited Elisa to step out into the garden with him — into a typical semi-formal elevated garden of an old mansion in Barcelona. He wanted to talk to her alone. Elisa stood undecided for a moment, but seeing the smiling and approving faces all around her, she could hardly refuse.

If one were able to transcribe into literary form the idyll of these two singular lovers on that radiant afternoon in the placid Barcelona of the eighteenth century, it would surely become one classic page, perhaps even an immortal page in the literature of love of all epochs. No other lover had ever shown such gentleness and artistry in words and gestures in wooing his beloved; no masculine heart had ever vibrated with more intensity. Nevertheless, the talented "lady's man" failed miserably in the struggle to win the love of the young, beautiful girl.

Once it seemed that the gifted suitor was very close to claiming a jubilant victory; however, Elisa, finding herself relentlessly harassed, used the stratagem of tactical withdrawal. She begged to be excused for a moment. Taking advantage of the temporary truce, Elisa ran to her bedroom to put her tumultuous emotions into order.

Elisa had arrived at the dangerous moment when her heart wanted, but at the same time did not want to give in to her besieger. Temptation was almost irresistible. But, unfortunately, Elisa gave too much importance to the under-the-surface influences which, since the day of her confession to Father Alonso, she had been receiving regularly.

Alone in her room, she found it hard to stop the racing which seemed to be taking place in her heart. She liked him — why deny it? For a moment she pretended that she had accepted the proposal and felt like the happiest girl in the world. Unconsciously, she glanced in the mirror and seemed to approve of the image of the happy girl who had just become betrothed. The next instant, however, she panicked. Another kind of heart throb shook her; she was crazy! That happy, exhilarated girl in the mirror could not be she! The sweet words of her suitor had turned her head! — no, she would not allow herself to be convinced; her decision had to be to reject the offer, and she absolutely would not change her mind!

Someone knocked softly at the door. Lucrecia and her kind mother were both there. "Elisa!" cried the aunt, wrapping her niece in her warm embrace.

The smile of happiness that had shone in Elisa's eyes had now disappeared. Aunt Lucrecia scolded her gently for having left her suitor alone in the garden, "Your betrothed — "

Elisa cut her short, "He is not my betrothed — and never will be!"

Lucrecia was shocked. Elisa's mother intervened, "Your aunt is right, daughter; you must return to the garden."

Gaspar had remained alone for some time, seated on the stone bench in the garden, realizing that his situation was not very promising. However, he smiled good-humoredly, somewhat amused at Elisa's sudden disappearance. He had understood her emotions, half-fear and half-anger. Even so, he was surprised at the persistent resistance of his beloved; in all his romantic experiences he had never known a woman with such stubbornness. He felt that he understood a woman's heart fairly well, and he almost had reached the conclusion that such resistance was not normal. Elisa certainly wasn't reacting humanly!

Engrossed in thought, Gaspar did not notice the appearance of Elisa's father who was now advancing toward him. "They left you alone, my friend!" he complained, by way of excuse.

Having no comment, Portolá smiled sadly.

"Elisa is too young," continued the worried father in the same tone of excuse. "You must pardon her; she'll be back soon."

"Don Oleguer," Portolá replied firmly and with great dignity, "I would like to hear from you, completely and frankly, if there is any reason why I should not be engaged to your daughter."

Taken aback by this sudden change, Don Oleguer responded almost mechanically, "Not that I know of." After a brief moment, however, he continued, "Of course, there is a great difference in age, and this is the first time Elisa has ever found herself in such a situation. Even so, the only reason I can see for looking unfavorably at your proposal is Elisa's natural mystic tendency. Elisa has expressed her desire to become a nun on several occasions."

Portolá could not hide his disappointment.

Don Oleguer hurried to explain, "Of course, the idea of becoming a nun may be a passing influence from the convent atmosphere. Only time will tell whether she will really continue with this wish. I think the prudent thing to do now would be to adopt waiting tactics and not to rush matters. Elisa is still very young and inexperienced; her attitude may change in time. I know how you feel; maybe the whole problem is that this is not the right moment. As for me, dear Gaspar, I would consider myself fortunate to have my daughter marry you. So, let's wait and hope."

Portolá was grateful for this frank declaration, but felt that he should insist. "The problem is, Don Oleguer, that I must know, one way or another and the sooner the better — if possible, today. A great decision I must make depends entirely on Elisa's decision. The captain general is waiting for my answer."

Don Oleguer realized that he must have a talk with his daughter at once and begged to be excused for a few moments.

Elisa, accompanied by her mother and aunt, was on her way back to the garden. Don Oleguer waited for them at the foot of the stairs. "I have to talk to you, Elisa. Please come with me."

At this moment, one of the servants announced the visit of the Reverend Father Alfonso.

"You talk to him, Amalia. I'll see him later. Come, daughter."

Father and daughter stepped into the library. Doña Amalia welcomed the aging monk, an old family friend. Meanwhile, Aunt Lucrecia rushed out to the garden to calm the impatience of the gallant captain.

While Don Oleguer and his daughter were talking intimately in the quiet and secluded library, the sly Dominican monk talked to Doña Amalia, ostensibly for a simple visit, pretending to be unaware that Elisa was at home that all-important Sunday afternoon in June.

Doña Amalia, of course, considered it useless to try to hide the reason for the excitement in the house that day. Besides, the cautious mother wanted to take advantage of Father Alonso's visit to consult with him and to ask for his service regarding Portolá's proposal to her daughter.

Father Alonso acknowledged that he was already aware of the affair, speaking carefully until he could learn the parents' reaction. Once he had learned that the decision was to be Elisa's own, the shrewd Dominic felt reassured. He did not need to know anything else; this was the key to his victory. He expressed apparently impartial sentiments, invoked Christian resignation and the will of God while surreptitiously watching through the lace curtains as the arrogant silhouette of the lieutenant of dragoons whiled away the time in the garden. Now he was observing him with more pity than hatred.

Through Aunt Lucrecia, Portolá learned of the arrival of the influential Dominic. He realized now that, since Father Alonso was Elisa's confessor, it must be he and no one else who was the origin of Elisa's powerful and mysterious resistance.

On the other hand, Lucrecia kept assuring Gaspar that she knew the tortuous ways of the girl's heart and that she could guarantee him that she was merely using a subterfuge to disguise the natural fear that love always brings to young ladies. "Young ladies are like that," Lucrecia insisted self-confidently. "Elisa's pretext is simply innocent coquetry to make her more desirable — I myself have used this device several times, although, alas! uselessly."

Gaspar had almost given up. The only gleam of hope left to him was the sober influence Don Oleguer might have on his daughter. His fortune depended now on the intimate talk Elisa and her father were having then in the library nearby.

When father and daughter emerged from their private conference, Elisa's face was pale and serious. When she discovered that Father Alonso was present, however, she felt relieved, considering herself saved. With spiritual counsel, she would find the support she needed so desperately to resist the powerful temptation. Father Alonso could help her too to maneuver out of the delicate position her mother's kindness had put her in when she had left the decision entirely in Elisa's hands. He could help her overrule the repeated requests from her father to reconsider becoming a nun, and to circumvent Aunt Lucrecia wild recommendations. Aunt Lucrecia was as enthusiastic about the wedding as though it was her own.

"Give Don Gaspar a reasonable explanation and an adequate answer, my dear daughter," Don Oleguer advised.

"Yes, father," Elisa answered submissively, "but, before I do, I'd like to have a talk with Father Alonso since he is here."

"It's not necessary, Elisa," interrupted Gaspar, brought back into the house by Aunt Lucrecia. Serenely, the "jilted" suitor added, "I fully realize the situation. I never like to force matters, and I have already caused too much upheaval." Then, addressing himself directly to Don Oleguer and Doña Amalia, he said, "I only request a final word with Elisa. Then I'll withdraw."

Permission was granted, and the couple stepped aside, halfway to the door of the garden.

"I regret the turmoil I have put you in, Elisa," Gaspar said sincerely. "I don't want to upset you any further. You need not speak or give me an answer; I can read your thoughts. Before leaving, though, I want you to know that I will always love you, no matter where I may be and no matter how many years pass. I know that you are under influences you cannot avoid now. Goodbye for now. We may meet again some day, some place. My heart will always wait for you. Here is the precious little medal of yours that I was holding as a token. If, by chance, you should change your mind and your heart is free to love, send the token to me, and I'll understand what it means. I would be happy at your side forever. Goodbye, Elisa."

The couple sadly returned to join the family. Elisa went to cry on her mother's shoulder.

Gaspar de Portolá, dignified and elegant as always, offered his hand to Don Oleguer, bent his head respectfully toward Doña Amalia, and turned toward Aunt Lucrecia who, eyes full of tears, went to him and took his hand in hers, expressing with her warm silence the sorrow she was feeling for the unexpected turn of events. The self-possessed lieutenant, with well-chosen words and with his natural arrogance, said, "My dear friend, when a monk's cassock appears, no matter how venerable it may be, the doves of love cannot be free to fly!"

The blow registered with Father Alonso, but he remained impassive. Don Oleguer fell into one of his typical silent moods. The revengeful Dominic could no longer see the human figure of the lieutenant, but rather the ominous sign " ⚎ ". He could not help twitching his nose as though offended by a sudden odor of sulphur, no doubt of mephistophelic origin.

Map of America, showing California as an island. Drawn by Henry Briggs in 1625, this map shaped the European view of the New World for well over a century.

Chapter Nine

That night Gaspar de Portolá suffered an unusual insomnia, an insomnia that was to recur persistently in the days to follow. Elisa's rejection had caused Gaspar a disenchantment and thoughtfulness which were new to him. The worst part, however, was that he was not able to recover by one of his usual diversions. On any other occasion or under different circumstances, the habitual seducer would have found oblivion with a new romance. This time, however, the system would not work; too much of his heart was involved for him to forget Elisa with any other trivial affair. It was now not a matter of personal pride, but rather of a really serious wound deep in his heart.

Gaspar made a firm effort not to fall into a state of depression, but he could not resist the temptation to attempt to analyze the reasons behind his disconcerting failure. For this reason he spent his nights in a state akin to delirium, reviewing endlessly the entire affair.

In one of these half-conscious moments, a resounding name crossed his thoughts like a fleeting, evocative idea. Then, every now and then, this same name claimed his attention, until, finally, it became a stirring, new hope of rescue. This name was not that of a different, more alluring woman, however. It was a name surrounded by mystery and legend, a name capable of firing anyone's imagination — "America!"

At first Gaspar de Portolá had to concentrate to grasp the full meaning of that very special word. He asked himself whether America would be the rescue he was seeking. Was America the new adventure which could heal the deep hurt? At this point, Gaspar usually fell asleep through mental exhaustion and his question remained unanswered.

On awakening one morning, Gaspar suddenly remembered that the term given by the captain general for making up his mind would expire in three days. The fateful word, America, came back to his mind, not as a foggy fragment of a dream, but clearly and concretely and full of meaning.

Maybe America really represented the beginning of a new life for him. In fact, what was there to keep him in Barcelona now? Without Elisa, what else remained — flirtations, insinuating smiles, shady affairs? Were such trivialities worth living for? No! It was time for him to shake off all indolence and laziness. The captain general was right; he was wasting his life miserably!

One afternoon at a social gathering an elegant lady indifferently offered him her hand to kiss as she exclaimed sarcastically, "I suppose that now all the handsome men of Barcelona will shun us to go to America to chase savage belles." Portolá stood perplexed as though she had read his thoughts.

The same evening at an aristocratic reception a prominent gentleman stated, "Now all the young scions of Catalonian nobility will have to respond appropriately to the magnanimous gesture of our king. Since he has now confirmed officially all the old privileges of Catalonia, it would be unwise not to make full use of them."

It seemed to Gaspar that the only vital topic of the day was America. In fact, this single word had stirred the popular imagination with a sense of novelty similar to that evoked when the New World was mentioned for the first time with the discovery of America. Gaspar began to have the impression that all the important people were pointing fingers at him, accusing him of indifference and apathy, and so agreeing with the accusation made by his good friend Marquis de Mina, the captain general.

Yes, he would go to America, Gaspar concluded.

For amusement, Gaspar wanted to try the affect his decision would have on his faithful and sensitive valet, Vincent. He smiled again, thinking about the amusing contrast between his nebulous ideas and the flat, matter-of-fact attitude of his genial squire. Gaspar realized that Vincent's ideas were not always impractical. Many times the valet had produced the spark which brought light to some knotty problem whose solution lay in some neglected corner which Gaspar had overlooked. Truly, Vincent was not one of the ordinary orderlies serving the officers of the Barcelona garrison; he had studied for the priesthood, and if some unfortunate circumstance had not led him to forsake his vocation, he would not now be reduced to the dullness of household chores.

The moment Vincent heard his master mention, as though casually, the idea of America, he exclaimed, heatedly, "America, if my master will allow me, I shall confess that I have been anxious for many days to hear this word from his lips. No doubt the youngest of the Portolás has finally heard the call from his illustrious ancestors. At this very moment Don Francesc de Portolá, and even more, Don Nicolas from the beyond, must be listening to their heir with tremendous pride. They must be saying that finally young Gaspar is a true Portolá."

Unwillingly, Vincent turned to glance rancorously at the motto added at the bottom of the family escutcheon. The persistent seminarist was about to hint to his master that the outrageous second half of that motto should be erased, but he did not quite dare.

Gaspar, understanding, smiled kindly. Then he remembered the vague doubts that were assailing him. He moaned, "A Catalonian in America — as a public officer for Spain."

Vincent immediately grasped all the implications of these patriotic scruples and found them natural. He reasoned, however, "Any Catalonian in your position, master, naturally would go to America to serve a foreign king, to serve a flag that is not that of the old kingdom of Catalonia. It is true that he will accomplish deeds as a vassal of another state, but it is not your fault that history has gone wrong and that the Catalonian kings no longer exist! Nevertheless, within yourself, master, you can continue to feel the pride of being a Catalonian, and as exactly that, to participate in the colonization of America."

Gaspar accepted his valet's reasoning in silence. Discreetly, Vincent continued, "My master could imagine that, as far as Catalonia is concerned, the discovery of America has just taken place — two hundred years later. The Catalonians will arrive in the New World precisely when the Castilian conquistadors are already exhausted and empty of initiative. The Catalonian drive may open new frontiers and find new kingdoms to discover and conquer in the New World."

The Catalonian nobleman sank into deep meditation. The arguments brought out by his well-read orderly had not failed to make some impression. Gaspar felt that Vincent's reasoning was logical, and he was led to consider the position of Catalonia in reference to the discovery and colonization of America. He recalled a recent lecture given by the young and already illustrious historian, Antoni de Campmany, at the Academy of Letters and Science of Barcelona. The well-known scholar had revealed that if Catalonia had been banned officially from intervening in the achievements in the New World, Catalonians individually had found means to participate in it since its very discovery. Campmany qualified the Catalonian participation in America as "a clandestine participation." He based this phrase on the fact that many Catalonians, in spite of all the interdictions which had excluded them from the greatest adventure in history, had succeeded nevertheless in reaching the shores of the New World. It was only logical that a people of such a maritime tradition and so characterized by its adventurous spirit would not resign itself to remain idle in the peninsula while, overseas, there were such adventures and achievements to carry out. The American adventure was only a continuation of the famous Catalonian expeditions and conquests that had been carried out around the Mediterranean Sea, in Sicily, Naples, Greece, and in other parts of that region.

By the simple changing of their family names to disguise the Catalonian nationality, many of the compatriots of Portolá enrolled in or stowed away in the galleys and frigates of the Spanish fleet and thus became part of the glorious caravans of adventurers on the way to the New World.

In Seville, for example, there existed what was commonly called the "ghetto of the Catalonians" where many Catalonian merchants, deprived of the right to do business with America, managed deals with the new territories even under the infamous name of denizens of that ghetto. This Catalonian underground produced extraordinary individuals, among them the noted pharmacist Felip Guillem who in the sixteenth century invented an instrument to estimate the magnetic variations of the compass, an invention which was immediately adopted by the Spanish navigators. Thus a kind of revenge was achieved by the Catalonians for the rebuff committed by the *Casa de Contratacion* of Seville against the learned Catalonian cosmographer Domenec Villarroel who was unjustly substituted by the Castilian Zamorano.

From the ghetto of the Catalonians came many of the sailors and soldiers who reached the forbidden America; they enrolled on the ships or in the armed forces with newly-adopted names and fictitious Andalusian or Extremenian nationalities. Thus they managed to circumvent the foolish, egotistical policy of the Catholic king and queen who had banned all foreigners from the New World, including, of course, all those people born in Catalonia.

Many of Gaspar de Portolá's contemporaries knew of illustrious names from Catalonia, Valencia and Majorca which had contributed to the great discovery. Aside from the possibility that Columbus (Colom) himself was probably one of the Catalonians who had disguised his nationality, a number of Catalonian scientists had also taken part in the preparations that made the Columbian voyages possible. Gaspar remembered such prominent men as Guillem de Vallseca, author of the *Mapamundi* used by Amerigo Vespuccio in his navigations, and the map maker, Jafuda Cresques (true name Jaume Ribes) who later became famous at the Portuguese court of Henry the Navegant.

As early as Columbus's second voyage in 1493 at least two prominent Catalonians appeared on board the caravels: Father Bernat Boil, head of the religious mission, and Captain Pere de Margarit, head of the military forces. Since that time, many Catalonians had found a way to reach the American shores, and Portolá imagined that they had accomplished many heroic feats under anonymous, practically incognito, identities.

All these examples and much thought induced Portolá to decide definitely to start a new life in the vast New World. If so many Catalonians had not hesitated to cross the wide oceans to America, even under the humiliation of having to hide their true identities, he could well follow their example. As a public officer of the Spanish state, serving a foreign royal banner, he, at least, could keep his pride, knowing that he was a Catalonian.

The very next day the elegant lieutenant paid a visit to the captain general to inform him of his acceptance of a post among the expeditionaries to America. His good friend and superior, Marquis de Mina, congratulated him warmly and assured him that his wise decision would be gladly accepted at court. The marquis was certain that Gaspar's appointment to a high position in the administration of the colonization of the Spanish territories in America would come in a short time from Madrid.

Gaspar left the palace of the Captaincy General feeling the elation of the man who, after long consideration, has finally made up his mind to take an important step. He hurried to his suburban residence to begin the elaborate preparations he would doubtless have to make.

On his way this lover of calm Barcelona began to feel nostalgia at the thought of abandoning his beloved city. Instantly this feeling of nostalgia became enmeshed with the remembrance of Elisa, opening again the deep wound in his heart. Along with the charm of Barcelona, he was going to lose, for no justifiable reason, the one true love of his life. He blamed himself now for having renounced it without violent, even brutal resistance.

A momentary, passing thought that there might still be a way to attempt a new effort came into his mind and revived in Gaspar a memory of his tender relationship with Elisa. It was Elisa's very naivete and the platonic character of the entire affair which finally persuaded him that it would be useless to attempt to force matters. Nevertheless he would not deprive himself of a sentimental farewell before going so far away from his beloved. Once in the remote wilderness of America at least he could carry in his memory a last beautiful image of his dear Elisa.

About two o'clock in the afternoon Gaspar arrived at his residence. He ordered Vincent to prepare the horses immediately. Vincent, already used to the sudden decisions of his master, did not bother to try to guess what was in his mind.

As the two horsemen advanced at a leisurely pace through the suburban fields and alleys, with don Gaspar in the lead, Vincent soon understood that they were on a sentimental journey. The general direction in which they were traveling clearly pointed to the small village of Pedralbes where the Gothic monastery stood.

The imposing group of buildings was now an historical monument. It had been founded in the year 1320 by King Jaume II of Aragon as a present to his wife Queen Elisenda de Moncada. On this sunny afternoon the mass of buildings was a cluster of gold. The massive tower, the stout structure of the church, the arched gallery and the crenelated walls, all in pure ogival style, stood with imposing majesty.

Don Gaspar and his faithful squire stopped at the arched gate of the monastery and dismounted as a sign of respect and veneration. Gaspar could not enter that ancient monastical abode without overcoming certain inhibitions. In ancient times the sovereign kings of Catalonia had passed through these arched approaches in sumptuous processions. The golden stones seemed only fit to welcome persons of the highest nobility. Besides, that enclosure now housed the shy and trembling Elisa and any indelicate act might acquire the character of profanation.

On their way Gaspar had reorganized his original plan of trying one way or another to secure a final meeting with his sequestered love. On reaching the place, he realized that he could not use any of the rash devices he would have used in any other amorous adventure in this religious and solemn environment. To gain time and to relieve his valet of the perplexity of seeing his master lost in indecision and scruples, Gaspar nodded his head and turned his horse to the side, indicating a new route to follow.

"Wait for me here," ordered Don Gaspar, handing the reins of his horse to Vincent.

A few moments later, the hesitant suitor found himself close to the iron grate, the back entrance to the convent garden, at the same spot in which he had had his abrupt meeting with Elisa. He felt sudden nostalgia, and a sudden guilt like that of a vulgar thief. He did not linger long; he walked away as though he were fleeing.

Gaspar turned around the wall of the convent and returned to the main gate of the monastery. With great dignity he walked up the stone-paved ramp and followed the flagstone path to the center of the main court. His own soft steps along the path seemed to him to be less profaning than the strident stamping of a horse's hooves.

Gaspar turned in the direction of the arched romanesque portal of the church. Presently this strange pilgrim was kneeling at the foot of the tall, golden altar with its magnificent carvings. He stayed in this pious position for some time, but discovered that he had almost forgotten how to pray. He began to feel frustrated and was about to rise when a melodic religious tune rang through the high vault. The intense vibration of the voices of a choir made him turn toward the origin of the chant, a small side chapel with a latticed loft where the nuns and pupils of the convent had come to sing the *trisagium*. He guessed immediately that Elisa would be among them. What an unexpected delight!

At this hour of the day with the rays of sunshine falling in a semi-horizontal position, the stained glass windows of the church projected a shimmering rainbow toward the little chapel and the choir. All these effects made the music seem more mysterious and almost divine. Gaspar moved into the obscure purple and red shadows of a pillar where he could remain without being seen. The long sinuous notes of the Gregorian chant as sung by the invisible women in the loft created a curious sensual sensation in Gaspar. The chant was a lyrical, symbolic invocation of the Lamb of God, and Gaspar seemed to detect that the nuns, as a group of impatient virgins, pronounced the name of the Divine Lover with the same fervor and nostalgia of a sweetheart who pronounces the name of her absent lover.

For a moment, Gaspar associated himself with the legendary figure of Count Arnau, who under the spell of the devil, fell in love with the Abbess Adelaida whom he visited by night, riding toward the abbey on a flaming horse. By some strange aberration the image of Elisa became mixed with that of the tortured Abbess, and Gaspar imagined her in that dark loft, trembling, transforming the verses of the *trisagium* into profane delirium of love. He could see her donning the white toque of the secluded nuns, pale with desire, feverish in her sinful flesh, invoking the Holy Lamb as a secret substitute for her worldly lover.

Then came the proper *trisagium* ternary in which the nuns' chant was answered by the pupils, and Gaspar felt as though he were the very essence of sin and the incarnation of all the evil on earth.

Holy God, Strong God, Immortal God
Deliver us of all evils.

If Gaspar had not been so utterly confused, no doubt he himself would have beat upon his breast intoning the *mea culpa*. Suddenly he became alarmed at what was happening to him. He, a perfect emulator of the sacrilegious Count Arnau; he who that very afternoon had come to the Monastery of Pedralbes virtually with similar purposes as those that had moved the legendary count; he who would not have hesitated for a moment to force out the grate of Elisa's convent cell to satisfy his love, forcibly, was feeling now like a weakling, full of repentance.

After a short while the *trisagium* was over, and from the loft a hushed padding of feet and friction of starchy vestments, followed by the small steps of the pupils could be heard, finally dying away along the long, solitary corridors. Gaspar, now wrapped in silence and still in the dark purple shadow, decided that this would be the final farewell from his beloved Elisa. Except for his longing, he would keep the memory of this moment as his only relic — one that he would carry with him to the far unknown vastness of America. Disheartened, Gaspar stepped from the shadow, languidly carrying his wide-brimmed plumed hat, and as he passed under the colored rays of the stained glass windows, he appeared to be a fantastically unreal, brilliantly-colored phantom.

Leaving the church and emerging into the full sunlight of the courtyard, Gaspar was momentarily blinded and felt as though he were coming

out of a dream. He attempted to reconstruct the images of that dream —
the darkness of the church, the fleeting shafts of multicolored rays of the
afternoon sun through the high windows, the dimness of the choir loft
and the imagined silhouettes of the nuns and the pupils as they projected
their melodious and lyrical voices toward the high vault. Suddenly as he
reconstructed his vision, he noted the image of a piece of sculpture
which disturbed him ominously. It was the figure of a woman lying on
top of a stone sarcophagus, that of the famous Queen Elisenda de Moncada, wife of King Jaume II of Aragon. Gaspar saw it in a symbol of his
own tragedy. Elisenda had renounced love and had secluded herself in
this monastery which ever since had carried the unhappy queen's name.

Elisa had committed a similar act of renunciation, and there she was
now, sequestered and lost to the world and to him. Gaspar became even
sadder, realizing that this was not a dream but a painful fact.

Composing himself, and trying to find a silver lining with his usual
natural philosophical tendency, Gaspar thought that in the field of love
there are many deaths, but there are also resurrections — we usually call
them miracles. So Gaspar de Portolá, as optimistic as ever, proclaimed
before that cold stone of the sarcophagus, that he believed in the ever-
recurring miracles of love.

Chapter Ten

The tripartite peace treaty of 1763, which had ceded American territories to England, created concern throughout the overseas Spanish possessions. The Viceroy of Nueva España in particular considered it appropriate to insist on his old favorite idea of recommending the creation of a regular Spanish army for the American territories. Finally Charles III, understanding the necessity, listened to the viceregal recommendation and ordered the creation of the Regiment of America which would be stationed in Mexico temporarily, but would constitute the foundation for an eventual regular army for the entire continent.

In order to proceed with such an important creation, the crown sent the able military chief Juan de Villalba to New Spain with secret instructions, but with ample authority to organize the new army. He was accompanied to the New World by five field marshals, a group of selected officers and a considerable number of troops. The rest of the army would be recruited in the respective territories.

It was among this group of selected officers that Don Gaspar de Portolá, now promoted to captain, traveled to America.

On August 20, 1765 the expedition gathered at Cadiz, the port which, together with Seville was designated as point of departure for all parties enroute to the New World. The port of Barcelona, opened in 1763 as a result of the new royal provisions, was authorized only for commercial traffic.

On that clear summer morning as Gaspar and his orderly Vincent walked down the streets toward Puerto de Santa Maria they were met by all the ragamuffins and idlers of the important Andalusian city. They were envied and admired by all the ne'er-do-wells.

"Say, Captain," yelled one of the boys, "take me as your *mozo de estoques!*" (sword boy)

"Do you think we are going to America for bullfighting?" Vincent answered haughtily and contemptuously.

"Then send me an Indian with plumes and all!" retorted the boy, not entirely frustrated as an adventurer.

The wide bay of Cadiz offered a brilliant spectacle. Beside the man-of-war *Galicia* which was to carry the Villalba expedition, there was a fleet of ships set to sail toward different seas. Among these were the much-admired man-of-war *Aragon*, the frigate *Industria* and the merchant marine vessel *Flora*.

On the deck of the *Galicia* which displayed the royal flag the officers of the expedition paraded under the bright southern sun in their shiny and colorful uniforms, dreaming about the fast-approaching promotions as soon as they got to New Spain. The very least they expected was a generalship, if not a promotion to viceroy. Bending over the lee side rail, they greeted and commented on every new expeditionary.

"That one is Captain Portolá from the noble family of Catalonia," commented an ensign to his colleagues. "I served under him in Portugal," he added, not without pride.

Portolá of the svelte silhouette and open, frank smile instantly gained the *simpatia* of his future traveling companions. As soon as he set foot on deck he walked directly toward the upper structure. He passed close to a group of waiting officers and greeted them spontaneously with a hand wave. He proceeded to present his credentials to Lieutenant General Juan de Villalba who declared himself happy to have him on board. Portolá delivered the personal letter addressed to Villalba and written by their mutual friend, Marquis de Mina, Captain General of Catalonia.

"I agree with our friend, the captain general," said Villalba as he finished reading the letter. "It is an honor for the expedition to be able to count on such a man as you," and he added, "As for me, since the first I have considered including your name in the list of expeditionaries as an omen of strength and glory."

Portolá answered modestly, "Be sure, General, that any glory which is to result from my humble actions will be simply proof of the intelligence and ability of your command."

"Thanks, Captain, thanks" said the lieutenant general, flattered. "I see that your reputation for generosity and unselfishness is warranted. With captains like you we could conquer any new world, if there are still some to be discovered. Hernan Cortés would have found a man of his own caliber in you. Now, at my side, I am afraid we shall arrive in America much too late for any grand adventures."

At the forecastle among the sailors and petty orderlies, Vincent, the shrewd ex-seminarist turned squire, was already master of his situation.

"I cannot see why you Catalonians are going to America — unless it's to put up a store," a young Extremenian, a possible descendant of the wild adventurers who accompanied Pizarro, was telling him sarcastically.

Vincent, smiling scornfully and mumbling some inaudible remark, finally replied heatedly, "The Catalonians have been called to America finally lest the whole empire dissolve between your fingers like brittle candy! Castilians, Andalusians and Extremenians are still living enraptured with the monopoly of having been the first to arrive in America. But, what have you done since Columbus? Only two things: to wipe out the native civilizations and to erect beautiful empty churches. You believe that to colonize is simply to appear in a desert land, unfold the flag, set up a cross and proclaim 'All this is ours!'

"You thought that by the simple act of coming to America, bringing a religion and a new language, you would have all the territory secured forever. But the Indians said, 'A religion? A new language? All right, leave them there.'

"The Indians will never become Catholics or speak your language. They will continue to worship their traditional idols and to speak in their own dialects. If they end one day by taking over the Spanish language, it will be to transform it, ultimately to a point that Spain will understand it no more."

Then, taking a breath, Vincent continued, "Colonization, that is to say civilization, means to build — to build roads, schools, stores and factories — all those things you reproach the Catalonians for."

Meanwhile, Gaspar de Portolá had established cordial relations with his colleagues on the *Galicia*. Most of them were younger than he and with much less practical experience. For this reason alone he commanded a certain respect.This fact added to his fame as an illustrious and sophisticated man, a fame which always preceded him, caused even the officers of higher rank to treat him with distinction. Even though Gaspar was used to this curious situation which was to repeat itself each time he changed environments, he felt some uneasiness this time in spite of the fact that he was trying to talk and act simply, almost humbly, so that he might be treated only as one more colleague.

The general topic of conversations aboard the *Galicia* was, of course, the unknown and remote America toward which they were traveling. The young adventurous officers talked about the New World in the glowing terms of the years of discovery. Gaspar listened to them and smiled discreetly.

One evening prior to sailing, Commander Villalba turned the after-dinner conversation into a semi-formal meeting and invited each member of the expedition to tell his particular point of view regarding America. As leader of the expedition, he was very interested in knowing the ideals and interests which motivated each man.

"What impels you to go to America?" he asked one of the officers directly.

The first answer was to set an almost general pattern: "I hope one day to become a Pizarro or a Hernan Cortés!" the young officer answered

impulsively. Then, as he heard the amused laughter of his comrades he
tried to explain, "The chances of promotion in the Peninsula are so slim
that America is our only hope."

"Curiosity was my immediate motive," another declared, adding, "I
have heard so much talk about streets paved with gold and silver that I
cannot wait to set my eyes on them."

"Only your eyes?" someone asked humorously.

Another expeditionary replied to the query of his commander somewhat reticently, "I must confess that I welcome this opportunity to go to
America because of the need I have for a change of scenery." He declared
that the monotony and uselessness of garrison life in a provincial city like
Burgos had become intolerable for him. He felt that America could
operate like a miracle, regardless of any possible painful reaction, dis-
sipating all dreariness and transporting him to a dream world.

There was an impression of a sort of mysticism under the melancholy
and restlessness. It was of such stuff that the anonymous early *conquistadores* were probably made, those men who were slow to react after
many years of idling in taverns, but who, hit by the whim of enrolling to
go to America as though to the ends of the world, were to astound all
humanity with feats never before heard of.

"And you, Captain?" Villalba finally asked Portolá.

Gaspar took a little time to answer, "To tell you the truth, Commander, I do not know exactly why I am am going to America." Then he
added dryly, "Maybe the only definite reason is my strict sense of duty."

"A very commendable motive; it tells a lot in your favor," Villalba
exclaimed, pleased. Somewhat intrigued, however, he insisted, "But no
doubt the idea of your going to America must have awakened some
intimate, personal yearning in you — "

"Possibly," muttered Portolá, rather curtly, and then condescendingly, "but I cannot identify it clearly, not yet."

"You must covet glory, honors, riches, of course."

"I am not quite sure."

"Not sure — strange — "

"You will understand. While I have been listening to my colleagues,
many times I have felt myself identified with their several ambitions and
dreams. Trying to reach a conclusion, however, I feel that not the glory
nor the riches nor the remote possibility of becoming another great conquistador can bring me any more thrill than this sparkling glass of wine
can bring to my lips. Maybe this is because I have a different concept of
America. My dear colleagues speak of America in the beautiful words of a
legend, the wonderful legend of the New World. I, however, have the bad
habit of trying to analyze and to reach a personal opinion about every-

thing. That's why I have come to a different concept of America — maybe an erroneous one, but my own."

Around the table the score of officers stirred a little in their seats as though getting into position for closer attention. Portolá continued.

"In my opinion, now, two hundred and seventy years after the discovery, we are in a third phase of colonization — a phase in which, frankly, I cannot see clearly what men of our characteristics and condition can expect from America. At first America represented a fantastic geographical adventure, a tremendously exciting stimulus for scientific discoveries to revolutionize all cosmographies. America, in fact, was to be the definitive confirmation of the roundness of the earth. America made true Columbus's dream — the dream of a geographer to reach the east by navigating west.

"In the second phase, the American enterprise became merely economical and one of military expansion. But America offered a surprise by proving to be a barrier to the Indies, and, not only this, but it also made unnecessary all the proverbial riches of the Orient because of the treasures America herself had to offer. The gold and silver from America surpassed in value the treasures of India. So, during these two phases America justly represented a paradise, a wonderful destination for any man with a nautical needle, a sword of the Holy Writ in his hands.

"At present, in this third phase and at this late date when this territorial expansion has built the largest empire on earth for Spain; when the Spanish conquest has been brought to the remotest latitude; when all sources of riches have been exploited or exhausted; and when conversion to Christianity has penetrated all the gentile population; frankly I do not see what kind of stimulus — what extraordinary yearning — America can awaken in us. So I find my greatest stimulus in the strict fulfillment of my duty. The greatest honor I can expect is to die, if necessary, in the faithful fulfillment of my mission as a dedicated military man. In regard to riches, all the fabulous gold of America I can aspire to possess will be, eventually, some strips of gold ribbon for my dress uniform!" They all laughed heartily.

This speech of Portolá's subdued the spirit of celebration somewhat at this gathering at the officers' mess. A singular silence filled the room, then each one began to feel, as did Commander Villalba, that they had been presented with a new concept, one which demanded thought.

A second lieutenant from Seville was to bring back the festive mood, "Jesu — these Catalonians turn everything into a drama! I'm going to America just to look around for some cute little Indian!" Laughter resumed.

Late that same evening while Portolá was taking a final stroll on deck he heard some steps behind him. He turned to see Commander Villalba approaching.

"Good evening, Captain!" the general greeted him. Portolá responded politely.

"Your little speech of this evening, Captain, rather worried me," the Commander confessed. And before Portolá could take the remark as a reproach, the general added, "But, I don't blame you — on the contrary! I know that you are considered to be a man of extraordinary practical sense. The best proof of this is the assertion you made tonight that the basic duty of a military man is to stick strictly to discipline and to the orders received. Exactly what America is lacking is authorities that do not overstep their orders. In that area your prospects are unlimited, although, frankly, I do not agree with your pessimism."

"Pessimism?"

The Commander continued, "Yes, in America there is still much to be done, and I assure you that you will find a large margin for unexpected enterprises. You may lack ambition, however, and ambition is what I would recommend to you."

"Thanks, General," answered Portolá politely, and then, rather heatedly, "I only ask that you allow me to add a few different words to my speech of this evening."

"I am listening."

"To be analytical does not mean to be pessimistic," Gaspar stated as a premise. "At the table this evening I made reference to ambition, but to high ambition, not petty greed for gold or silver, to a jump in rank, or even to the reward of an *encomienda* or some material grant.

"I have mentioned a third phase in the colonization of America, but in order not to bore you and my colleagues, I did not elaborate on the idea. My point of departure in this new concept is that Spain has never looked to America as a possible field for human progress, I feel that once the third phase of the venture was reached, Spain is now under obligation to contribute to the civilization of America. The conquistadors have exploited the rivers and lakes of the colonies, the mines of their mountains; they have fortified coasts and cities, have built temples and palaces, have set up an administration equal to that of a metropolis, but there is an American element which remains untouched: Man.

"The little that has been done to influence the human element is in the direction of a religion to be accepted blindly, and sometimes to be imposed by force or by terror. I ask myself if it is not time to bring to America some of our modern ideas, and in turn to assimilate and to develop some of the native characteristics, some of them as old as America itself.

"Sometimes the colonial Spanish empire gives the impression of being an enormous territorial bundle of property belonging to the Spanish Crown only through some official writing on a piece of paper. Theoretically, Spain has brought an European civilization to America, but by means of a royal decree, typical of all the other Spanish decrees which invariably end with the manifest or implied recommendation. *"obedezcase pero no se cumple"* [let it be obeyed but not complied with]."

The General interrupted, "You see, Captain, you fall into pessimism again!"

"No. What I have just said is proof that I am moved only by a new and superior ambition. Let me tell you, General, that in going to America I will not be satisfied to become a great captain or even one of the typical conquistadors with all the glory of old times. I have a vague idea of what I want and of what I think can still be done in America, and in the achievement of this ideal I will not be satisfied to play any secondary role. Far from it — either all or nothing. I have never been interested in halfway measures. On my family coat-of-arms there is a motto, added personally by me, which defines exactly my pessimism as well as my optimism. It reads: "King or Nothing!"

Chapter Eleven

On board the *Galicia* there was extraordinary activity. She was about to sail. All the members of the Villalba expedition had been mustered in. At the prow the clarions announced that the moment had come to hoist sail. The second in command, Chief Officer Elguero, began to shout commands energetically. Don Jaume Sassola, captain of the frigate, an old skillful navigator, appeared on the deck in all the vestments of authority. On shore people were watching the complicated maneuvering of the rigging in amazement. Sailors climbed the ropes to the top yards with astonishing agility. It seemed in no time that the tall masts, shortly before bare and bald, were displaying the graceful contoured lines of sails greedy for wind.

"All canvas to the mizzen topsail!" shouted the head crewman to the lagging sailors who were busily rigging the main mast.

The military members of the expedition, almost all men from inland areas, watched with astonishment as the sails swelled with the first gusts of wind. Their enthusiasm swelled their breasts, too, with legitimate pride.

All interest then passed from the ship to the shore, to the breakwater dock. The mooring lines had been unlashed. A fresh easterly wind had risen, and as the sails caught this breeze, the vessel moved uncertainly at first. Soon the pilot's hand made itself felt and the *Galicia* was headed for open seas. Very soon the graceful frigate, her prow pitching into the bright golden reflection of the declining sun, now almost set on the calm waters of the bay of Cadiz, was bound for her long voyage.

Everyone's eyes turned once again toward the white city and its adjacent harbor. The expeditionary officers said good-bye to their motherland, knowing that the nexy day's dawning would break with the light of a great adventure, in the distant light of the new world, the unknown, America the marvelous, the so deeply-desired and anxiously-awaited destination.

From the time of Columbus it had been well-known that three natural sea routes existed which might be used to sail from Europe to the western hemisphere. The characteristics of these three routes had been favorable for the discovery of America. A simple glance at any sailing chart reveals the existence of these three routes — and these three only

— by which the old world could sail to discover the new. The first of these routes, or channels, is formed by the great arctic current which flows from the Davis Strait toward the waters of Greenland until it loses itself in the more powerful Gulf Stream current. The second is created by the extraordinary strength of the trade winds which are caused by the combined action of the sun's heat and the daily revolutions of the earth. These trade winds blow all through the year between the two tropics in a westerly direction toward the southeast north of the Equator, and toward the northeast south of the equatorial line. The third route, or the great equatorial current, is formed by the trade winds which rise on the coast of Africa and die on the coast of Brazil on the delta of the Amazon River.

The *Galicia* followed the second of these three routes. Now she was already sailing on high seas with the favorable winds previously anticipated. On the ninth day, the frigate passed the Islands of Tenerife and Grand Canaria. From there she would allow herself to be carried by the favorable flow of the trade winds which would carry her to the shores of America itself.

In the popular language of the crew the channel of favorable winds which persisted for over one thousand miles was called "the Gulf of the Dames", no doubt because of the gentleness of these sweetly perfumed tropical winds blowing from the palms on the warm shores.

After sailing along the coast of Africa toward the south for five days, the *Galicia* crossed the tropic of Cancer and reached the Cabo Verde Islands, From there she headed her prow toward the deep green waters of the high seas to actually begin cruising through the immense vastness of the Atlantic Ocean.

While the small Spanish frigate was floating like the half shell of a nut lost in the middle of the aquatic disc which the ocean becomes as soon as one loses sight of land, there was plenty of time on board to note the smallest incident and comment on the majestic monotony of the voyage.

The group of young officers, laymen in knowledge of sea matters, roamed aimlessly along the bridges and decks, repeating endlessly and tediously all the old sea-faring tales and fantasies. One of them evoked the ancient terror of navigating beyond the Columns of Hercules as narrated in the ancient Greek literature. He was forgetting that for more than two centuries these mysteries and terrors had been dispelled by the Columbus caravels who had substituted *"Plus Ultra"* for the ancient, ominous warning, "Do not sail further."

A young ensign with ambitions in the literary field spoke of the fantastic continent of Atlantis submerged beneath the intense blue waters. The eager young man gave precise details about the world of the Atlantans as though he were lecturing about a positive geological theory, forgetting

that the myth of Atlantis had been invented by Solon for political convenience. The tale had been based on a corrupt version of Nimrod's
narrative and the poetic vision of Plato, six centuries before the birth of
Christ.

Nevertheless, the topic of Atlantis filled long hours with pleasant and
colorful conversation, somehow lightening the idle existence on board.
The ensign carried on his fantasy, asserting that in early ages Europe and
America had formed a single continent, and that gradually this unity was
destroyed until Atlantis remained a vast island running from Iceland to
the Azores. Finally this large island mysteriously disappeared and gave
birth to the legend of Atlantis. The tale has such evocative power that it
has survived through the centuries.

Even after the discovery of America by Columbus, the shores of the
New World were mentioned as being the shores of the Atlantis world.
Some modified the old legend to suit their convenience and to fit the
new theory. Bacon created a new fantasy, placing the old Atlantis in a
region in the Pacific. However, the illustrious British author, contrary to
the theory of the Greeks, suggested that Atlantis was devastated by a flood
and later repopulated by a barbarian race called Americans, rather than
having been submerged because of a terrifying earthquake.

Inevitably conversation turned toward the stories of horrifying
storms and shipwrecks on the seas. Many of the "landlubbers" had faced
death undaunted at least once on the battlefield, but now, at the suggestion of a turbulent sea, they became pale as cadavers. Chief Officer
Elguero, on passing and hearing the fearful comments, endeavored to
calm the young officers by predicting the most favorable meteorological
conditions and a calm and perfect crossing. Unfortunately, however, he
made the mistake of warning the young expeditionaries that it was not
the turbulent seas that worried the navigators in those seas and latitudes,
but rather that the worst misfortune a sailing vessel like the *Galicia* could
encounter in these tropical seas was a despairing dead calm. This complete stillness of wind and water was worse than the most ferocious
unchaining of the elements.

Elguero remembered a trip many years before to Cartagena of the
Indies on a vessel of the windward fleet when he had endured the agony
of four weeks of total calm. The frigate had remained completely
stationary in a sea of hot-steaming viscous liquid.

"It was a hot sultry day in the middle of June," he explained. "The day
began with a gradual brightening which little by little defined the con-
tour of objects, but rather like a murky halo increasing in radius but not
in intensity. This strange aureole became a thick wall wrapping the burning sun all day long, allowing neither sunrise nor sunset. The sun

appeared and disappeared intermittently as though through the warm fumes of a boiling cauldron. The sea was shiny, flat and oily with still, dead reflections like those on a dull mirror; it was grey as a pearl of dubious orient with intermittent rosy light as though from some distant, but invisible fire. The intense aquatic disc seemed to be floating at the center of a universe of fog and vapors.

"The ship itself was a sad sight. The sails hung flaccidly from the masts like gigantic lifeless leaves from desolate dead trees. The silence was thick with stillness; nothing stirred or breathed in the sky, on the sea, or on the ship. The absolute stillness and absence of any noise gave the impression of suffocation, making us feel as though we were inside a giant glass bell from which all air had been extracted to create a vacuum.

"Besides causing this physical uneasiness, everyone aboard, from the master to the least ship's boy, gradually began to fall into great mental depression. The first day we assumed that it was a passing calm, not infrequent in tropical waters. The second day the dense haze which had made the sky indistinguishable from the sea suddenly disappeared, but not from a flowing breeze, rather like vapor which had melted. This change brought some hope, but during the days which followed, in the persistent immobility and stillness of the ship, one got the impression that the sky and sea were two opposite enormous discs, threatening to smash us. Some times one almost wished that this comic cataclysm would happen, mercifully. Day after day, for over three weeks, not the slightest change occurred in the exasperating stillness of the atmosphere. For the first time in my life, I really grasped the meaning of the word 'eternity'.

"Simultaneously, in the mind of every individual aboard," Elguero continued, "a series of fearful ghosts began to roam because of the unavoidable feeling that there was a physical impossibility of ever reaching port at all. There were phantasmagoric images of a ship adrift on the salty span, with drinking water and all food exhausted; of the monster of scurvy watching in the darkness awaiting the propitious moment to strew the ship's decks with stiff bodies.

"During those days and nights of horrible hallucinations, always within the despairing calm and quietness, one felt his mind subjected to the exacting balance of the eve of Judgement Day. How one remembered then the tiny sweetnesses of life that before he used almost to despise! Like little crumbs left at the edges of the tables where sumptuous banquets had taken place, one now gathered the remnants of memory which tasted so exquisite. One remembered the pale cheek of an aging mother which as an adult one had so often neglected to kiss! With what filial tenderness he would kiss it now! One remembered the loving, solicitous wife, so often ignored during moments of indifference and coldness; or the playful, happy child and the chance for caresses so often shunned.

"Remembered too, with a vividness which almost hurt, were the small spectacles of nature formerly almost ignored: the sweet summer breeze through the silver elm trees; the clear blue, luminous water of a mountain brook bouncing among pebbles and twigs; the almost inaudible flute music of the wind through the grass of the meadow; the twittering of birds in the clear perfumed coolness of an early morning — all these memories under the smashing pressure of a sky empty of air or clouds, on a sea empty of currents or waves, in scorching tropical heat and mortal silence and stillness!"

After this depressing evocation, the young officers began looking at the sky apprehensively; they seemed to feel a kind of suffocation as though air were missing, so impressed were they by the vivid description Officer Elguero had painted of the mishaps which sometimes transforms the shapely seaworthy ships into pathetic silhouettes on the immensity of a deadly immobile sea.

During the first days of the cruise, Gaspar de Portolá had struck up a friendship with the Captain of the frigate, the old Majorcan navigator Jaume Sassola, who turned out to be a good travel companion and a *causeur* of most unsuspected interest. The friendship began casually although it was obvious that mutual sympathy began spontaneously between the two.

One day Master Sassola found Gaspar leaning on the poop rail watching the foam of the ship's wake.

"You seem to like the sea, Captain," the old man remarked.

Gaspar was somewhat startled since he had been distracted from pleasant reminiscences evoked by the greenness of the playful water going by.

"As much as a poor landlubber may like it!" exclaimed Portolá. He added quietly, "The sea tells me very little. Rather it perplexes me since I am from inland."

"Sometimes that does not matter," responded the master, "very good navigators come from dry land."

"I know only fresh water of a river — a river that does not hold boats."

"Where do you come from?"

"Balaguer, on the Segre River."

"So you are Catalonian. Like the Majorcans, you should know a lot about the sea. You come, as I do, from a race of old navigators!"

Portolá was pleased to learn that the master was Majorcan; he felt that he should have guessed it by his family name. Both were from territories of the same nation, the Catalonian countries. This fact alone helped to make their friendship more solid.

Many afternoons Portolá went up to the command deck where Chief Juan de Villalba, as a permanent guest, usually slept during his siesta. Without awaking his superior, Portolá resumed his talks with Master Sassola whose stories of sea-going adventures delighted him enormously. The subject was new to him, and his interest in and curiosity about the sea and navigation began with his first talks with the loquacious Majorcan.

As always, Portolá secretly resented any reproach, no matter how slight, such as the master's comments on his ignorance about maritime facts, coming as he had from a sea-going race. This ignorance annoyed him, and to judge by the careful attention he was to pay to the master's words, it seemed that the captain of dragoons was trying to catch up on sea knowledge during his short stay aboard the *Galicia*.

One afternoon, not without some embarrassment, Portolá requested the master to tell him some of the maritime deeds of their ancestors. Sassola smiled, acquiescent, but flattered. Without realizing it, Portolá had given an invitation to the master to talk on his favorite subject, the subject on which he was expert. Because of his expertise, the conversation acquired the character of a lecture more than that of a casual talk.

"You must certainly know," began the master, "that once the Italian Admiral Roger de Lluria, serving the Catalonian navy, asserted emphatically that, 'Not a single fish in the Mediterranean would dare to swim in it without bearing on its sides the red and yellow colors of the Catalonian flag.' "

Portolá smiled, amused.

"This boasting," continued Sassola, "was more than justified. As early as the ninth century Catalonia had a navy of her own. With it she attacked and defended herself against the pirates who tried to land on her shores. In the eleventh century Ramon Berenguer II, Count of Barcelona, extended his official protection to all ships entering or leaving the harbor of Barcelona and as far along the coast as Cap de Creus on the north and Salou, south of Barcelona. These first protective measures made possible the sending of a powerful fleet against the Moors of Majorca and Valencia, territories which later were to become part of Greater Catalonia because of the union of the three kingdoms.

"In 1296 Pope Boniface VIII nominated Jaume II of Aragon-Catalonia the standard bearer and admiral of the Armada which was to sail for the conquest of the Holy Lands. The same king, in 1322, equipped a fleet comprising sixty ships for an expedition to Corsica and Sardinia, islands which had been ceded to him by the Pope in exchange for Sicily.

"During the thirteenth and fourteenth centuries the Catalonian merchant marine was large enough to be a rival to that of the Italian republics with which she vied for the commerce on the Mediterranean.

"Due to this wide maritime expansion, Catalonia had to establish consuls in almost every port of the Mediterranean, from Marseilles to Tunis and as far as Salonica. In Barcelona there were large arsenals for shipbuilding of all sizes, shipyards considered to be the most remarkable in Europe.

"Catalonia was one of the first nations to issue laws of the sea. During the reign of Jaume I, the Conqueror, the *Book of Sea Consulates (Libre del Consolat de Mar)* was promulgated. It was a collection of traditional practices and laws of the sea for all the Mediterranean. This code was put into force in Barcelona at the end of the thirteenth century, and immediately after was adopted by Venice, Genoa, Pisa and other commercial maritime powers. Its prescriptions have regulated basically the commercial maritime traffic in southern European waters up to the present time.

"Our independent rulers were the first in Europe to institute mail-carrying ships between its dependencies overseas. In 1440 Alfons of Aragon, in continuous battle with Italy, recognized the danger of the existence of remote states of the Catalonian-Aragonese Crown without direct news from the metropolis. Immediately he equipped two large galleys which inaugurated the mail service between Valencia and Naples.

"However, the field in which Catalonia proved to be much ahead of all the other Mediterranean nations was that of the knowledge of navigation. As early as 1286 the famous poligrapher Ramon Llull, in his book *Felix de los Maravelles de l'Crbe (Phoenix of the Wonders of the World)* stated that the compass was an essential nautical requisite: *'Chartam, compassum acum et estellam maris.'* That is to say, the sea chart, the compass, the magnetic needle, and the rise of the winds.

"In map-making, Catalonia and Majorca were in top place during the entire Middle Ages. The first chart made in Majorca bears the date of 1323. Later, in 1339, appeared the celebrated *Mapa Mundi,* drawn by the Majorcan Angel Dulcert. It is drawn over parchment and measures 1.45 meters long by .75 meters wide.

"The Dulcert chart was followed by the *Carta Catalana* of 1375. This noble chart indicates the Rose of the Winds with thirty-two rhumbs instead of the thirteen currently indicated. For more than a century, from 1553 to 1657, Catalonians and Majorcans worked diligently in making nautical charts while, at the same time, perfecting maritime instruments. The astrolabe, for example, the ancient instrument used for establishing the position of the stars in relation to the North Pole, was known and manufactured in Catalonia, mainly in Perpignan, early in the fourteenth century. King Pere, *el Ceremoniós,* mentions it in one of his letters dated 1352.

"The Catalonian kings had personal interest in maritime matters. Remember that there was a large section devoted to geography, astronomy and the sciences auxiliary to navigation in the private library of King Marti, l'Huma. An old inventory of this library indicates that there were twenty collections of harbor charts *(Catalan Portulari),* four of them on parchment and four on a wooden board. Among the books and documents there were two dealing with the astrolabe, four on the properties of the planets, three referring to eclipses of the sun and moon, and a variety of treatises on astronomy, geometry, almanacs, specifications and all kinds of ships, and many works on foreign maritime science, all translated into the Catalonian language.

"With all this background, it is logical to suppose," the master continued, "that Catalonians and Majorcans contributed effectively to the discovery and colonization of the New World. It is well-known that Amerigo Vespuccio used the Catalonian *Mapa Mundi,* drawn by our compatriot Guillem de Vallseca, and that other map makers from the Principality and the Islands contributed with their charts to the Portuguese discoveries. Among these one must mention Jaume Ribes to whom the Portuguese Henri the Navigator entrusted the management of the National School at Sagres."

These accounts by the scholarly master of the *Galicia* kept Gaspar de Portolá fascinated for many hours during the long voyage. The ship, after alternate periods of calm and cross winds, on the thirtieth day of navigation, September 21, came within view of the first isles of the Antilles, those of San Martin and La Aguja, the first step toward the Americas. This view of land produced the same natural excitement aboard as that produced by sailors in mutiny or in the desperate state of anxiety of the sailors aboard Columbus's caravels.

With the proximity of land, the surface of the sea had become smooth and benign, the pale green becoming less uniform and delicate. It was now green and blue, streaked with shades of yellow and mauve. In the early morning and late afternoon it was iridescent. Animal life was plentiful. Flocks of sea gulls and pelicans filled the sky with sinuous gliding and shrieks of joy. Flying fish were a fascinating novelty for the Europeans who made a game of watching them. To be convinced of the proximity of land, it was not necessary for one to accept only the swift passing of the sargassos of peculiar ochre color which the ship had been encountering since many miles out. Now entire trunks of palm trees and full branches of tropical vegetation came near the sides of the frigate as though in salutation from the nearby land.

After three days of this gentleness the *Galicia* came in sight of Puerto Rico, the incredibly, incomparably green island, a true revelation to the European traveler that tropical lands can be tender and soft and not always violent. With majestic, stately slowness the svelte frigate heaved toward the glorious bay and the port of San Juan where she would stop for water.

Replenishment finished, two days later the ship headed into the same waters into which Ponce de León had once, full of hope, set forth in search of the fabled fountain of youth which was never found. After skirting several islands and sand banks of fleeting beauty — the same islands Christopher Columbus considered to be the earthly Paradise — the expeditionary ship made way toward Campeche and the Yucatan peninsula across the Caribbean under a heavy downpour of rain.

Soon the battery of cannon of San Juan de Ulúa, outside the Port of Veracruz, was able to announce the salute in military protocol, the arrival of the sturdy frigate, carrying the Villalba Expedition in which Gaspar de Portolá was travelling.

The ship arrived on the first day of November in 1765. The voyage had lasted exactly sixty-nine days. The travelers aboard the *Galicia* could see the merchant vessel, the *Nueva España,* anchored in the bay. She had sailed from Cadiz twenty-seven days earlier than the *Galicia*, and had arrived the same day in Veracruz. She carried a cargo of mercury, indispensible for the exploitation of the silver mines, a magic attraction for the Spaniards. A tropical calm had delayed the cruise of the auxiliary vessel.

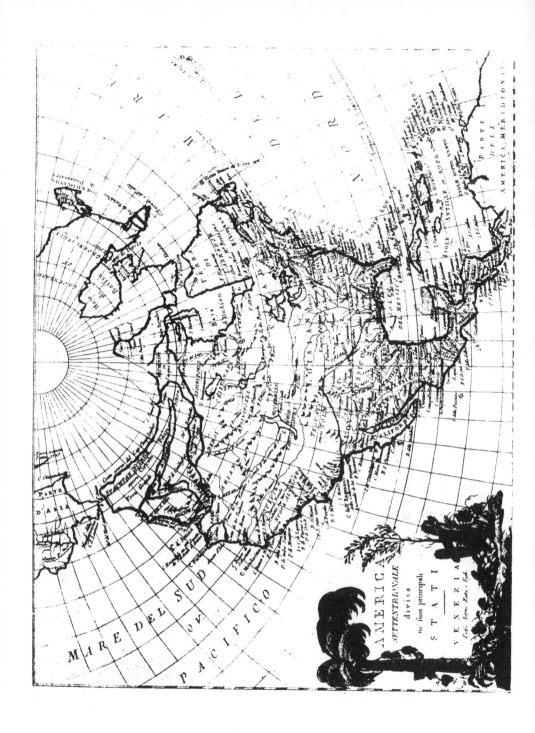

An Italian map of America, drawn in 1785.

Chapter Twelve

The bells of the cathedral of Mexico City rang with the usual air of festivity each time a ship anchored in Veracruz, bringing mail and fresh news from Spain. This time, however, Viceroy Joaquin Montserrat, Marquis de Cruílles, detected in the bells a special quality which filled him with pride and joy.

The newly-arrived ship was not bringing him any particular royal franchise like those usually eagerly awaited; rather, she was bringing him something better, the assurance that, finally after many repeated recommendations from him, New Spain could count on a regular army of its own, an army which was absolutely essential for the security, not only of the colony, but also for the rest of the Spanish territories all through the Americas. On board the just-anchored *Galicia* were Lieutenant General Juan de Villalba and one skeleton general staff which would constitute the basis for the future army.

From behind the curtains of the main balcony of the palace, the Viceroy stared, dreamily, at the now empty and disorderly plaza. In the not-too-distant future, he mused, the wide Zócalo would become alive and colorful with marching formations and military parades, demonstrating a fast, combative power that would end forever the present depressing spectacle of the small and ragged viceregal gaurd.

Cruílles, even though he knew that Juan de Villalba was carrying definite and strict instructions, meant to have his will felt in all matters concerning the formation of the new army. He, more than anyone, knew the elemental needs of that army, and he intended to fight to the last to see that new Spain and the other colonies would possess an overseas military body fully adequate for the needs and the dignity of the crown.

Assuming that by that time the mail pouches brought by the *Galicia* had reached his office, Viceroy Cruílles abandoned his dreams and proceeded toward the administrative aisle of the palace. He was anxious to set eyes on the royal prescriptions for the organization of the army, almost certain that the directives would reflect the erroneous point of view of the dignitaries of the metropolis.

In the outer office, the young lieutenant in charge of opening and classifying the mail addressed to the viceroy was seated. Before him was the sealed envelope which had arrived on the *Galicia*. He had already set aside those letters which were marked "secret", to be attended to personally by the viceroy. He opened a voluminous bundle which contained the administrative papers. He picked out a list containing all the names of the men in the Villalba Expedition and was about to dismiss it after a casual glance. Then his eyes fell on the name of Gaspar de Portolá, and the young officer reacted vehemently, with badly-disguised annoyance. Immediately, however, he smiled with vicious delight. Almost as a miracle, he saw an old expectation of his family fulfilled: to meet Portolá again face to face.

The young lieutenant, now adjutant to Viceroy Cruílles, was no other than Lieutenant Ruiz Mendez who took part in the grotesque duel with the shrewd captain of dragoons in Barcelona. Having been assigned to the New World, Mendez had displayed enough ability and had been fortunate enough to be recommended for the very privileged post close to the viceroy.

Considering Portolá his eternal rival and enemy, Ruiz Mendez, after reading him name on the list of the Villalba expeditionaries, felt that the time had arrived when he could effect his long-awaited revenge. Now the tables would be turned; Mendez felt in command of the situation. Portolá was a greenhorn in New Spain while Mendez, counting on the influence a secretary can always exert on his master, felt confident that he could cast a shadow on Portolá's future career.

When the viceroy entered, Ruiz Mendez informed his Excellency about the various affairs and mentioned the list of the members of the Villalba Expedition. Marquis de Cruílles showed instant and warm interest and took the list, together with the sealed envelopes marked "secret." Such an interest in the list visibly annoyed the adjutant. He dared state, "In the list appear some *notable* officers," and disguisedly sarcastic, "among them the notorious captain of dragoons, Gaspar de Portolá."

"I already have some references on him," said the Viceroy simply.

"He is an old friend of mine," lied the lieutenant.

"A distinguished warrior, and, I understand, a truly charming man," responded his Excellency.

"Also famous for his battles on the fields of feather!" ventured Mendez, thinking painfully about Lucia.

Viceroy Cruílles smiled, and them commented, "A gallant military man is usually victorious in all fields!"

The viceroy then walked into his private office, beginning to plan the protocolary reception due the freshly-arrived expeditionaries. The entrance of a new regiment into the capital of New Spain called for a welcome party full of pomp and grandeur!

On arriving at the Port of Veracruz, Gaspar de Portolá felt quite impressed. The resounding salvos from the fort at San Juan de Ulúa gave him a vague impression that in each cannon report, a faint and small echo was intended especially for him, saluting his arrival in America. If there was anything Gaspar hated, it was any indifference about his own person. For him, it was pure logic that he attribute secretly to himself any homage paid in general on enterprises in which he participated.

Gaspar had noticed that things were accomplished in America with a solemnity quite unknown on the Peninsula. The call of the local authorities aboard ship, their strict observance of rank and of protocol had seemed somewhat provincial, it is true, but everything was surrounded with an archaic pomp which was properly fitting.

The first sight of land and of the town of Veracruz had disappointed him somewhat. Lacking the exuberant vegetation of other tropical lands, this section appeared to be some desolate corner of an abandoned world. Only a little farther into the bushy jungle, however, the graceful archways of the Provincial Palace testified to the typical ostentation of the Spanish institutions overseas.

Gaspar found compensation, however, for the disenchantment of the land, by turning his eyes toward the calm waters of the bay where the Windward Fleet was anchored. Here was an indication that the old sea power of conquering Spain was not yet entirely spent. Among the nearest vessels, Gaspar identified the frigates *Asia* and *Bizarra* as well as the merchant schooners *Astuto* and *Veloz* with their delicate and arrogant design.

The trip from Veracruz to Mexico City proved to be monotonous and tiresome. However, the excitement of the arrival in the capital of New Spain was more than compensating. Houses, buildings, promenades and streets were bedecked for the great occasion. The celebration was for nothing less than the first appearance of the American Regiment, especially arrived on the *Galicia* to serve as the foundation for the overseas army! Viceroy Cruilles had made a point of surrounding this arrival with great solemnity and festivities. A holiday had been declared, and the main event would be a parade such as had never been seen before in the New World. Windows, balconies and along the streets were thronged with people. Everything was ready for the great welcome.

Shortly after nine o'clock in the morning, the blaring trumpets announced to the entire city the nearness of the troops, approaching along the Veracruz *calzada*. Excited shrieks of children added another herald to alert the citizenry, arriving in great numbers to throng the sidewalks. The bells of the cathedral and the rest of the churches continued their festive ringing.

The parade participants advanced proudly along the established course amid enthusiastic acclamation. At the head of the parade appeared the ensign bearing the royal banner followed by the strident band of bugles and drums. The officers of the various battalions forming the regiment were next, and finally, Lieutenant General Juan Villalba rode smilingly, surrounded by his staff of field marshals and other high ranking adjutants. Gaspar de Portolá cut a striking appearance mounted on a white horse. He was noticed immediately, particularly by the ladies of the court. Sensing that he would soon be a much-talked-about subject in the colony, everyone asked his name. One lady, carried away by her enthusiasm, proclaimed loudly that this rider was by far the most handsome captain in New Spain.

As the parade reached the Grand Plaza and faced the Viceregal Palace, the brand new Regiment deployed skilfully and elegantly. Viceroy Cruilles from his improvised throne on the special platform built for the official welcome, smiled with pride, seeing his old dream beginning to come true.

The welcome, following protocol, began as Don Juan de Villalba and his group of field marshals and high-ranking personnel advanced to the foot of the dais. Lieutenant General Villalba ceremoniously climbed the three steps to receive the accolade of the viceroy amid general applause. Next, the judges of the *Real Audiencia,* the mayor, the councilmen, the officers of the Holy Inquisition and other authorities of the entire colony presented their respects to the high-ranking members of the expedition.

Immediately following these ceremonies, the religious ceremony at the monumental cathedral rising on the east side of the Zócalo took place. The illustrious Archbishop of Mexico City officiated, and all the authorities and prominent people were present. All day long the city was wild with popular celebrations, with dances, games, races, cock-fights and folkloric entertainment at the Plaza del Volador. There were cavalcades of flower-bedecked canoes on the Canal de la Viga and as far as Xochimilco. Bands played all through the day in the plaza of the cathedral and in other public squares and parks.

The viceroy invited the members of the military expedition to an informal afternoon party at the terrace and patios of his sumptuous palace. The garden was decorated with artistic floral garlands.

The peak of the festivities was the Grand Ball in the evening at the residential halls of the viceroy, an event which would be joyfully remembered for many years in the annals of the colony.

It was during this important fiesta that Gaspar de Portolá shone with the usual prominence, enjoying the attention which was so personally flattering to him. The ladies who had already noticed his smart bearing in the morning parade made every effort to find a pretext to be introduced in order to enjoy his eloquent gallantries, or to catch a fleeting spark from one of his flirting glances. Gaspar had his hands more than full trying to pay attention to so many charming ladies at once and to share a dance with each one. Furthermore, Gaspar realized that he must step carefully here at the residence of the viceroy, some ten thousand leagues from the familiar metropolis and away from the court environment and the worldly salons of Barcelona; true tact must be used.

In attendence at this Grand Ball were many prominent and well-known ladies, respectable wives of important dignitaries, of husbands who were not accustomed to the gallant promiscuity which was natural on the peninsula. Gaspar could feel the stares of many distrustful husbands and would-be rivals; so he proceeded cautiously, with measured words, allowing only some truly special ladies the glance which conveyed what the lips would not dare to say.

As Portolá advanced toward the center of the hall to initiate the first waltz, all eyes concentrated on him with an admiration which increased with each step of the dance. Portolá had brought with him, for the first time in New Spain, the manners and style of elegant France which the Bourbon dynasty had introduced into Spain with its accession to the throne of Spain. The majority of the military men and public officers present had come to New Spain during the reign of the House of Austria, and Gaspar brought to them a peninsular reflection previously unknown to them. He and the expeditionaries from the *Galicia* represented new blood and the first breath of modernity to arrive in the colony since the time of Philip V.

Under these circumstances it is easy to understand the degree of popularity and notoriety Portolá acquired in the viceregal society, particularly since the Grand Ball had been organized by Viceroy Marquis de Cruilles for him and for his valiant colleagues.

The morning following the Ball the distinguished captain of dragoons of the newly-formed American Regiment, went to the palace to present his respects to the viceroy. It was a surprise to Gaspar to find as adjutant to His Excellency the rancorous Lieutenant Ruiz Mendez whom he had already forgotten. When the fastidious adjutant attempted to humiliate Gaspar by making him feel the authority of the position he held by having him "cool his heels" at the ante-chamber of the viceroy, the good-natured aristocrat smiled with full consciousness of his own superiority and waited patiently and silently. Gaspar knew that the silly illusions of his former rival would soon come to nothing.

As a matter of fact, Viceroy Cruilles welcomed Portolá with delight and treated him royally. A detail which, among others, Ruiz Mendez had not taken into account was that the viceroy and Gaspar were fellow citizens of Barcelona, and that Portolá carried letters of recommendation from mutual friends and the latest news from Catalonia for which Cruilles was yearning after his long absence from Barcelona.

After the protocolary visit, Portolá left the palace with a sarcastic smile on seeing the revengeful lieutenant burning with rage and resentment.

Gradually Gaspar de Portolá adapted himself to the uneventful life of the colony, measuring every step and calculating the consequences that any misstep might bring. With such cautious treading, it was not difficult for him to keep his proverbial prestige intact; on the contrary, his reputation grew day by day, particularly among the feminine world in which the original evaluation persisted: that he was "the handsomest captain in New Spain."

The impression that the courtly man of the world had gathered regarding Mexico was not very flattering — not that the physical aspect and general conditions of the capital had disappointed him since he had not really tried to imagine them previously. It is probable, however, that perhaps unconsciously he had expected other things. In general, he had the impression that he had arrived in an important, populous provincial town with all the attributes and pretensions of being a capital, but, nevertheless, it was a town lost in the dust and neglect of a third-rate Spanish provincial city with the habits and social life of the past century.

Nature itself, the landscape, the general aspect of the land, with the exception of the exotic attraction of the volcanoes, failed to establish that one was on virginal American soil — instead of the violent red of virgin and intact soil, the land had an all-over dull grey color of ashes or pulverized coal, appearing like terrain trodden and calcinated by the passage of a thousand generations. Even the vegetation appeared rickety and dusty with aloes, cacti and maguey growing as phenomena of a bare and exhausted land. Apparently the Valley of Mexico, with the Lake Texcoco in the center with neither water flowing in nor water flowing out, was merely a basin, a sort of concave hull, into which any residual waters trickled for centuries, transforming the top soil of the valley into a sea of dry mud now and then later leaving it purulent or arid. Hence, the gray and wasted aspect of the soil, like the surface of the ancient marshes or lakes, long since evaporated and dried-up.

What was most depressing to Gaspar was the visual appearance and the tumultuous character of the city — its crowded and jumbled population. On the thoroughfares appeared a constant stream of beggars, ragged denizens, Indians and specimens of half-castes degenerated by poverty and exploitation. Among these there roamed a trickle of workers carrying heavy loads on their shoulders; vendors of dubious victuals and rejectable merchandise; monks with burlap sacks on their way to beg for stale bread; quacks, penitents, pilgrims of all sorts; scrofulous and lymphatic children; vagrant dogs; starved goats and muddy pigs; donkeys infested with sores and boils and sundry stray animals moving about the ragged crowd.

The ancient canals, preserved as a relic of old Mexico and formerly constituting graceful city streets, appeared now as pestilent sewers with floating bodies of dead cats, rubbish of all sorts of discards, even occasionally a human body, dead as the result of some unspeakable crime. Along these canals, on overladen canoes, were carried into the city all manner of things: vegetables, flowers, wood, stones, sand, and even beams and building materials to be sold in the public markets. The result was a sort of poor-people's-Venice appearance.

Through the depressing processions along the streets, occasionally an ostentatious carriage would appear carrying a stately lady dressed in rich and expensive Manila silks with her native maid, dressed in bright and flashy colors beside her wearing several pieces of costume jewelry. After witnessing these contrasts, Portolá asked himself how the colony could survive with such extreme division of classes, both of them parasitical, without a middle class to balance, and an organized peasantry for the systematic farming of the vast seas of abandoned land.

By night the city was a no-man's land. In complete darkness except for a few lamps set out by conscientious citizens or a lantern here and there carried by a passer-by, it was truly daring to venture abroad even in cases of extreme necessity or emergency. Here and there one stumbled into high piles of rubbish or stepped into deep puddles of mire, or worse, met with the surprise of a bandit's stepping from the darkness.

On festival days the capital experienced a transformation. Occasionally the viceroy took his family on a richly adorned boat from his palace to the Convent of San Francisco by way of the canal that crossed the city from east to west. There were stage shows and concerts, attended by the entire colony, at the Coliseum. Holidays, too, were the days appointed for visiting the convents, and there was unusual traffic of stately carriages carrying elegant ladies, and placid church dignitaries and arrogant civil servants with plumed hats and uniforms with golden stripes.

Mexico City had many lavish mansions, palaces and public buildings which made the general poverty of the population and their flimsy dwellings even more striking. Even around the viceregal palace and off such important streets as Plateros and Santo Domingo there were crumbling slums, the results of the capricious planning of mere chance.

The majority of the population was formed by members of religious orders — friars and nuns and all denominations were secluded by the hundreds inside thick-walled buildings under tall belfries where the bells rang incessantly for the slightest reason, or for no reason at all. Along the streets at any time, a great variety of religious vestments of all kinds and all colors appeared: the black tunics of the Benedictines, the brown habits of the discalced monks, the white cossack with black cape of the Dominicans, those of the Mercedarians with a long red cross on a white stole. Church-going was a general, inevitable practice — an unwritten obligation.

With an over-abundance of dubious merchants, mostly half-breed, and the corruption of public functionaries who were always plagued by debt, the way of life in the colony was not a strictly honest one and morals were openly relaxed. Women of the streets had an open field for their activities, but commerce with them was conducted with great secrecy and a good deal of hypocrisy.

In this unusual atmosphere, Gaspar de Portolá had to find his own way to adapt and to thrive. Of course, after his thorough analysis of the entire panorama and its prospects, the clever captain of dragoons was soon to meet with success. A few short months after his arrival in New Spain, Gaspar had become, not only the undisputed idol of all the ladies, but also the favorite or protegé of His Excellency the viceroy — that is to say, his fellow-countryman Joaquim Montserrat, Marquis de Cruilles.

Chapter Thirteen

Carrying almost unlimited powers, the *Visitador General,* Don José de Galvez, member of the *Consejo de Indies,* had arrived in New Spain on July 18, 1765. The enormity of these powers in addition to the prerogatives the Visitador attributed to himself, rightly or wrongly, caused him to be antagonistic and brought about the constant opposition of Viceroy Cruilles who felt thwarted and divested of the supreme authority he himself was supposed to represent in New Spain.

This contingency had apparently affected the military and political career of Gaspar de Portolá adversely since, after having been in the New World for almost a year, he had not been assigned to any important post, nor had any of the golden opportunities promised by the captain general in Barcelona materialized.

On August 23, 1766 Viceroy Cruilles was removed from office, taking with him, for the moment, all hopes of immediate prospects for Portolá. However, almost simultaneously, the news came that Marquis de Cruilles was to be replaced by Marquis de Croix who came to Mexico in the same high position. On the one hand, Portolá was losing an avowed protector and compatriot; on the other, however, an old personal friend and companion in the campaigns of Italy and Portugal was to be his replacement. Needless to say, the lucky captain of dragoons was to find in the new viceroy the same private and official considerations he had enjoyed with the former viceroy.

In spite of the change in masters, Lieutenant Ruiz Mendez continued in his position as private adjutant to the new viceroy, only to continue secretly to bear the humiliation of the constant success of his rival in the intimate circles of the Marquis Charles de Croix, former major of the Flemish Guard.

Because he had never been very good at appreciating the strength of opposing forces, Portolá failed to estimate correctly the capacity for intrigue of his enemy Ruiz Mendez. At the very moment, due to the close cooperation between Galvez and de Croix, a series of important projects were in the making. Furthermore, Mendez now could count on a powerful ally which pure chance had brought to him as a godsend for much needed assistance. A short while before, the intolerant Dominican Father Alonso had arrived in New Spain. Less than a year before in Barcelona, he had intervened in the proposed wedding of Gaspar and Elisa, and now he had been appointed the private spiritual advisor and confessor for the viceregal palace. Obviously his influence would not be small.

Father Alonso's presence in Mexico now constituted a menace of which Gaspar de Portolá was unaware. Very soon the ominous sign, ♯ , cause of former misfortunes, would become here in Mexico too a moving shadow, stealthily attempting to darken each step made by the nobleman from Balaguer. Of course, Portolá was nonchalant and blasé enough to laugh at such dangers, even if he were aware of them. The new viceroy too, having been educated in Flanders under the free-thinking trends of French society, felt no concern for this kind of thing. Nevertheless, Father Alonso, inside the palace, could cause irreparable harm to Portolá.

Beside the intrigues within the palace which might affect Portolá's career, Father Alonso had a weapon capable of reaching Portolá at any distance, just as it had done before when he was about to be married. This formidable weapon was the confessionary. Portolá would probably have smiled scornfully and self-confidently if someone had come to him with such an idea. No doubt he would have asserted that any insinuation in the ears of anyone, man or woman, made for the purpose of alienating his affection, would produce exactly the opposite effect. Perhaps Portolá was correct only in so far as women are concerned. Considering the nature of woman, no doubt the insinuations or suggestions of Father Alonso made in the intimacy of the confessionary would startle the decorous ear of a stately lady; however, they would also stimulate the general belief that the daring young wooer was in league with the devil.

All speculations aside, a plot against Portolá was already being woven in the antechambers of the palace where at the same time many bright perspectives were beginning to open. During his visit to New Spain, one of the most important projects entrusted to Don José Galvez by the king of Spain was of a truly transcendental nature. It was in fact the most dangerous decision ever made by the Spanish Crown under any dynasty. Final instructions had just arrived in Mexico in a tightly sealed envelope marked TOP SECRET. In fact, these instructions had been considered so secret that the king had ordered his secretary to write on the envelope this ominous warning: "Under penalty of death, do not open this sealed envelope until exactly June 24, 1767 at dusk."

Within the palace there was subdued talk and nervous uneasiness over these final secret instructions. By way of some subterranean channel it was known that these unusual instructions had been compiled in Madrid in extreme secrecy, in the chamber of the king himself. The further precaution had been taken of having the instructions written in several copies by children from the orphanage, too young to understand what they were writing. No one, however, had any idea of what the sealed envelope might contain.

As the days passed, waiting for the appointed day, June 24, expectancy and nervousness increased all through the palace.

Finally the evening of the historical date arrived. Viceroy Marquis de Croix and the Visitador General Galvez locked themselves behind securely guarded doors. The envelope was opened only after following the written directions to the letter. The text consisted of a royal decree, but what a decree! A copy had been sent simultaneously to all the civil and military authorities both at home and overseas. It was a decree expulsing the Jesuits, the *Compañia de Jesús,* from Spain and from all its possessions. It was written in unusually violent terms, and read:

You are vested with all my authority and my royal power to proceed, well-armed, immediately to the convents of the Jesuits. There, you will arrest all persons and within twenty-four hours you will escort them as prisoners to the Port of Veracruz where they shall be put aboard ships ready there for this purpose.

Simultaneously with the arrests you shall seize and seal the archives of the community and all individual papers, not allowing any of the arrested to take with him anything except the prayer book and the personal clothing indispensible to the journey. Should a single Jesuit remain in your sector after this embarcation, whether he be sick or even dying, you personally will be punished by death.

(Signed) The King.

Both Galvez and de Croix realized the enormous sensation this expulsion of the Jesuits would cause. They considered the delicate mission to which they had been assigned. They knew that this king's decree would stun international society. It was logical that King Charles III demand that its execution be swift with absolutely no room for delay or failure.

Early the following morning, June 25, 1767, a squad of armed men arrived at the doors of the Maximum College of Saint Paul and Saint Peter in Mexico City. The force was led by the Visitador José de Galvez himself. A few hours later the Jesuits were escorted as prisoners to Veracruz.

The same morning Viceroy Marquis de Croix published an edict informing the populace of the promulgation of the decree, warning the citizenry, under penalty of death, not to obstruct in any way the execution of the royal instructions. The edict prohibited any conversation, private or public, on the subject of the decree, and warned especially about mentioning it in meetings, public gatherings of any kind, or in private parties orally or in writing.

A major difficulty in complying with the edict was the fact that Jesuit establishments in New Spain were located largely far from the capital city. The majority were located in Sonora, Sinaloa, and in other provinces of northern Mexico. There were some located in the peninsula of Baja California as well. Any action in such distant locations could not be taken with speed, and a man of tact and energy, a man who could be both diplomat and fighter — an exceptional man, in short — was desperately needed to act as commander in charge of the mission of fulfilling the requirements of the edict.

Galvez and de Croix began shuffling names. It was not an easy task to find the appropriate man. Could this man even exist in Mexico?

Within the palace the imminent assignment to the remote territories as far as Baja California was discussed secretly and with mixed emotions — it was an important assignment, but extraordinarily difficult and tough. The general feeling was that the man who undertook such a mission would derive from it more discredit than glory.

Ruiz Mendez had an idea. The thorny aspects of the matter sharpened his capacity for intrigue. Smiling craftily, Ruiz pondered the name of Gaspar de Portolá. To suggest his name for a mission with such prospects of failure would be machiavellic revenge against his rival. If nothing else, a mission hundreds of miles away in the wilderness, would keep Portolá far from the glamour of the court, exactly where Ruiz wanted him to be.

Mendez, however, did not quite dare make the suggestion himself directly to the viceroy. The matter was supposed to be a great secret of state. He would need some higher-up. Suddenly the name of Father Alonso came to mind. He would be the ideal collaborator!

After long and secretive huddling with Mendez, the crafty Dominican monk requested and audience with the viceroy. He appeared before Marquis de Croix and the Visitador José de Galvez together and considered the coincidental presence of the latter a special stroke of good luck.

Father Alonso went directly to the heart of the matter. It was a matter of such importance and pertinence, he said, that he would spare any preliminaries. However, as a sort of preamble he explained that his special position in the palace had led some of his friends to request his good offices to intercede in favor of a particular person. Finally, he added, the request had been made by someone of particular prominence whom he did not wish to disappoint. By mere chance, this person had heard of an important mission, and felt that he could recommend an officer who would be most apt and appropriate.

"And — the name of such an officer?" asked the viceroy, somewhat impatiently.

"He is a distinguished military man — " and rushed by the impatient looks of the two men, he burst out, "the captain of dragoons, Don Gaspar de Portolá."

On hearing the name, Galvez and de Croix exchanged knowing looks.

They were in accord; it was an excellent suggestion. Why had they not thought of him?

The effect produced by Portolá's name did not escape the alert Father Alonso. Fearing that because of their enthusiasm the two men might dismiss him, accepting point-blank the suggestion, the shrewd monk hastened to initiate the insidious plan he had proposed to Lieutenant Mendez on agreeing to become an accomplice. An old hand in this kind of plot, the monk wanted to make certain that, even if Portolá's failure and discredit should not materialize as a result of the delicate mission, he himself would achieve another sort of gain in the well-planned scheme. By using his habitual system of seeming to be reticent, he could harm the military and political career of Portolá in the long run. Therefore, he continued.

"Of course, this party as recommended is not perfect, as his prominent friend would have us believe in asking me to intervene in his favor. His Excellency and the Honorable Visitador General well know that no one is perfect! That's why, on my own account," he continued, "I made a point of investigating the qualifications of Captain Portolá. And I did well. There are some flaws in his personal background."

"For example?" interrupted de Croix.

Father Alonso slowly took from under his habit a neatly folded paper, opened it slowly, and handed it silently to the viceroy. Both authorities eagerly read the paper, and unable to understand it, almost immediately asked, "What is it?"

Father Alonso merely pointed to one corner of the document, drawing the men's attention to the cabalistic sign, the H with the cross under it, with which we are already familiar.

"I don't understand it!" exclaimed de Croix.

"It's a copy from the personal file of Gaspar de Portolá at the Holy Office. The symbolic sign is the stigma weighing upon the genealogy of the Portolás," Father Alonso explained.

Somewhat annoyed, the visitador general demanded, "And what is the meaning of it?"

Father Alonso who had been waiting for just such a question, now threw himself into an elaborate tale concerning the anagram. He finally summed it up by saying, "It is the flaw, secretly designated by the Tribunal of the Holy Inquisition, to identify heretics."

Soon after, Father Alonso withdrew from the viceregal chambers fully convinced that he had compromised the career of Gaspar de Portolá enough for as long as he would remain in New Spain. This time, however, not really knowing the nature of the mission, Father Alonso was to be proved entirely wrong.

Because of the kind of men both de Croix and Galvez were, and because of the nature of the mission to be accomplished, the insidious data revealed by Father Alonso favored rather than harmed the recommended officer. The proof is that immediately after the monk's withdrawal, again behind locked doors, the two statesmen exclaimed with sincere enthusiasm, "Gaspar de Portolá, of course! He is exactly the man we need! Gallant soldier, strict in duty and discipline, tactful, pleasing in disposition but at the same time firm in action, and besides all that — a heretic! A more qualified man could not be found to carry out the expulsion degree! And this holy man dares to insinuate that Gaspar de Portolá is not perfect!"

That afternoon, Gaspar de Portolá emerged from his residence dressed in his brilliant uniform, wearing all his insignia and sparkling accessories, those proper for an act of service. He was living in a small mansion with a baroque facade, located near the convent of San Francisco.

As he stepped out to the entrance, he found the street completely flooded due to the recent heavy shower which was usual almost every summer afternoon, falling on the city with almost tropical fury. At the corner of the street, the usual picturesque spectacle which took place on such days was going on — people were having great difficulty negotiating the crossing. Portolá, amused, almost forgot his appointment at the palace because of his interest in the fun a crowd of street urchins were having as they watched courageous pedestrians trying to cross, only to find their feet in the rushing water.

Prominent people came by and tried to cross with almost comical dignity. An elegant lady approached and the ragamuffins and on-lookers relished, in advance, the embarrassing situation in which she would soon find herself. Portolá himself smiled mischieviously. the lady in question, however, seemed a determined person, and did not seem to care whether the guileful audience thought or did not think that she was or was not aware of the trap. She raised her silk dress a little, exposing many pleated petticoats and a fairly well-shaped ankle, and placed her tiny foot in its shiny patent-leather shoe on the first stepping stone of the crossing. A premature slide on the muddy stone warned her of the danger, and she retracted her step swiftly and just in time. Portolá had no heart to leave the lady in her distress any longer. He approached her and offered to help her across even if it were in his arms. He said that he himself had to cross the street.

The lady, obviously not particularly modest, assented with a pleased smile, accepting the offer of the gallant officer. Gaspar took the frail lady in his arms as though he were carrying a baby, and protected by his high black boots, crossed the swift torrent with serene, confident firmness. Just before reaching the opposite sidewalk, Portolá stopped in the middle of the whirling waters with the precious load in his arms and asked her, "And what will be my reward?"

Without a thought, the lady rewarded him immediately with a kiss on the cheek. This unleashed a shower of applause from the big audience of ragamuffins. With a graceful bow, Portolá deposited the lady in a safe place and for a short while stood watching her as she went away down the street.

Then Gaspar remembered the official paper he was carrying under the breast piece of his uniform; he had almost forgotten it. He took it out to read it once more: "Viceroy Marquis de Croix and Visitador General José de Galvez request your presence at the palace today at 15:00 for an official consultation."

Portolá glanced quickly at his pocket watch, and crossing Plaza del Volador, rushed toward the viceregal palace.

After the consultation which lasted well over two hours, Gaspar de Portolá found himself assigned an extraordinary post with such ample and exceptional powers that it seemed impossible to even have been dreamed of. The interview had been very different and far from the ordinary one he had expected. He sensed the unusual nature of it as soon as he stepped into the palace. Because of the feeling, he adopted quite a different manner than when he paid a visit to his illustrious friend. At once he noticed that Visitador Galvez was standing looking very grave and serious and not in a mood for light conversation. Gaspar listened with utmost attention to the careful words of the viceroy and to the later interjections of the visitador.

Finally the text of the extraordinary Decree of Expulsion was read to him in its entirety. He could not hide the tremendous impression it had on him. He noticed particularly the passage of text which stated that the mission was to be carried out "firmly and even with the use of arms if so needed." This passage gave him a measure of the kind of power which was being entrusted to him.

Before the two high authorities dismissed him, Gaspar de Portolá was informed that with that specific mission, he was receiving the nomination of the important post, newly created, of Military Chief and Governor General of Baja California.

When the svelte captain of dragoons stepped out of the palace that late afternoon in June of the year 1767, he wore a smile of triumph — a truly legitimate smile of triumph for the first time in his life, probably.

Chapter Fourteen

Gaspar de Portolá, a strongly self-disciplined man and a man who never turned back on any enterprise, no matter how difficult, accepted the special mission and the post of governor general of Baja California without the least hesitation. Since he was fully aware, however, of the wide reach of this delicate mission with which they were entrusting him, after a brief reflection, he imposed certain conditions. The step they were taking was one without precedence in the history of Spain; the expulsion of the Jesuits meant sword against the cross, a formula diametrically opposed to traditional policy. Furthermore it called for the use of force.

These peculiar circumstances, Portolá alleged, demanded firm, but cautious action. Therefore, he demanded that together with the full authority inherent in the assignment, he also be given complete freedom concerning the means to carry out the mission.

Viceroy de Croix and Visitador Galvez accepted Portolá's terms, agreeing that he would have an absolutely free hand in the manner of execution. The visitador general further called Portolá's attention to the fact that the post of military head and governor general of Baja California carried with it full authority in all territories within New Spain from which the Jesuits were to be expelled.

The terms accepted by both sides, José de Galvez expressed curiosity concerning the basic ideas Portolá had in mind for the execution of the radical degree of expulsion. Completely self-confident, the virile captain summarized his entire plan in a single sentence: "If the decree, as I understand it, signifies the Sword against the Cross, my feeling is that the general strategy should be not to make use of the sword at all."

Heavy silence filled the viceregal chamber. Discomfort prevailed for a few moments until finally Galvez dared to exclaim, reticently, "If you can accomplish the mission the way you say, it will prove that you are not only a very able man, but also a genius!"

Turning toward the viceroy he added, "Do you believe, your Excellency, that such a genius can exist?"

With a cordial smile at Gaspar, de Croix answered seriously, "Yes, I am convinced of it!" Then he stepped forward and extended his hand to Gaspar who returned the hand shake effusively.

Portola set forth immediately to begin preparations for the difficult assignment. His first move was rather surprising. For any other military man, the first logical step would have been to visit the chief of the local garrison in order to muster necessary forces. Portolá, on the contrary, being endowed with sensitivity and tact which was rare in the barracks, headed toward the convent of San Fernando, the center of the Franciscan order in New Spain.

Portolá asked to see the local superior. He had several minutes to wait. Since the Father Guardian was absent, a minor official came out in his place. He was a short, pale man of very modest demeanor and humble appearance. His smile was meek, but his deep brown eyes were extremely expressive. He was Father Junípero Serra, President of the Franciscan Missions in Mexico. He greeted the handsome military man reverently.

After announcing his name, Gaspar knelt to kiss the knotted cord the monk wore around his waist.

Father Junípero showed vivid interest in the captain whom he already had become acquainted with through rumor. Portolá began to explain the purpose of his visit, speaking in Spanish.

"You may speak Catalonian," interrupted Father Junípero, "I am Catalonian too, from Majorca."

Portolá was pleased and went directly to the point: "I come to request help from your community, Father."

Father Serra smiled serenely, but not without a malicious sparkle. He hastened to say, "It is not every day, Captain, that prominent people like you come to the church for help!"

Gaspar apologized sincerely, "It is true, I do not have much of a reputation — some even say that I have dealings with the devil, but I assure you, Father, that this is only ill will toward me. Besides, I do not come for a personal matter; I need the help of your venerable order for the king and for the state." Then Portolá informed Father Serra of the secret nature of his mission.

Already aware of recent events in relation to the members of the *Compañia de Jesús,* Father Serra had no difficulty in understanding the tremendous importance of the noble captain of dragoons. He immediately invited Gaspar to follow him into a small office annex of the Capitulary Hall where the good-natured monk listened to the friendly military man with extreme attention.

Summarizing, Portolá concluded that his plan consisted of marching toward the expulsion of the Jesuits from Baja California and the north of

New Spain, not with a battalion of soldiers, but with a group of Franciscan monks.

"Considering the different character of the two Orders," Portolá explained, "everyone will understand the meaning. This alone," he continued, "will change the violence of an expulsion — always detestable, no matter how justified — into a quiet substitution. The king and the state are not interested in attacking the church in any way; it is only a matter of overthrowing the political power of the *Compañia de Jesús.*

The cautious Father Serra made no comment. He limited himself to assuring Captain Portolá that he would transmit his request to Father Guardian as soon as he returned from his inland trip.

Two days later, the Guardians of the Franciscan Community at the Convent of Saint Francis received the official visit of don José de Galvez whom Portolá had informed of his preliminary talk with Father Serra. The Father Guardian accepted with great honor, and secret relish, the request of the visitador general to furnish to the military head of the expedition the group of Franciscan fathers Portolá had requested.

Father Serra was appointed head of the group of religious men, and because of the urgency of the departure, he was ordered to cancel his previously planned return to the Mezquital province where Father Serra's commendable missionary work was being conducted. He was in the convent of San Fernando at that exact moment only for the purpose of giving account to his superiors of his spiritual achievements in that province.

The thought of Baja California filled Father Serra's heart with new dreams and yearnings. He knew the task the Jesuits had begun there, and, in truth, in his evangelical zeal he had often felt legitimate envy. On that day Father Serra prayed with special fervor, asking God for the inspiration and the ability he would need for the pursuit of the task he was about to undertake.

"California," the remote land of legendary virginity! The thought brought tears to his eyes. Father Serra had read the notices written by the Jesuits Marcos Barriel and Jacob Baegert and knew the possibilities the land of infidels offered. The *Compañia de Jesús* had barely touched the surface of the enormous evangelical work to be done there. Even with his inborn natural modesty, Father Serra knew that he could go no farther. The Jesuit tactics, as the authorities hinted, consisted primarily of developing the minds of the natives for utilitarian purposes. Father Serra knew that more durable and abundant fruit could grow in the hearts and souls of the converted.

The Indians of Baja California in particular could be converted easily into the Christian faith because of their primitive and virginal state of mind due to the complete isolation in which they lived in that vast and distant peninsula. Contrary to the faiths or beliefs of many of the other Indians in the American continent, the natives of Baja California did not profess any religious belief. Their explanation of the mysteries of the creation of the world and the other fundamentals of existence was based on an association of ideas. Some scholars have asserted they they revered the holy black raven named Xangisxiux, but, in actual fact, it did not have the attributes of a god. Their culture was primary and obscure.

Different from the Mayans who knew mathematics, the Pericues, the Utxis, the Ikas, the Guaicures, the Pauros and the Otximis of Baja California could not count beyond twenty, using fingers and toes. If they needed larger figures they threw handfuls of dust into the air, showing the utter impossibility of reckoning any calculation.

Historical traditions were not remembered. Nomad life had kept them from religious worship. These peoples had no inclination toward agriculture and lived almost entirely from possible hunting. This way of life allowed no love for the soil, nor any hope for anything to come from the gods. These Indians believed themselves to be descendants of birds or stones, and when they died, their relatives broke their spines so that they would never return to the world of the humans.

When the first Spaniards to arrive in Baja California began to decipher the native language, they learned that the Indians associated the arrival of the white man with a recent eclipse of the sun and subsequent earthquakes. Because of these events, the Indians believed that the white men were from a supernatural world until they saw the Spaniards killing birds and other animals; then they were convinced that these were just ordinary men like themselves, but different in some ways.

The Baja California Indians were humble and peaceful; no scholar mentions ferocious instincts in any of the tribes. These characteristics of his future converts sent Father Serra into dreams and passionate fantasies, those of a practical idealist.

The date of departure was near. The Guardian Father of the convent of San Fernando gathered together all the community one morning and selected a special group among them. He addressed them thus:

"Dear Fathers and Brothers, go forthwith with the blessing of our Holy Father Saint Francis; go to work for your mystic task to the territories of California which have just been assigned to our Order; be happy that you are going with our Lector, Father Junípero Serra, whom I appoint president of these missions. I can add nothing else but that you maintain obedience to him and pray to God for him and for his good work."

Father Guardian awarded Father Serra the written patent of his authority, and the eyes of the humble Franciscan sparkled like those of a saint. All the community, led by the group of the selected ones, fell to their knees and prayed to God for the new venture of the missions of California which had just been entrusted to them.

Chapter Fifteen

A wide-spread legend existed concerning the fabulous riches stored in New Spain by the industrious pupils of Saint Ignatius of Loyola. One heard of productive exploitation of mines, principally silver mines, to which it was said, they devoted their entire, exclusive attention. Popular word also had it that the Jesuit missions in unexplored Baja California were merely pearl fisheries conveniently camouflaged. The crown had issued no permit to the *Compañia de Jesus* for pearl fishing, but it was assumed that the installations on the deserted peninsula were more for earthly ambition than for evangelical and spiritual purposes.

At any rate, no one knew the real truth, and even Portolá prepared his expedition influenced by this cross section of popular supposition. It did not take long to gather the minimum armed force to take with him. The group of Franciscan monks was also ready to join his expedition in an agreed-upon location in the northern territories.

On November 30, 1767, the ship carrying Portolá and his men cast anchor in San Bernabé harbor, near Cape San Lucas, Baja California. The soldiers on board, filled with the notion of the immense riches of the Jesuits, relished in secret anticipation the looting of these missions. At the Mission of San José del Cabo, the first mission they were to find, they suffered their first disillusionment. They found the mission virtually in ruin, and the only items of any value were a few modest church ornaments and a few domestic utensils. This same disillusionment was awaiting them at the mission of Santiago. Their last hope was the installation at Loreto, actual capital of the peninsula, where the greedy soldiers were sure all the riches from the exploitation of the mines and the pearl fishing were to be found.

Portolá arrived with the well-planned purpose of acting cautiously and diplomatically. After setting up general quarters at La Paz, thus transforming the place into the official capital of Baja California, he began a visit to the surrounding territories in order to have a general idea of its true geographical situation. On inspecting the Jesuit holdings, although he discovered their system for keeping out all white people who were not missionaries, Gaspar found that the over-rated silver mines, in fact had turned out to be unproductive. As for the pearl fisheries, these too turned out to be pure legend, blown-up by the tales of fishermen who occasionally landed on these barren, deserted shores.

The Jesuits had confined themselves to guarding the territory zealously from intruders, stating that their only purpose was the conversion and civilization of the natives, and that their task would certainly be hindered if the crown were to allow other white colonizers with crude utilitarian and material purposes in mind to enter.

Portolá spoke to his sixteen missionaries who took care of the several Jesuit establishments on the peninsula. He spoke to them more as a friend than as first governor of the territory, thus drawing some respect and liking if not true friendship, from those who were soon going to become victims of the drastic decree of expulsion.

From the peninsula, Portolá crossed to Sonora, on the other side of the Gulf, in order to visit the missions of New Galicia and New Vizcaya. There he found the same conditions of poverty and destitution. Everywhere he went he gathered more information which destroyed the legend of the fabulous earthly riches hoarded by the Compañia.

At Alamos de Sonora, Portolá had the opportunity of having long conversations with the illustrious Jesuit of Catalonian origin, Rafael Capmany, who greatly enlightened the Governor in regard to the tasks and intentions of the Compañia in Baja California.

Faithful to the strict discipline of the order, Capmany heatedly declared that during the sixty-nine years' stay of the Jesuits on the peninsula, they had devoted themselves to the commendable work of colonizing that wilderness. The missionaries had established maps and maritime charts of the coasts, both of the east and the west as well as of the neighboring islands; had explored inland up to Parallel 31 of the northern latitude; had founded twenty-three missions and the chapel of Jesús del Monte; had built a number of stonework buildings; had taught the natives not only religious fundamentals but also various crafts; had opened a real network of pathways connecting the various missions with one another and with the provincial home at Loreto; had started scientific research and ethnological studies on the population; and had even established an initial irrigation system to help in planting the few arable lands around.

Portolá, also faithful to the official ideas of the state he represented, argued that given the international and militant character of the Compañia, it was only natural that these non-publicized tasks be looked on with suspicion, and that they be considered to a certain point, if not subversive, at least rivals to the work of the state itself.

Portolá, at any rate, declared that the expulsion of the Jesuits was not caused by their particular work in Baja California, but that it corresponded to a general movement throughout the European Catholic countries in which the fear existed that the Compañia was preparing a vast revolution to overthrow the absolute monarchs of all European countries. This explained the fact that such countries as Portugal, France and more recently Naples, had also decreed the expulsion. Facts in America, Portolá continued, had proved also that the evangelical work of the Jesuits often took on a political aspect, as attested to by the rebellion in Paraguay fomented and supported by the Compañia.

The Catalonian Jesuit restrained himself from discussing the subject further, and only smiled self-confidently, although he considered the reproach to be a direct hit.

Capmany exclaimed pointedly, "Can the Compañia help it if the more awakened indigenous populations begin to be aware that on some more or less distant day they may end by being subjects of the Spanish state?

This time, in his turn, Portolá abstained from commenting. He himself had to agree with the logic of such reasoning. In years to come, noted historians would remark that the task of the Jesuits was, in fact, the first seed — intentional or not — sown in America in favor of the emancipation of the American republics.

The quick visit ended, Gaspar de Portolá, officially as governor, returned to Baja California and served the Decree of Expulsion on Father Duerne, Guardian Father of the provincial homeof Loreto, who was to take care of the notification of all missions and establishments of the order.

Contrary to what one might have expected, the decree did not cause any turbulent disturbance other than natural surprise. Missionaries had endured many years of silence and self-denial, of hard life in an unproductive enterprise, and in a way, they saw in the decree of expulsion and in the the arrival of Gaspar de Portolá a sort of provincial event which would relieve them of that miserable existence.

Portolá himself was astonished at this reaction, or better, by this lack of reaction. With the frankness and simplicity for which he was noted, he declared later that a simple letter, written by the king, inviting the lean rank and file soldiers of the Compañia to abandon the territory, would have been sufficient.

Nevertheless, in the high levels of the aggressive order, indignation was wild, and unleashed a bitter verbal attack against the Decree of His Majesty. Portolá weathered these sudden storms with well-thought-out calm and tact. His indomitable sword remained idle inside its sheath, as previously planned. Moreover, his restrained action became an important personal success. The angry dignitaries of the Compañia, and even more so the simple missionaries, while giving vent to their anger toward the hated monarch, were understanding of the position of the strict and loyal soldier. Not for a moment did they consider the idea of making Portolá's task more difficult. At the same time, Portolá displayed very human understanding of the unfortunate plight of the monks.

The climax of the mutual comprehension between the expulsers and the expulsed took place on Fedruary 3, 1768 at the harbor of Loreto at the time of farewell. The Jesuits boarded the *Concepción* escorted by the military deputy José Lasso. As the ship sailed away, the soldiers knelt along the pier while the natives gave signs of genuine sorrow and regret. Portolá could not help uttering an exclamation of pity.

When the notification reached Mexico City that the drastic decree had been executed, both the viceroy and the visitador general were amazed at the ability and tact with which Portolá has disposed of such a thorny problem.

In Madrid, the king himself, on reading the report from José de Galvez, could hardly believe that, because of the efforts of the brilliant military man, the Jesuits had abandoned their installations in Baja California not with anger, but with tears in their eyes.

Chapter Sixteen

The *real* of Nuestra Señora de Guadalupe at La Paz, with its humble church and small fort, had been founded by Father Eusebio P. Kino, the first Jesuit missionary in Baja California, in 1683.

Now, in 1768, Portolá, as governor, had converted La Paz into the capital of the Peninsula and made the *Real* of Guadalupe his official residence. Today he inspected the remodeling work just completed and, although the place was going to be called the Palace of the Governor, it did not display any great luxury, but maintained its air of a convent, a simple severity which pleased Portolá. The wide windows open to the bright sun and to the deep blue sky of the southern latitude was more in keeping with his quiet, sober nature than the artificial pomp of most of the official palaces.

From the facade side, the new governor and military head could watch the growing California town with its small port open to the east, located almost at the extreme tip of the peninsula. Across the gulf, mostly in San Blas, there already was a civilization trying to reflect the luxury and life of the capital of the colony. There the flow of paper work and red tape with orders and counter orders from the viceroy and visitador (and whoever else in the long line of public servants in Mexico City) continually arrived.

Gaspar felt that he preferred the independence and savage solitude of La Paz. Here there was no superior to obey, or worse, to flatter, and almost no subordinates to order or reprimand. Through the windows of the rear of the palace, he would watch the small troop of soldiers bivouacing at the *Real*. The appearance of this set-up gave the impression of power rather than of musical comedy, and Don Gaspar felt himself to be like a little king.

Vincent, his faithful orderly, appeared at the door. "Did His Excellency call?" he acquired ceremoniously, but with a mixture of comic familiarity. Then he added, "Or is it more proper to say, 'His Majesty'?"

The Govenor smiled good-humoredly.

Vincent insisted, "Now, my master, you really are the 'King of California.'"

In the same mood, Portolá commented, "A king without a kingdom!"

He then walked toward his work table to check a long list of instructions to be given for the final details of the palace installation.

Vincent, always obstinate, ventured the last words, "The best kingdoms are those that exist only in the imagination!"

Portolá felt as though his loyal servant, through some form of telepathy, had guessed what he was thinking. The Californias were, in fact, only imaginary kingdoms — far from both Madrid and the capital of peninsular California itself.

The vast region annexed to New Spain was not much more than a line of bare promontories and flaming dunes where the precarious wild vegetation and the more or less ferocious animals shared the inclement scorching sun with a native population, primitive and raw to the brink of irrationality.

Since the time Hernán Cortés, in 1535, had explored the gulf between the burning peninsula and continental New Spain, very little progress had been made in Baja California. Cortés had suffered there the total failure of his ambitious dream of finding in Baja California the solution to the mystery of the Indies, the problem first set forth by Christopher Columbus on discovering the new world. The great discoverer had been convinced that America was only an advanced extension of Asia, and his landing had proved him wrong. In spite of that, Cortés was not quite certain that the American continent on the Pacific side was not, after all, connected to the Asiatic continent.

Cortés began his exploration of the western slopes from the Gulf of Tehauntepec north, but all denied his stubborn belief. His plan consisted of navigating first toward the farthest north and then east and south to follow the contours of the Indies. This he imagined to be the configuration of the connection between Asia and America.

The navigators of his time spoke of a large canal separating the two continents. Even if this were true, Cortés was sure that he could find the mouth of the canal. His sailing went well until the three ships of his expedition went astray getting into the Gulf of California, later called the Sea of Cortés. After a year of errors and misfortunes, confusion reigned in the mind of the conquistador. The mouth of the Colorado River at the upper end of the Gulf looked more like the sea than a river, and, to his eyes, this made California an island.

This unexpected prospect discouraged him from further exploration. Probably the ambitious discoverer feared that by entering those northern waters, he might open the door to a world of labyrinthian surprises. Called to attend to more important matters, Cortés decided to return to Mexico City and abandon the wild project of modifying the primary geography of those days.

After repeated expeditions by several navigators, among them Casanat, Cardova, Carbonell, Font and others, the small colony of La Paz was definitely established by 1634. Some natives were baptized and some inland excursions were undertaken as far as provisions allowed. A little north of La Paz, the colony of San Bruno was founded, and not much farther, that of Loreto.

During the sixty-nine years of the Jesuit occupation, during which time sixteen died, the population of the territory increased very little. Baja California continued to be an almost deserted and barren peninsula, interesting only because of the legends of fabulous riches to be found there.

With the provision of the post of first governor, occupied by Gaspar de Portolá, the Spanish state inaugurated the first peninsular civil administration, with the curious fact that there was nothing to administer.

The directives received by Governor Portolá for the performance of his duties were rather vague. One of the basic recommendations was that he should "maintain that province under the obedience to the King, keep the territory in peace and notify the Crown of any happening what-soever." The instructions forwarded to the viceroy were not much more concrete. He was urged to keep sending there able personnel for "the promotion and management of commerce, mine affairs and matters con-cerning population."

The irrelevancy of these general orders served to give Portolá even more the impression that he had *carte blanche* as though he were sitting on a throne in some fantastic and imaginary kingdom.

The first six months in his incredible "kingdom" were spent in mak-ing the Real of Guadalupe habitable, and in making the small port of La Paz somewhat functional. This gave the soldiers and a good number of the natives something to do. The public works and supplying the popula-tion were to give unusual activity, at least, to the harbor. Soon the pro-visional pier and the small bay were visited by ships coming from San Blas, across the Gulf, carrying building materials, furnishings and provisions.

At the same time the work was progressing, Gaspar devoted part of his time in study of his subjects and the lands included in his limitless jurisdiction. He was appalled by the low state of civilization of the native population. Even though their physical appearance did not differ much from that of the continental Indians, their mentality was so primitive as to border on bestiality. The natives lived in the typical *jaceles* of all New Spain, but amid such poverty and filth as to offend the senses. Adult males and children went naked; the women wore only a very brief straw apron.

Their staple food consisted mainly of a sort of *atole* made of yucca shoots and some wild roots with the occasional addition of a lizard or other reptile of dubious nutritive value.

In spite of the beginnings of Christianity spread by the Jesuit missionaries, the Indians around La Paz and other sectors of the peninsula maintained their ancient superstitions. They worshipped Changischinx, the holy raven, and had their priests who were at the same time their medicine men. The latter were recognizable by their capes made from the hair of the dead. On holidays most of the Indians painted their bodies with yellow and red, obtained by grinding colored rocks.

The landscape was just as poor and desolate. The vegetation, mostly cacti, was more a plague than a blessing. Agriculture did not exist, simply because of the complete absence of water. If any arable lands were to be found, they were in arid wildernesses. The rest of the country was solid rock, extensive dunes and dried-out soil scorched by thousands of years of implacable isolation.

In spite of the outlook, depressing in both the humane aspect and in nature's display, Portolá did not feel any disillusionment whatsoever for a single moment toward his acquired "kingdom." On the one hand, he took into account the perfect bliss of his subjects because of their total lack of needs and their own ignorance, to the point where he almost envied their absolutely free existence on the very edge of civilization. On the other hand, regarding nature, Portolá's eyes were too bent on imaginary embellishments to allow him to be depressed by the immediate landscape. Far beyond, the blue silhouette of the high mountains in the middle of the peninsula spoke to him of virginal heights never trod by any human, the exploration of which he had not renounced. Then he turned his eyes toward the sea, and in the primal solitude of the bays and caves, along with the savagery of cliffs and reefs he anticipated adventures never before experienced.

As the work of restoration came to an end, on March 13, 1768 the group of Franciscans who were to take charge of the missions vacated by the Jesuits arrived at La Paz. The group was composed of fourteen minor monks headed by Father Junípero Serra. Among the group were other Catalonians from Majorca, Fathers Joan Crespi, Fermi F. Lasuen, Francesc Palau and others. This gave Governor Portolá the impression that his "kingdom" was enriched by the formation of a small colony of residents of Catalonian origin.

This arrival, however, did not modify the administrative chores of the governor at all, nor did it decrease his authority a bit. On the contrary, if, on one hand, the missionaries left the protection of the impoverished native population under his care, on the other, in his role of protecting the missions, including the overseeing of the civilizing labor of the evangelical monks also, Portolá had become a sort of lay Bishop, or as he humorously termed it, a sort of honorary General Sacristan, a distinction which he felt was not devoid of irony.

Aside from the arrival of these valuable collaborators, no other important event marked the first year of Portolá's stay at Baja California. The sleepy colony continued to thrive in its original placidity and solitude, almost as in the remote days of its primitive foundation. Without administrative problems, since there was nothing to administer, and without military conflicts because of the peaceful, submissive nature of the peninsular Indians, the affable governor could enjoy an almost idyllic life.

It had not taken long to discover that, if the barren soil and volcanic rocks of the flat lands refused any attempt at adventure, contrarily, the sea and mountains, with their unexplored ravines and calm blue waters of the coves, were an unlimited field for sport and surprises. Very soon, the principal topic of conversation was the more or less gigantic size of the last marlin hooked, or the last deer bagged by the sporting governor on his daring excursions in the untamed altitudes or in the hidden seaside nooks — hunting and fishing expeditions which the ingenious Gaspar de Portolá organized lavishly, as a minor absolute monarch might have done if lost on an island in the middle of the Pacific, in a fabulous non-existent kingdom, but nonetheless real in his fertile imagination.

ENSENADA

SAN VICENTE

VELICATA

•SAN IGNACIO

LORETO

LA PURISIMA •

LA PAZ

CAPE SAN LUCAS

Baja California, the "kingdom" Portolá ruled from La Paz.

Chapter Seventeen

This time of peace in the drowsy kingdom, however, was not to last long. One fine day a long list of recent appointments of eminent persons to New Spain arrived in La Paz. Among these appeared the name of the honorable don Oleguer de Siscar, a recent arrival in Mexico City, assigned to the high position of president of the *Real Audiencia* of Mexico. The illustrious magistrate came accompanied, according to the list, by his distinguished wife doña Amalia and their young daughter Elisa.

Gaspar de Portolá felt a jolt to his heart. All at once he forgot his position as governor and supreme authority in Baja California, and felt himself to be again the happy, gallant bachelor of his good days in Barcelona. As though there had been no lapse of time, he lived again the emotions of his first meeting with Elisa at the rear grille of the convent garden in Pedralbes, a memorable night that was to mark the most important turning point in his life of adventures.

Gaspar felt buried in a turmoil of thoughts wanting to be considered at once, although he could discriminate each one with total clarity as he concluded that, after all, Elisa had not become a nun; that he could again rekindle his lost hope; that their sad farewell in the garden, a painful image that had tortured him for years, now vanished like a swift shadow of misfortune; that he could now see Elisa again as radiant and beautiful as ever; that he was now again on the way to reconquer Elisa's heart.

Suddenly he had forgotten all about California and his fabulous kingdom. He began planning what to do. It did not take long; he had only to listen to his heart's desire — he had to see Elisa, that was all.

He called Vincent and ordered him to make the preparations for a trip to Mexico City. They would leave at once.

Chance, however, did not favor the impetuous lover. That very afternoon a dispatch arrived from San Blas announcing the imminent arrival of Visitador General don José de Galvez with an important commission for the governor.

Gaspar felt as though his hands and arms were tied with numbing ropes; he could do nothing but wait for the arrival of general visitador.

After having visited Sonora, Sinaloa and the rest of New Galicia, in the north of New Spain, the active special envoy from the king boarded a ship at San Blas, the most remote Spanish naval base, by then already a rival to Acapulco. Two days later, early in the afternoon, this ship entered the tropical bay of La Paz.

On a four-oarsman barge, flying with regimentary colors, Governor Portolá accompanied by the head of the guards and the majordomo of the palace, approached the ship and climbed aboard to present his respects to envoy from the crown. Upon landing, Visitador Galvez was honored with a colorful parade which went along the causeway by the sea, from Governor's Palace to the old mission. Once having welcomed him at the official work chambers, Gaspar did not lose any time in pressing the visitador general into revealing the nature of the mission that brought him.

Galvez, although somewhat surprised by such impatience, since the subject was a pressing matter, went directly to the point.

"A message from Viceroy Marquis de Croix, received upon his arrival at San Blas, enclosed an urgent order of the greatest importance just received from Madrid. The Marquis of Grimaldi, the Minister of Foreign Affairs, had learned through the Spanish Embassy at Saint Petersburg, that Empress Catania of Russia had a plan to send an expedition to invade and occupy Alta California and other unexplored territories north of the Gulf of California or Sea of Cortés." These lands had been considered to be Spanish possessions since the sixteenth century.

Visitador Galvez explained to Portolá that Alta California was actually an unknown, unexplored territory. Although it was considered to be a Spanish possession, the data available was very vague. It was not known for sure whether California was an island or part of the North American continent. Navigators like Cabrera Bueno, Rodriguez Cabrillo, Francesc Gali and Sebastian Viscaino had made timid explorations by sea, but no one had explored it by land. Vizcaino mentions "the great port of Monterey" with its wide bay in the "form of an O," so wide, he asserted, as to be capable of harboring the entire Spanish Armada. However, the existence of this great port and wide bay had been known since then only in a very inaccurate and hazy way.

Portolá found this colorful narrative fairly interesting, but did not get enthusiastic. His mind was wandering to Mexico City and to the romantic figure of his longed-for Elisa.

Visitador Galvez continued: "I have concrete instructions from His Majesty regarding the watchful measures to be taken all along the western coasts of Alta California. The king's order to Viceroy de Croix provides for the sending of an armed expedition to protect that territory against invation and insult from any foreign nation; to keep the territory in peace and to promote mining and trade and initiate the Christianization of the native population. The first objective is the occupation in the name of Spain of the famous 'port of Monterey.' "

Gaspar de Portolá, without need of any formal request, offered himself to command this important expedition. Visitador Galvez was more than happy. Since the beginning he had taken this for granted, but he was prepared to exert pressure if necessary.

The matter settled, nevertheless, Gaspar, with his mind set on Elisa, requested a leave of absence for two months. Personal affairs of extreme importance required his presence in Mexico City for such a period.

Galvez was disconcerted. He retorted that the king's order did not allow any delay, and at any cost and with any kind of sacrifice, the Russian invasion of Alta California was to be prevented. Galvez, with sincere emotion, appealed to the sense of duty and to the patriotism of Gaspar de Portolá.

The governor remained silent for a few moments and pondered all the aspects of the unexpected situation. He had to choose between his military honor and the feelings of his heart. He lamented that such an urgent commission had come up at this moment. Finally he concluded that he had no choice and agreed with the visitador. The latter showed great satisfaction and then and there formally appointed the gallant nobleman from Balaguer commander-in-chief of the armed expedition, and, in advance, governor of Alta California.

That evening when Visitador Galvez retired to his private apartment, leaving the governor to debate alone over his personal and official affairs resulting from the new situation, Portolá decided to attend to the matters he considered of utmost importance — to decide what to do about Elisa. He studied the situation coolly. It was regrettable that bad luck and other mysterious forces always seemed to conspire against one on the eve of attaining complete happiness. He concluded, however, that if the matter of Elisa had remained in abeyance for three years, nothing would be changed by another few months of delay. It was most essential, then, that he communicate with his sweetheart.

Gaspar began to write a long sentimental message. Once completed, he read and reread it again and again, allowing his emotions to enlarge every tender and evocative passage. He sealed it, very moved. He rang and Vincent appeared. With the impossibility of going himself, Gaspar had decided to send Vincent to Mexico City with the specific mission of taking a message directly to Elisa and returning quickly with an answer.

This matter out of the way, Portolá felt great relief. He was not a man of regrets or useless lamentations, and, even if he felt sorrow over being deprived of some anticipated joys, since he was a fatalist, he now wiped the matter from his mind. His military duty was now his only concern. Besides, he had committed himself, and his word was sacred. He could now devote all his efforts to matters of the mission, with the feeling in the back of his mind, that a new dawn of hope was beginning to appear in the sky for his love.

Portolá studied intently the new and extraordinary enterprise that was set before him. To begin, he pondered the overall importance of it. Truly, the mission to which he had just been assigned constituted the exceptional opportunity that only three years before in Barcelona his good friend Marquis de Mina, Captain General of Catalonia had foretold. His going to Alta California as Commander of the armed expedition and as the first white man to explore by land that unknown and immense territory, made him a new conquistador, another Hernán Cortés, a new Pizarro, in effect, the king of a new Eldorado.

At this point Gaspar remembered his old uncle, don Nicolas de Portolá, who had put such high hopes on his young nephew's destiny. He remembered too his venerable father who had insisted on his son's attachment to a military career. Both would now feel proud of the last descendant of the noble house of Balaguer. Dreamily, Gaspar turned to look at his family coat of arms and at the daring motto, "King or Nothing!" he had added to it in a moment of adventurous ambition. Now he thought that the fulfillment of the motto might not be an impossibility after all.

Sudden depression set in. Gaspar would go to the discovery and exploration of California, not on his own, not as a proud scion of his heroic ancestors, but merely as a functionary of Spain, in the name of a king who, at heart, was not his. Uncle Nicolas had spoken to him about this sort of humiliation, but he had never grasped the real significance of the thought. He might conquer a kingdom, yes, but he would not be able to impart to it the stamp of his nationality nor the virile accent of his native language.

This led the future conquistador to think of the many Catalonians who, since the discovery of the New World, had had to participate in the colonization of America in a humiliating manner, if not in a clandestine way. This explained the fact that Catalonian participation had not appeared in the chronicles or in authorized history books. The latter were official accounts, written for the Spanish kings who would never have admitted that "foreigners" such as the Catalonians were actually participating in the great American adventure. For a moment, Portolá feared that, no matter what his deeds might be in California, even his name would never appear in future chronicles because of the sin of being a Catalonian.

He became a little reassured on considering that his very transfer to

America was due to the new regulations of King Charles III, which in truth were amending the repeated interdictions from previous Spanish kings banning the Catalonians from participating in the colonization of the New World. Nevertheless, he felt the affront of the injuries exerted over his fellow countrymen. For a moment he wondered about the different course the colonization might have taken if the practical and industrious Catalonians had participated openly. Maybe even today in some colonies of the New World, Catalonian would be the language spoken.

Just recently, Portolá remembered, a number of Catalonians had been able to move to America legally without being excluded as "foreigners" even if officially tagged as Spaniards. Like he himself, most of them had come to New Spain. Among these were eminent personalities like Joaquim Montserrat, Marquis of Cuilles, who from 1760 to 1766 had been the able Viceroy of Mexico. There were also many monks and even simple soldiers, among these the companies of "Catalonian Volunteers," also known as "Miquelets", which were, in a way, the modern version of the famous "Catalonian Almogavers" of the time when Catalonia was a free and sovereign nation.

The thought of these companies of Catalonian Volunteers gave Portolá an exciting idea. He asked himself, "Would it be possible to find enough Catalonians in New Spain to carry out the exploration of California with the exclusive help of my compatriots?"

If it were possible, he thought enthusiastically, the conquest of California could become a Catalonian achievement! It would be a unique precedent in the history of the colonization of America!

Gaspar began eagerly to compile the list of Catalonian elements of his knowledge in New Spain. To start with, in La Paz he had the group of Franciscans headed by Father Junipero Serra, most of whom were from Majorca or from Valencia, both Catalonian countries. He had with him in La Paz too the head of his armed forces in Baja California, the Majorcan captain Ferran Ribera i Montcada. The master of the ship *San Antonio,* Joan Peres, was also a Balearic seaman. To his memory came the name of the engineer and mapmaker Miquel Constanso, who resided in Mexico City. These elements and other similar ones together with the "Miquelets" of the companies of Catalonian volunteers, would be quite sufficient to carry out the expedition in a way that it would acquire a Catalonian character.

Gaspar hinted to Visitador Galvez about his desire to select himself the men to accompany him to California. Galvez considered this to be a normal request, and when Portolá explained to him his plan of surrounding himself with the greatest number of Catalonians possible, Galvez approved the idea. As a good Andalusian, the visitador admitted his warm sympathy for Portolá's countrymen. He even suggested other names of Catalonians residing in New Spain, and, on the spot, he dispatched an order to Colonel Elizondo of the garrison at Guayman, to embark to Baja California a body of twenty-five men of the Free Company of "Catalonian Volunteers," under the command of Lieutenant Pere Fages, to be put under the orders of Governor Portolá.

Gaspar de Portolá was pleased at the new turn things were taking and considered the California enterprise with growing interest. He considered the Spanish thrust in America nearly spent, and for a moment, dreamily ambitious, thought that this fully Catalonian enterprise could establish a new pattern for a novel concept of colonization and civilization. He did not know, however, that this was to be in fact the last such enterprise carried out by Spain in the New World, and so, he, a Catalonian, was to become "the last Spanish Conquistador in American territory."

Chapter Eighteen

U pon arriving at the capital of New Spain, Vincent, Gaspar's diligent orderly, proceeded discreetly to the residence of don Oleguer de Siscar. The illustrious magistrate, president of the *Real Audiencia* of Mexico, was really pleased to hear from his distinguished friend Gaspar de Portolá. Vincent explained to the eminent gentleman from Barcelona the high position now held by his master who was now considered to be like a minor king in the distant and quiet Baja California. On learning the object of the long trip and about the mission of romance entrusted to Vincent regarding his daughter, don Oleguer, with Catalonian frankness, could not repress this comment.

"I am really proud to see that I was not wrong about the faithfulness and constant affection of Gaspar for Elisa."

In confidence, good naturedly, don Oleguer confessed to Vincent that it was on his pressing advice that, after all, Elisa decided not to become a nun. Then he mentioned his appointment as magistrate in New Spain as a providential event to reawake in Elisa's heart the hope that some happy day she would see her former suitor again.

At this moment of intimate revelation, the door of the library opened suddenly, and Vincent stood amazed on seeing before him the former school girl of only three years before, now transformed into a beautiful young lady. Vincent was so spell-bound that he failed to notice the male figure beside her. When Vincent turned his gaze toward the young officer standing a few steps from don Oleguer's daughter, he was surprised to see that it was Lieutenant Ruiz Mendez who, it seemed, was bound to be the eternal rival of his master.

Elisa kissed her father tenderly on both cheeks, and don Oleguer told her that he had something very important to tell her. On hearing this, Ruiz Mendez discreetly took leave and withdrew. the happy father then pointed toward Vincent and said to his daughter, "Look, Elisa, a visitor for you!"

Elisa was confused. She did not know the man before her.

"Vincent brings you pleasant news," added don Oleguer.

Respectfully, Vincent stepped toward Elisa and delivered his master's message to her.

Elisa opened the envelope and looked for the signature immediately.

On reading it she suddenly turned pale, and then as suddenly blushed pitifully. She tried to pretend because of Vincent's presence, but she was so disturbed that she did not realize that she was not even reading the message.

"You are so happy that you didn't even look to see what Don Gaspar has to say," joked her father.

Tactfully, Vincent intervened saying, "If you allow me, I will leave. I will be back tomorrow for the answer."

Once Vincent had left, Elisa jumped into her father's arms.

"Don't you want to read the letter?" repeated the old man, this time with curiosity apparent.

Elisa laughed, "Oh, yes, father — but alone! And I will let you read it too — afterwards!"

Both laughed, and Elisa, after kissing her father once more, rushed to her room.

Anxiously, Elisa read and reread several times each word of the tender letter of Portolá. The letter was written in simple language without rhetoric. Elisa found in it the tone of Gaspar's talk to her first at the grate in the garden and then at the stone bench. This time, however, in writing, the romantic words of her gallant suitor did not bring her the former fear and trembling. She was no longer a school girl. Now she was a sophisticated lady of the viceregal entourage and was used to being courted. She laughed now at the childish awe Portolá's words had produced in her those first times.

Elisa picked up her pen and went to her delicate dressing table and set herself to write a long, elaborate letter. Remembering the worldly advice given her by other ladies of the court, she planned to be cautious. Elisa began her answer by warning Gaspar that she was now a different Elisa from the one he had known in Barcelona, so different, in fact, that he probably would be surprised. Of course, she had not forgotten him. What woman could ever forget someone who had dared jump over the high walls of a convent to talk to her? However, now —

At this point Elisa realized what she was doing. Was she merely trying to flirt? Suddenly the passionate words of Gaspar's letter, like a flame that suddenly revives, flared up and shook her emotions. Now she detected the voice of sincerity in that fervent message of adoration. She suddenly understood that this writing was not a play with words — it was love, the love of her life, love which was knocking for a second time at the door of her heart!

Elisa got up quickly and tore the letter she had started to write. She felt ashamed of herself. Instead of a banal letter, empty in meaning, she would send Gaspar the answer he was waiting for. She went to a small desk at the corner of her room, took from a drawer the little medal of Our Lady of Mercy that Gaspar once wanted to keep as a token, and put it into an envelope which she sealed immediately. This was the answer she was going to send Gaspar. The right and sufficient answer — the answer he expected!

In the meanwhile in Baja California all preparations were being completed for the extraordinary expedition. The men selected by Portolá had been gathering, completing the shortage in the military ranks or in the crews of sappers, guides, interpreters and muleteers. Visitador Galvez held continuous meetings with all these groups and was coordinating everything. During a decisive meeting of everyone concerned, the final plan was set: the expedition would be divided into two branches, one to go by land and the other by sea, with Gaspar de Portolá as commander-in-chief of both, while acting at the same time as the first governor of Alta California. As director of the spiritual aspects of the enterprise, Father Junipero Serra would accompany Portolá. Several Franciscan fathers would go along with Father Serra for the purpose of Christianizing the Indians and to establish missions.

During the following days, the southern tip of the Baja California peninsula witnessed the most energetic accomplishments of all its history. Loreto, La Paz, Cape San Lucas and San Blas across the Gulf were the main centers of this unusual activity. At San Blas the brigs *San Carlos* and *San Antonio* were being fitted, and at the wharfs of La Paz and Cape San Lucas the provisions brought from Loreto and other points of the peninsula or on the continent were being stored. These remained under the care and responsibility of Captain Ribera i Montcada appointed commissary of the expedition.

The cargo being accumulated included, besides church implements such as chalices, crucifixes and chasubles, all kinds of tools and farming gear, seeds for vegetables and grain, corn, flax, varieties of flowers as well as shoots and graftings of all kinds of European trees to be introduced into the new territory.

To be safe and to make the enterprise doubly effective, it was decided to send two sections of the expedition by sea and two by land with the appropriate distribution of leaders and men. Galvez was satisfied with the progress of the preparations and Portolá acted with swiftness and energy even though he was worried by the delay in Vincent's arrival with Elisa's answer, without which he would not like to undertake such a long and dangerous journey.

There were some snags. The Gulf of California or Sea of Cortés had a bad reputation, and chose this time to prove its capriciousness. The brigantine *San Carlos*, with its seven sails, was poorly built as were most of the vessels of the era. Because of this and the rough seas, early in December she arrived at La Paz in a leaky and unseaworthy condition, having met with a storm crossing the gulf. Galvez inspected the distressed ship and declared that it was in need of many repairs before being fit to sail again. It was found that its chief need was caulking, or even better, a coating of pitch over the bottom, but pitch was unavailable. A man of resource and rare expediency, Galvez conceived the idea of improvising a similar substance from a native plant, and to everyone's amazement, the solution worked. The ship was reloaded and soon became seaworthy again.

On January 25 the *San Antonio,* under the command of Captain Joan Peres arrived at San Lucas more or less in the same sad condition as the *San Carlos.* It also had to be unloaded and careened, its bottom coated with the pitch substitute. These readjustments took nearly a month.

Although time was working in favor of Portolá, the long and eagerly awaited reply from Mexico City was not there. This fact increased his impatience and worry, especially when all preparations were nearly completed. It was useless to think of a new excuse for requesting a postponement from Visitador Galvez.

One day a second message arrived from Madrid confirming the Russian plan of invasion of the territories of Alta California. The king's order insisted on the necessity of taking immediate measures "without the loss of a single day" to thwart the Russian intentions.

Then came the day that everything was ready. Galvez could not wait to see the expedition on its way. He considered it a credit to his organizational ability and gave it enormous importance. "His illustrious Lordship, His Most Catholic Majesty King Charles III of Spain, qualifies the undertaking as *Sacred Expedition* of don Jose de Galvez, and thus it will probably be known in history."

The visitador summoned Portolá and all the other leaders to a meeting to establish the date of departure. Governor Portolá called on him first to disclose again his personal problem and the need of waiting for the return of his orderly Vincent from Mexico City. He begged for a few days' delay. Galvez, in his dilemma, had no altenative — the king's orders demanded priority. The date of departure was set.

With great regret in his heart, although with a strict sense of duty, Governor Portolá accompanied by Visitador Galvez and their entourage traveled to Loreto where the official ceremony was going to take place. The *San Carlos* and the *San Antonio,* followed by the auxiliary ship *San Jose* loaded with provisions, had sailed with favorable winds some weeks before. On the *San Carlos* traveled the lieutenant Pere Fages with his company of Catalonian Volunteers, the engineer Miquel Constansó, the surgeon Pere Prat and the Franciscan Father Parron, sixty-two men in all, including the crew and the troops. The *San Antonio* commanded by Joan Peres did not carry troops, but its crew and two missionaries, Joan Vizcaino and Pere Gomez, were aboard.

One of the land sections, the one which would act as spearhead, under the command of Ribera i Montcada, had left Velicatá in the north of the peninsula a few days before. Included in this group were Father Joan Crespi, the chronicler of the expedition, another missionary, a map maker, three muleteers, forty-one Christianized Indians and twenty-one "soldados de cuera" from the presidio at Loreto — called thus because they wore coats made from several layers of leather and carried shields made from several thicknesses of rawhide to protect themselves from possible arrows of the Indians.

Finally, on March 9, 1769, the main branch of the expedition was ready to march at Loreto, under the command of Gaspar de Portolá himself. This group included Father Serra, the historian Francesc Palou, the missionary Miquel de la Capa i Cos, sergeant Jose Francisco Ortega, four muleteers, two servants, nine or ten regular soldiers, and forty-four Christianized natives. In all the four sections of the expedition were composed of 219 men, 200 head of cattle, 187 horses and mules for carrying packs and tilling the land, for slaughter and for husbandry.

The farewell ceremony took place at the old Loreto Mission, formerly occupied by the Jesuits. Visitador General don José de Galvez presided over the event. Father Junípero Serra conducted a High Mass, followed by a general Communion and the blessing of flags, troops, and the remainder of the expedition. The ceremonies culminated in a heated patriotic speech by the visitador.

Don Gaspar de Portolá, commander-in-chief of the four sections of the expedition, rode his horse to the head of the column, and solemnly gave the order of march. The last thing he did, however, was to turn his head toward the south, in the direction of La Paz, in the vague hope of seeing his orderly returning from Mexico. A message of love from Elisa could remove the deep regret with which, in spite of everything, he was leaving Loreto.

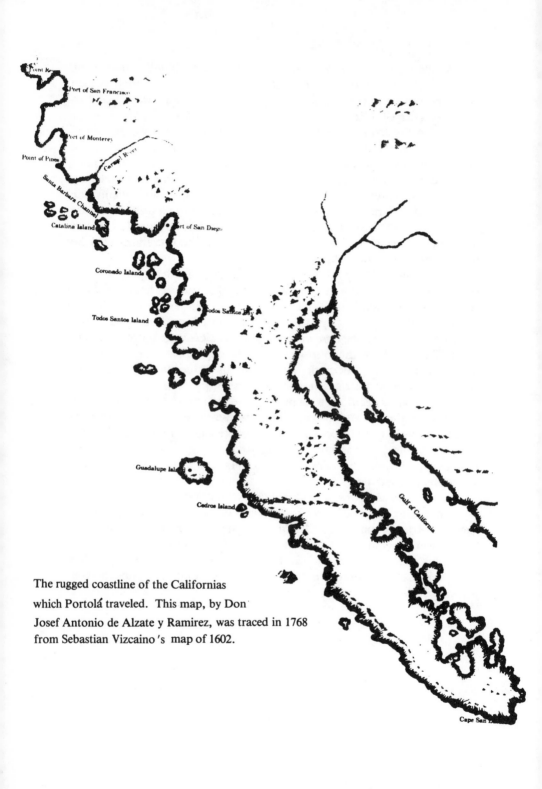

The rugged coastline of the Californias
which Portolá traveled. This map, by Don
Josef Antonio de Alzate y Ramirez, was traced in 1768
from Sebastian Vizcaino's map of 1602.

Chapter Nineteen

After a short stay at Velicatá where a mission was founded, the Portolá expedition traveled for one hundred and fourteen days through the arid lands of the California peninsula. Because of Father Serra's injured leg, caused by an old would he had received at the time of his first arrival in Mexico, now aggravated and swollen, the march was even slower and more painful. Father Serra could barely walk, and Gaspar de Portolá, to relieve his agony, proposed that the priest return to Velicatá, but the dedicated religious man flatly refused. Portolá ordered a litter built, but the enduring and humble Franciscan refused to be carried by human effort. Finally one of the muleteers applied an ointment used for mules, bringing relief so that the Father could continue to march.

During the course of the long march, the expeditionaries established their first contacts with the Indians who generally proved to be peaceful and friendly in spite of their astonishment at seeing these bearded white men, carrying long sticks which made deafening noise and riding the strange animals which they were seeing for the first time. At first the Indians had the idea that the men were the sons of the horses they were riding.

As they proceeded northward the expeditionaries found the terrain wilder and more abrupt. The natives they met were completely uncivilized and very poor. Men and children were completely naked while women wore only scanty straw aprons. The Indians took advantage of any distraction to steal any of the white men's possession they found. They found Father Serra's eye glasses and even tried to steal Gaspar de Portolás's boots. Fortunately both items were recovered in time.

The terrain was imposing and primeval, covered by scrubby vegetation and populated by rarely seen jackrabbits, deer, and mountain goats.

When provisions began to run out, the struggle was even harder; some of the weaker Indians belonging to the expedition either died, or moved by fear or sheer hunger, deserted.

Toward mid-June, Sergeant Ortega and a soldier from the advance mission arrived in San Diego and announced to the missionaries and troops there that Portolá's columns were near. Captain Ribera i Moncada sent a small patrol to meet the commandant and Father Serra and to escort them to the camp established by the first section of the land expedition in Alta California.

Meanwhile the *San Carlos* and *San Antonio* had anchored in San Diego Bay after coping with no small difficulties. The sea expedition had been much less fortunate than the land ones. The flagship, the *San Carlos*, after awaiting favorable winds off the coast of Baja California for days and days found itself, to the great dismay of Captain Vila, almost without drinking water. Most of the barrels of water were leaking, and many were already empty, and finding potable water was not easy. Sickness began to spread on board; most of the navigators came down with scurvy. Many sailors and some of the Catalonian volunteers became very ill, and some died. Captain Vila took advantage of the first favorable winds to head toward the north, following the course established by Cabrera Bueno and Vizcaino one hundred and seventy-five years before. On April 26 they reached the coast of New California. Looking at the heights of the Sierra Madre, Captain Vila remembered the Sierra Nevada as seen from the coast of Motril in Andalusia.

The *San Carlos* sailed as far as Catalina Island across from San Pedro Bay before the captain realized that he had bypassed San Diego. After turning back, the flagship entered her port of destination on April 30 at about five o'clock in the afternoon. There the *San Antonio,* which had preceded her by a few days, lay at anchor with everyone concerned about the delay of the *San Carlos.* The two ships exchanged the regimentary gun salvos. It was learned that the small ship *San Jose* had foundered in heavy seas, with all provisions aboard.

After the arrival of the new expeditionaries, Captain Ribera with the aid of Engineer Constansó and Surgeon Prat, transferred the temporary encampment to a more convenient site. In order to obtain potable water, it was necessary for the white men to begin talks with the hostile Indians. After many misunderstanding and much diplomacy, the Indians consented to lead the new-comers to a nearby spring. This place proved to be ideal for the new camp since it had abundant water and some vegetation with aromatic plants. Among the plants were sage, rosemary and even rose bushes. Surgeon Prat combined the plants with medicinal properties, and he used these herbs to treat some of his patients.

On June 29, shortly before noon, Commandant Portolá and Father Serra, leading their column, were sighted from the camp. They were welcomed with shouts of joy and salvos from muskets.

The news of the many sick and dead, both on land and on the high seas with the loss of the *San Jose,* saddened Portolá. After reviewing the forces, he found that all, without exception, including soldiers, sailors, officers and the religious personnel who had arrived by sea, were more or less affected by scurvy. A total of thirty deaths was recorded.

In spite of the sad state of affairs, enthusiasm did not diminish, and Gaspar de Portolá called a general meeting to organize the march toward Monterey. The Captains of both the *San Carlos* and the *San Antonio* declared that their ships were not in sailing condition, due chiefly to the lack of able men and of provisions.

In view of this fact, it was decided to accomplish the march by land instead of by sea as had been originally planned. It was decided that the *San Antonio* would return to San Blas with the sick men on board, to return with a cargo of provisions. She would then proceed directly to Monterey to join the land expeditionaries again. The *San Carlos* would remain in San Diego with Father Serra and a few armed men while Portolá and the body of the expedition would undertake the long trek toward the north to explore and occupy Alta California, with the main objective being that of securing for Spain the port of Monterey.

Remaining in San Diego, Father Serra who was concerned with the Christianization of the new territory could begin looking for a suitable place in which to found the first California mission. On his way northward, Portolá would collect information about the vast unknown land which they were penetrating for that very purpose. As a beginning, Portolá ordered the capture of a few Indians of the tribes in the San Diego area.

One of these captured Indians turned out to be one of the main *caciques,* a man of intelligence and imagination. With the obvious purpose of discouraging and disorienting the intruding foreigners, this chieftain gave a fantastic description of the unexplored territory. He told of an Amazon queen who had absolute power over all of Alta California, and about a very ferocious tribe which lived under water. Other stories included an account of a desert tribe which sat under the shade of their own enormous ears, and of another extremely evil group, all bald-headed from birth, which was the terror of the high hills and canyons.

Portolá smiled at such fantasies and turned to other less imaginative captives who gave him some elementary geographical data. One of these Indians said that another arm of the Colorado River which they had just passed ran at the north of the territory. The wide waterway flowed lazily around the mountains and finally disappeared into the great northern sea.

It was in this atmosphere of mystery and vagueness that the final arrangements for the march toward Monterey were made. Before the departure of the expeditionaries, Father Serra, who had not yet found the right place for the establishment of the mission, said a field Mass beside a scrubby mesquite bush on a branch of which hung the bells intended for the future mission.

On the conclusion of the Mass, the scanty forces which were to undertake the arduous march fell into line for review. Besides the Commandant, Governor Gaspar de Portolá, these included Captain Ribera i Moncada, Sergeant Ortega and his twenty-six *soldados de cuera*, Lieutenant Pere Fages and his small group of Catalonian volunteers, Engineer Costansó, six muleteers, fifteen natives and Fathers Gomez and Joan Crespi, the latter diarist of the expedition.

Those remaining in San Diego until Portolá's return were: Father Serra; Captain Vila of the *San Carlos*; Surgeon Prat; a guard of eight *soldados de cuera*; five able sea men; a few sick sailors; a carpenter; a blacksmith; eight Christianized Indians from Baja California; and three boy servants — a total of forty persons, including the sick. The forsaken flagship *San Carlos,* invalided by lack of crew, remained in the harbor —a ghostly phenomena in the solitary bay which was seeing a ship anchored in its waters for the first time.

As the moment of departure approached, Portolá, just as at the departure from Loreto, felt a heavy weight in his heart. He was leaving again, sad at not receiving news from Elisa. At the last moment, however, one of the encampment guards fired a shot of alert. Two horsemen had appeared at the top of the hill. Portolá almost shouted for joy. While everyone was astonished, asking themselves who these riders might be, Portolá did not need to wait for them to get closer — he knew that they were Vincent, his orderly, and his escort, an Indian servant.

When the loyal orderly reached his master, he was completely exhausted. Almost breathless and unable to speak, he smiled at Don Gaspar as he handed him an envelope addressed in fine handwriting. While everyone wondered what the urgent message might be, the commandant opened the envelope and removed a small golden medal. After kissing it, he turned to Father Serra and asked, "Father Junípero, will you kindly bless this medal for me?"

The devout Franciscan saw with pleasure that it bore the image of the Virgin of Mercy, patron saint of Barcelona. He blessed the precious token of love, kissed it, and returned it to the happy governor of Baja and Alta California.

Portolá thanked the president of the missions, and Father Serra wished good luck to the departing commandant. The drum roll began, and Commandant Portolá unsheathed his sword and gave the command to march.

The courageous column began the trip northward, becoming the first white men ever to tread, explore, and discover the hitherto-unknown hills and valleys of until-then-uncharted California.

Chapter Twenty

The colorful cavalcade formed by Gaspar de Portolá and his men advanced northward through California, opening what was to be known later as "El Camino Real" or the most important north-south road of the golden state.

The Portolá march was to prove very important in the field of discovery. Years later, a historian would write: "Along more than six hundred miles of virgin and difficult terrain, the expeditionaries lifted the veil of mystery that was lying over California, discovering valleys, brown mountains, bright flowers and strange populations, who for the first time saw white men arriving by land."

The explorers advanced with their commandant at the head of the column, cutting a gallant and svelte figure on his white horse. Gaspar's head was covered by his tri-cornered hat with its white feathers, and he was wearing a tight-fitting blue woolen jacket with yellow cuffs and golden epaulettes, a white patent leather bandolier, and high French riding boots, bell-shaped above the knees. His eager hands held the reins lightly, and his sword hung from his belt. Serenity shone in his face, framed by his heavy, well-trimmed black beard and enlivened by his restless, gentle eyes which sparkled with strange liveliness as they were kindled by the dreams of adventure and as he marvelled at the virgin spectacle before him.

Directly behind Gaspar came the other officers wearing their colorful uniforms which revealed the French influence in the style introduced into Spain by the new reigning monarch. Among Portolá's staff, the most striking figure was cut by the sturdy Lieutenant Pere Fages who had a determined face with small lively eyes and an almost sneering smile, characteristic of his sensual and matter-of-fact nature, broad shoulders, thick heavy hands and powerful arms.

Behind Lieutenant Fages, in double file the six Catalan Volunteers rode proudly, wearing the typical gear of the ancient *guerrilleros*. Then came the pack train with supplies, drivers, and muleteers, Engineer Miquel Costansó in charge as quarter-master and manning the sappers and scouts. On resigned mules, rode Fathers Joan Crespi and Gomez, alternating their prayers with observations and comments which were to appear later as data in the historic diary of the expedition.

Vincent, the commandant's faithful and resourceful orderly, shifted here and there along the column conveying orders and recommendations from his master and chief, his mobility and unconventionality as picturesque as his verbosity.

Behind the pack train and cattle and horses, came the regular troops wearing their long leather jackets and arrow-proof shields, under the command of Captain Fernando Rivera i Montcada, characteristically pessimistic in appearance, thickly bearded, but a true watch-dog seriously protecting the rearguard.

The short column of men and animals, despite the brilliant color in flags and uniforms, was a mere tiny touch of color, lost in the immensity of drab landscape with the changing blue or mauve of the high hills; the alternating greys and greens of the plains, changing according to the flow of the capricious rivulets; and the occasional glimpses of the blue Pacific, far beyond toward the west, like a background, indefinite, but permanent.

Portolá and his men advanced cautiously, step by step, rather fearfully, but with the awe of one who steps onto forbidden ground, rather than that of apprehension for unexpected dangers. The virginity of the land made it seem a kind of holy ground.

Portolá occassionally felt as though he were back in Catalonia because of the mild climate, the eternally bright blue sky, the ever-shining sun, the color and shape of the mountains and the arid-land characteristics of some of the vegetation. Nevertheless, he could not avoid feeling that, at the next bend or around the next rock any kind of strange or unknown wonder might appear — such was the excitement under which they advanced. Once in a while the appearance of a familiar shrub or a small animal — a bush of sweet-blooming broom or a startled lizard — made the men exclaim, "Just like at home in Catalonia!" or "Like Majorca!" This similarity increased the wonder along the march.

At the end of the day, to recover from physical fatigue, and ease the spirit of excitement, the commandant ordered well-deserved halts. The distance between water points, however, was what actually governed the distance of the daily march. They usually set up camp during the early afternoon in order to explore the area, do some hunting, or to chase away the occasional coyotes or wolves which might prey on the animals or stampede the cattle and horses.

The early evening hours were peaceful, restorative periods. The principals of the expedition sat with their commander and friend around a big camp fire, made from dry underbrush gathered nearby. The conversation was varied, but because of the unusual circumstances under which they found themselves, each was of unusual importance. Of course, the most frequent topic was the character and meaning of this expedition.

"So far," Portolá commented, "the territory does not appear to be an island at all, as recent geographers have been claiming."

Costansó, as technician in these matters, often intervened, "Most of the geographers are merely day-dreamers — either they make their claims at random from the coziness of their bookish studios, or as victims of some cosmic theory which usually has no reference to fact. Talking from experience, I can say that geography is not written with ink, but with the juices of shoe leather. A good geographer must be a good hiker."

"What surprises me," commented Father Crespi, diarist of the group, "is that since the Vizcaino expedition in 1602, Spain has totally neglected this territory. Like all the other navigators of the Manila galleons, Vizcaino limited himself to timid explorations of the coast lines. I cannot understand the lack of interest of the crown in this magnificent territory which is apparently as large as Spain."

Everyone turned toward Portolá. The commander smiled weakly, and after a silent moment of thought, concluded that it was easily explained. The Spanish colonization impulse began to decline at the beginning of the eighteenth century, either through fatigue or the fear that more was being bitten off than could be chewed. As leader of the expedition, however, he could not express this opinion, so instead he explained.

"The captains of the Acapulco galleons had a single interest, to discover sheltering harbors on their route to Manila. On the other hand, the court at Madrid acts only in view of concrete and simple ideas. The crown has neglected California, perhaps, for the simple reason that until now no one has stated the possibility that these mountains are loaded with gold. It has taken the menace of Russian occupation of this territory to send us here to explore and occupy the land."

Fages asked, "And, incidentally, what is the origin of the name of California?"

Costansó spoke up again to explain, "This is also a product of fantasy. In the fifteenth century there was a popular novel titled *Las Sergas de Espladian* in which an imaginary country is mentioned. It is called California and it is described as an earthly paradise. In Cortés's time someone applied this fictional name to this territory."

Candidly, Pere Fages confessed, "In my ignorance of Latin, I figured that California meant *forn de calc* (Catalonian for *lime kiln*)."

Someone agreed, "To judge from the heat and the composition of these mountains, the idea of a furnace is very adequate."

Early the next morning the column resumed its march. The main objective was "to reach Monterey at all costs" — a goal ratified in every mind and on everyone's lips. Another important, though secret consideration was the fear that marching conditions were becoming more and more dangerous because of fatigue and progressive diminishing of supplies. Every four days a more prolonged halt was made. The time was spent mostly in discussing plans for the advance, tracing the geographical maps and compiling the diary.

Several different diaries were being kept, as was customary then. Father Crespi was the official chronicler, registering the general aspects of the venture with the purpose of informing the visitador general and the ministers of His Majesty. The zealous Franciscan, however, gave special emphasis to spiritual aspects and to the possibilities of future apostolic work. Costansó applied all his interest to recording geographical, physical and natural data of the territory. Portolá wrote a strict military account, almost limited to hours of march, distances covered and names of explored places. The general obsession about locating the port of Monterey, however, caused other important details to be neglected.

On July 18 the expedition reached a cool, pleasant site which, later, in 1778, was to be the location of the Mission of San Luis Rey. On the 20th and 22nd, respectively, two natives were baptized, both close to death, one of severe burns.

On July 24 they sighted from shore the islands Sebastian Vizcaino had recorded with the names of San Clemente and Santa Catalina — names they were to keep.

Anong the wild vegetation encountered were many flowers. Many slopes were like carpets of mauve or yellow. There were few Indians in that area, and the few they met were not hostile.

On July 28 they found a fairly wide river which the padres hurried to give the name *Rio del Dulcisimo Nombre de Jesús.* However, after a day of repeated earthquakes, the soldiers changed its name to *Rio de los Temblores.* Later this river was to be known as the Santa Ana. On August 1 they reached the banks of another river which they named *Rio de Nuestra Señora de Los Ángeles de Porciúncula.* This became the site of the present day city of Los Angeles.

The expeditionaries deviated from their northwesterly course to go inland. After crossing a chain of mountains, part of the Sierra Madre system, they entered the wide valley which they called the Valley of *Santa Catalina de los Encinos,* much later to be known as San Fernando Valley.

Before crossing the mountains, they stopped at the foot of the hills where several large pools filled with a black bituminous substance called their attention. Later this was to become the center of a large oil development and a rise where antediluvian mammals were found in a well-preserved condition in the black tar. Portolá advanced the theory that the enormous amount of thick black substance *(brea)* from the core of the earth was the cause of the earthquakes.

At the western end of the valley, they had to cope with the ascent of the craggy Santa Susana mountains which they negotiated half afoot and half on horseback. After the twisted system of mountains, they reached the Santa Clara river whose course they followed westerly toward the ocean. They arrived at *Pueblo de las Canoas,* so-called for the special type of boat built by the native Indians, the Chumash, part of the population of the Santa Barbara Channel. The expeditionaries found traces here of a higher development of civilization than that of previous tribes encountered. The Chumash were friendly, and, in contrast to other earlier encounters, showed a sense of curiosity. One explanation might be that this was a sea-going population affected by the open, universal spirit inspired by the sea.

When the expedition reached the wooded lands of the mountains where later San Luis Obispo was to be founded, they met another type of native. Although inferior in civilization to those of the Santa Barbara Channel, these inland inhabitants had wider tribal organization. Their apparent chief was an elderly Indian with a goiter-type protruberance on his neck. The soldiers nicknamed him *"el Buchón."* His authority seemed to be powerful, although the customs of the small mountain society seemed to be very relaxed. The soldiers, particularly, took advantage of the situation by boldly accosting the native girls, to the scandalized eyes of the Franciscan fathers who concluded that the devil had passed that way. The Santa Barbara Channel Indian girls had been timid and modest, but the women of the *Buchón* territory, approached the soldier's camp at the *Cañada de los Osos* spontaneously and accepted the gallantries and less refined advances of the rude soldiers.

This began a kind of romantic interlude in which a more ambitious white man of the expedition succeeded in gaining the heart of the daughter of the chief, himself. This incident evokes the idyll of the Indian Princess Pocahontas and the English Captain John Smith during the colonization of the eastern United States.

Gaspar took advantage of this romantic period to talk at length with Vincent on the subject of Elisa and the details of his commission and his stay in Mexico City.

Vincent explained the astonishing change in Elisa to a beautiful, grand lady, admired by the entire Viceregal Court. He related, too, the conversation he had had with Don Oleguer de Siscar, Elisa's father. These details delighted the man from Balaguer and quickened his desire to return soon to Mexico City. During this intimate confidential period, Vincent decided that he could not hide from his master any longer the fact that Captain Ruiz Mendez seemed determined to supplant Don Gaspar in Elisa's affections.

Portolá listened to these unhappy details in complete silence, but he obviously became restless and impatient, and abruptly ordered the entire column to fall in and resume the march toward the bay of Monterey.

The soldiers regretted leaving that "paradise" so soon, but the Franciscans thanked God for the relief. They left the woods making the sign of the cross and without turning their heads to look back in fear of actually discovering the devil sneering at them.

Chapter Twenty-One

The white men's stay in the *Buchón* dominions created open rivalry between the religious fathers and the laymen. It had begun at the start of the march when the soldiers objected to the persistent naming of all the places which were discovered by religious names. "At this rate," joked the soldiers, "Very soon the church calendar of listed saints will prove insufficient."

From that time on, the growing rivalry became a race in the naming of places — the Franciscans would call a certain site *Santa Rosa* and the soldiers would call it *Corral,* another was first called *San Luis,* to be changed by the laymen to *La Gaviota; Santa Clara* became *Bailarin, San Roque* became *Carpinteria* and *Angel Custodio* became *Las Almejas.* The feud, if this differing philosophy can be so called, reached its climax, not during the expedition, but a short time later when Pere Fages became governor of California, succeeding Portolá. Father Serra and his missionaries carried on a war without quarter against the agnostic lieutenant of the Catalonian Volunteers.

Through ever-increasing difficulties, the expeditionaries continued their march north along the coast toward their immediate objective, Monterey. The advance became slower and slower because of the broken terrain, and the cold at night was becoming severe. The uncertainty of the location of their objective made their steps less certain. The "famous" port of Monterey began to seem a legend and a geographical puzzle of the times. Navigators to Manila had often mentioned the large bay and its port in the shape of an "O", but both Cabrera Bueno and Vizcaino had located it in a very vague latitude. This vagueness was to cost much labor and many useless efforts for Portolá and his men.

On September 13 the expedition camped in a narrow canyon at the foot of the Santa Lucia mountains, named by Vizcaino himself. A scouting group led by Ribera i Montcada was sent to find a pass through the mountains. They needed picks and crowbars to force the way, but two days later the persistent sappers had succeeded in opening a passage.

With many of the expeditionaries ill, the ascent was certainly difficult, but they were to discover that the way down was to be even more dangerous. They advanced at the rate of one mile a day. On the way they rested in a small hollow or basin where the missionaries later were to found the mission of San Antonio de Padua.

On September 20 they left this camp and continued climbing and descending mountains, each one as difficult to negotiate as the one before. The passage was so difficult, with the cold weather and the sick men, that Father Crespi registered this territory in his *Diario Histórico* as the "Wounds of Saint Francis."

After a four day halt at the summit, they undertook the descent, and on September 25 the caravan arrived at the course of water called today the Salinas River and called by the missionaries *Rio de San Elisario*. Following the course of the river, they reached the sea coast again on the thirtieth, after making a big detour. Their assumptions that the river was the one Vizcaino had named *Rio Carmelo* was the cause of grave consequences. Because of confusing the Salinas River and the Carmel River, the expeditionaries became completely confused. Places which would have been easy to recognize became mystifying reference points, finally making the entire group incapable of identifying any geographical data.

On October 1, Portolá, Costansó, Crespi and five soldiers climbed a hill from where they discovered a point of land advancing into the sea, and which they correctly judged to be Point Piños. On the other hand, Ribera i Montcada with a group of eight men explored the shore southward, toward Point Piños, and although he found a small *ensenada* between the Point of Pines and another point south of it with an arroyo emptying into it and some small lagoons, he returned to camp declaring that no port was to be found.

In fact, the Portolá expedition was facing the "Port of Monterey" which they had been seeking and which they now did not recognize. Ribera i Montcada unknowingly had explored the Carmel bay and point and the estuary of the Carmel River, all of which is part of the great bay in the shape of an "O" mentioned by Cabrera Bueno. The expedition was the victim of a confusion or bewilderment which seems unexplainable today, but was the kind suffered by many explorers — for some strange reason they doubted the fact that what they had before their eyes was the great bay they were seeking. Costansó had recorded that it was at latitude 37°20' while Cabrera Bueno had placed the Bay of Monterey at latitude 37°.

Because of these grave doubts, the expeditionaries fell into a state of utter depression. Fatigue, lack of provisions, and the too-long span of time in the wilderness — they were on the 78th day of march since leaving San Diego — weighed heavily on their spirits.

Portolá, a practical man, more humanitarian than authoritarian, decided to put an end to the dangerous situation. Democratically, he called a meeting of all the leaders so that each might express his opinion and propose a solution. He himself was the first to speak.

Portolá stated the results of the explorations: that which was to have been a great bay had turned out to be a small ensenada, and that which was supposed to be large lakes were small lagoons. They analyzed the situation coldly: food was getting scarce, seventeen men were ill and demanding the assistance of many others, and winter was practically upon them.

Costansó insisted that they proceed as far as latitude 37°30' either to locate the port of Monterey or to prove that it did not exist.

Fages agreed with Costansó and asserted that up to that moment the great port had not been found. Ribera i Montcada, the pessimist, believed that the great port did not exist.

In conclusion, Portolá proposed that after a few day's rest, they resume the march until the port was found. Everyone agreed and a document was written up and signed by all.

On October 7 the expedition resumed its march along the coast, headed north. Twenty-three days later they arrived at Angel Custodio Point. Eleven of the men were so ill they had to be carried on stretchers. The winter scourge had begun, Portolá and Ribera i Montcada became ill, and there was a general epidemic of diarrhea. This, however, had the virtue of curing those who had been affected with "scrubby" for which there was no other remedy.

When on October 30 the party reached latitude 37°31' they still had failed to find the mysterious Monterey Bay. They saw only a series of large rocks jutting out into the sea near the coast. There the Pacific Ocean in all its immensity spread out before them. There was no use in trying to continue along the coast; mountains made it impossible.

The expeditionaries had no other recourse than to turn inland, even more disoriented by the absence of the great bay they were seeking so uselessly. Then they discovered that a long bay, inlet or cove, opened before them, just below the promontory they were on, with what seemed to be the mouth of the inlet extending from there to distant white cliffs and a high point on the northeast side advancing into the sea. Portolá and his men stood facing what later was to become the Golden Gate and the wide San Francisco Bay — one of the largest ports in the north Pacific.

The expedition recognized immediately that this was an important discovery, but obsessed by the elusive Monterey Bay, they did not give it its deserved importance. Therefore they stubbornly continued walking toward the port in the shape of an "O", their immediate objective, hoping to find there awaiting them the auxiliary ship *San José*, which, having missed the bay of San Diego, might have continued directly to Monterey with the supplies and provisions she was carrying from Baja California.

Even greater confusion was to result as the caravan continued when some of them insisted that Monterey Bay was further north. To make things worse, some Indians they met told them about having seen a ship sailing in those waters. So, lured by the hope of obtaining provisions, they doubled their efforts to locate the bay.

Several scouting parties were organized, and on November 6 they camped in a creek emptying into the San Francisco Bay which they called San Francisquito Creek. This camp was barren, lacking food, game or otherwise. They managed to survive for many days on acorns.

By the 10th all the scouting parties had returned, disillusioned. They had found only desolate mountains and a few not-entirely-friendly Indians, everything except the port. The imagined presence of the *San José* anchored in the bay was a mirage of hungry men. A decision had to be made before they all died. Portolá summoned a new *junta* of them all. The general conclusion was that it was useless to continue the search northward, and that the logical move was to turn back. Portolá made some objections, but finally acceded.

A thousand conjectures haunted these tenacious explorers concerning the disappearance of the famous bay whose existence had been recorded by the illustrious navigators of those waters in past centuries. The only plausible reason they could reach was that because of some cosmic disturbance, the promontories surrounding the bay had sunk into the sea, or that the bay itself had been covered by sand or had been destroyed by the stormy sea.

The same afternoon on which the junta was held, the caravan resumed its march. Retracing their steps, they arrived twenty-six days later at Carmel Bay. There they camped until December 10, making new explorations still to no avail.

The confused men had walked all around the shore which formed the bay at Monterey, had slept two nights on the beach, and had never been clear enough to detect that they were standing on the very site they had so laboriously and untiringly sought. On returning to the general camp at Carmel Bay, they all insisted on declaring the disappearance of Monterey Bay.

South of Carmel Bay there was no way to continue along the coast. The caravan had to undertake the arduous ascent of the Santa Lucia mountains once more. There was abundant grass for pasture for the animals, but the men would miss the fish, clams and mussels which had relieved their hunger for awhile.

Before leaving Carmel after the celebration of a sad Mass which seemed more a requiem, the disillusioned men planted a cross by the shore with the following inscription: "Dig here and you will find a message." The buried message was a short discription of the explorations which had been made and a request to any ship master happening to sail in those waters, to follow the coast and to let his ship be seen. The message ended by declaring, "This land expedition from San Diego turns back at this point ... forced by hunger."

The misery and privation were so acute that the expeditionaries ate sea gulls when they could catch them, and even slaughtered one of their mules "of which only the Catalonians and the Baja California Indians ate."

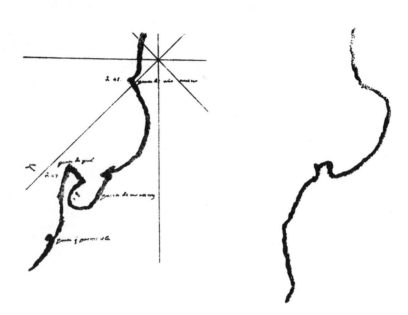

Left: Monterey Bay as drawn by Vizcaino.

Right: Monterey Bay, as actually seen by the Portolá expedition.

Chapter Twenty-Two

Meanwhile, in San Diego, Father Serra was not being much more successful with his enterprise — that of evangelization and conversion of the California Indians. As soon as Gaspar de Portolá and his men had started for Monterey on July 14, the zealous president of missions had begun his activities by founding his first mission. July 16 was chosen as the appropriate date to mark such an historical event. Early that morning the stake that was to mark the site of the Mission of San Diego de Alcalá was planted. The few men whose illness allowed them strength enough to stand weakly, helped in the construction of a few wooden huts for which they fashioned straw roofs. One hut was designed for religious services while awaiting the building of a regular chapel, and another, the largest, was destined to become a hospital.

The Indians watched the proceedings from a prudent distance; the least timid ones approached the fathers when they attempted to entice them with trinkets and gifts. The bulk of the tribe, however, kept at a distance awaiting a moment when the white men might turn around so that they could steal something.

The daring of the Indians increased as days went by, even reaching the point of stealing the sheets from under the very sick men. Cloth and every find of fabric were special objects of their greed, and they committed any sort of audacious act to get a piece of material. When one of the soldiers fired a shot and stood with his gun ready to fire at them they began to laugh and stood jeering, yelling "Boom, boom!", probably because they did not yet realize the deadly power of those noisy detonations.

The insolence of the Indians increased to the point where it became necessary to make the decision to enclose the mission within a stockade, greatly displeasing the Indians. Encouraged by the apparent peacefulness and goodwill of the white men, the Indians armed themselves with rocks and clubs, and on August 12 launched an attack against the encampment which lasted two days. One of the Franciscans was mortally wounded. The rioting Indians even attempted an assault on the *San Carlos* which was anchored in the bay. They cut the mooring ropes and tried to reach the ship in their canoes and to board it under the cover of darkness. This boarding was stopped, thanks to the vigilance of the watchman.

Returning good for evil, the Franciscan fathers increased their gifts, offering the Indians part of their scant provisions. The natives, hungry as they were, persisted in refusing the food, convinced that this food was the cause of the illness which affected the white men.

Finally the missionaries succeeded in employing a young Indian who had learned a few Spanish words to act as an emissary to propose to the Indians that they bring an infant which would be baptized and raised in the mission in the Christian faith as though he were a white man. To the immense pleasure of Father Serra, the emissary soon returned with an infant in his arms. The fathers began at once to prepare the ceremony of baptism to the growing curiosity of the Indian population. All went well with the ceremony until the moment arrived to pour the holy water on the infant's head. The Indians became so alarmed that they snatched the infant from Father Serra's arms and ran away to the great consternation and disillusionment of the fathers.

A few days later the expeditionaries under Portolá's command who had left San Diego six months earlier came within sight of the mission stockade. Even though they had failed in their objective to locate Monterey Bay and had suffered many hardships, Portolá was proud to think that he had not lost a single man. The returning men announced their approach with a salvo of musketry, and the encampment celebrated wildly.

The report of the precarious situation at San Diego caused Portolá great concern, and since he was solely responsible for the enterprise, he felt that he must take drastic action. The great number of sick men, the hostility of the natives, and the lack of provisions all pointed up the danger of their position. The *San Carlos,* lacking a crew, remained anchored in the bay, as idle an an invalid. The *San Antonio,* long ago redispatched to Baja California for provisions, had not returned, and the *San Jose* had never reached San Diego and was presumed lost at sea.

Portolá ordered a complete inventory of all provisions, and decided that the stores could not last them until mid-March; therefore, he announced that the expedition would return to Mexico if the ships had not reached San Diego by then. Since he held complete responsibility he could not tolerate such great and useless sacrifice of lives for an indefinite goal.

The firm decision of the commander created great consternation and visibly upset the Franciscan fathers, particularly Father Serra who, in spite of the fact that he had not been able to baptize a single native to this point, still continued to dream about converting the heathens of the territory.

Both Father Serra and Father Crespi remained stubbornly set on remaining in San Diego, and began a kind of conspiracy based on the argument that Providence would not allow their newly-begun evangelization to be abandoned. They even put a rumor into circulation that the commander had only sentimental reasons for wanting to return to Mexico City — the desire to be reunited with his beloved Elisa.

Gaspar de Portolá, a man of great integrity and concious of his duty, although human enough to understand weakness in others, paid no heed to this pettiness, and continued firm in his determination which he considered to be the only logical solution. In the meanwhile, the missionaries had begun a Novena addressed to Saint Joseph, begging for his heavenly intervention. At this point Portolá, an earthly, practical man, sent Ribera i Montcada and twenty men with horses and mules to the Mission of Velicatá in Baja California with orders to return as quickly as possible with all the provisions available. This was an obvious example of his firm intent not to abandon the expedition, if it were at all possible, even though he persisted in his interest in returning to Mexico City after the successful accomplishment of this duty.

On Saint Joseph's Day, March 19, the Novena initiated by Father Serra ended. All eyes turned toward the open sea beyond the bay as though awaiting a miracle. March 20 was the date set by Portolá to undertake the return. On that day no sails appeared on the horizon. Even so, Portolá did not give the order to break up the camp, nor did the order come on the twenty-first or twenty-second. Finally, on the twenty-third, the sails of a ship appeared far out in the sea, approaching the bay — it was the *San Antonio!*.

"Miracle — miracle!" shouted the men.

Whether a fugitive-imagined sail had appeared in the half light of sunset on Saint Joseph's Day as a premonition to Portolá, or because him warm heart caused him to grant grace, Gaspar had, of his own accord, willingly decided to postpone the order to return for four days. Now he joined in the general joy and enthusiasm, celebrating the arrival of the *San Antonio* as a tacit omen of the future success of the entire expedition — both for colonization and for evangelization of California.

The *San Antonio,* as already known, had returned to San Blas during Portolá's absence from San Diego, and, after loading abundant provisions, was ordered to sail directly north toward Monterey to meet Portolá and his expedition. On reaching the Santa Barbara Channel the ship cast anchor for a water supply. Natives informed Captain Peres that a group of men on horses had passed that way recently, headed south. Captain Peres did not understand the reason for the return of what he guessed to be the Portolá expedition, and hesitated between proceeding north on course toward Monterey, or turning back toward San Diego. The loss of an anchor forced his decision, and caused his providential arrival at San Diego on the crucial day in time to prevent the abandonment of that port, and with it the occupation of Alta California.

The arrival of the *San Antonio* rekindled Portolá's enthusiasm, and he felt again that he was the commander who, on leaving La Paz, had sworn to "fulfill his mission or die", adding that not to fulfill it would mean disloyalty to "God, to the King and his own honor." He saw clearly that now the conquest and occupation of Alta California could be accomplished with full safety for the men under his command.

Portolá gave orders to make ready immediately for the resumption of the long trek toward Monterey. Consequently on April 16, after the gathering of all the equipment and elements, The *San Antonio* sailed northward once again, one day in advance of the departure by land of the newly-formed column, again commanded by Portolá, which was to repeat the feat which was unexplainably unsuccessful the first time.

In spite of the uncertainty of locating the elusive Monterey Bay, the march was resumed with the definite plan of establishing a *presidio* on some nearby site. Portolá instructed Captain Peres to proceed directly to the sea inlet discovered by Sergeant Ortega the previous November, that is, to the entrance of the small inland sea, the Bay of San Francisco, discovered by Portolá himself. From there, the ship would turn south, exploring the coast as far south as Point Pinos.

On the *San Antonio's* second trip north, Fray Junípero Serra, surgeon Prat, and the geographer Miquel Costansó traveled. The latter had accompanied Portolá to Monterey by land the first time. Also aboard were Father Crespi, Lieutenant P. Fages with twelve Catalonian Volunteers, seven regular soldiers, five converted Indians, two muleteers, and several ship's hands.

Sergeant Ortega remained assigned to the San Diego Mission together with two Franciscan fathers, Parren and Gomez, twenty regular soldiers and twelve Indians from Baja California. The *San Carlos* remained anchored in the bay, under Captain Vila, its first mate, and twelve sailors.

The new land expedition reached Point Pinos on May 24, thirty-seven days after its departure from San Diego. This second march turned out to be much faster, with fewer accidents than the first. When the expeditionaries reached the foot of the cross they had planted by the shore, they found it undisturbed, although bedecked with bows and arrows, spears, feathers, dried meat, fish and shells deposited by the natives as offerings to strange, unknown gods. Portolá ordered camp set up there.

That same afternoon as Portolá, Fages and Father Crespi contemplated idly the placid expanse of water before their eyes, the perfectly smooth surface broken only by the capricious diving of some seals and an occasional whale crossing on the horizon, they exclaimed almost at once, "But — *this* is the Port of Monterey we have been searching for! The port such as described by Vizcaino and Calbrera.' " In fact, they had before their eyes "the great bay in the shape of an 'O'," although Cabrera had committed the error of placing Point Pinos as running northeast-southwest instead of northwest-southeast.

Their wonder was not so much at their finally finding the Port of Monterey, but at their having missed it the first time when, just as now, they had had it before their very eyes.

Chapter Twenty-Three

When, seven days later, the *San Antonio* anchored in those sparkling waters, the ship was welcomed with the joyous announcement that the mystery of the *"gran puerto de Monterey"* was finally solved. This very one was the large bay for which they had been yearning so long!

On June 3, 1770, all the members of the expedition gathered around a huge live oak tree which towered above the shore and the bay. They were about to proceed with the official occupation in the name of Spain of the Port of Monterey, and with it, all the territory of Alta California. The ceremony consisted of religious rites, officiated over by Father Junípero Serra before an altar bedecked with branches of pine. The Majorcan missionary, donning the white linen alb and the gold embroidered stole, intoned the *venite creator spiritus,* sprinkled that lonely spot in the wilderness with holy water, and began the mass which ended with a *salve* and the proverbial *Te Deum laudamus.* To this point the ritual of the conquest by the Cross was taken care of.

Next, the ceremonies were taken over by the bearer of the Sword, probably the first Spanish *Conquistador* to occupy new territory without having made use of the blade! Gaspar de Portolá performed the formalities prescribed for such an occasion. In the name of Charles III, he took possession of the territory. With his sword he saluted the royal pennon, plugged out a handful of grass, picked up a few rocks and scattered them in several directions, and thus incorporated the fabulous land of California to the Spanish Crown — the land explored, occupied and colonized, against all precedents in the New World, by a scion of the Catalonian nobility, together with a group which included seventeen other Catalonians who heretofore had been banned as "foreigners" from Spanish adventures in America.

The ceremonies concluded, Portolá had much to think about during the peaceful days that followed. He asked himself whether his mission in Alta California had really ended, or whether his mission implied continuance with the work of colonization. Personal motives caused him to think not. In the first place, his urgent need to see Elisa again called him to Mexico City. On the other hand, he reasoned, once he had fulfilled his military obligations, once he had terminated the strict mission of occupying and taking possession of the territory, his presence there was unnecessary. Of course, subjectively, his sudden return to New Spain would appear to be an abandonment of that kingdom he had conquered with so much effort. Should he remain there, he would be actually its true king, if only by delegation from the Spanish monarch. However, after weighing all the facts, he came to the conclusion that California was at that time an empty kingdom. Ruling there as governor and supreme military chief would make him a king, but at the same time, he would be nothing.

Secretly too there was a sadness which blurred the whole glorious enterprise. Portolá concluded that he was in California acting as a Spanish public official, serving a king that was not his own! How different it would have been if he could remain there in that high position as a Catalonian subject, as a true, authentic representative of an independent Catalonia, as a representative of his fatherland, as glorious and heroic as in the era of her sovereign kings!

Cutting short his dreaming and analyzing the situation closely, Portolá concluded that he was again facing an opportunity to choose between the mediocrity of being not-quite-a-king or nothing at all. He decided in favor of the latter. He would return to Mexico to gather the superficial laurels of the moment and to resume his placid and elegantly useless life. Other more ambitious men, probably more able but less sensitive, could continue the colonization work which virgin California certainly needed. For instance, Lieutenant Pere Fages, a Catalonian of different social origin, was a most capable man to create the beginnings of civilization in Alta California. He had the natural elements to initiate agriculture which one day would make the territory an abundant garden. He had horses, agriculture equipment and mules to till the soil; he had seeds and tree cuttings and sturdy farm hands, men who were healthy and strong in mind. Also, there was Father Junípero Serra, idealist and spiritual dreamer, and his faithful missionaries who were willing and able to channel the wayward and unpredictable force of the native population.

At this point, Portolá had reservations concerning the ideas of the zealous missionaries. Although these Franciscans were of more humble and healthy nature than the Jesuits who had been banned from Baja California, he feared that these religious men could constitute a hampering factor in the task of colonization if handled by such a practical and realistic man as Fages. Portolá thought about the spirit then prevailing in Spain among religious orders, and he was afraid that the missionaries might convert the California native population into a submissive, virtually castrated society, kept in original ignorance, made to depend exclusively, as in Spain itself, on the daily dole, the bowl of soup distributed every day at noon at the door of the convents to the lower Spanish classes.

When Portolá informed Lieutenant Fages and Engineer Costansó of his decision to return to Mexico, they were completely surprised. As his only excuse, the governor and commander in chief exclaimed with one of his typical smiles, "I have not come to America to till the soil!"

Long and serious conversations were to follow. Without any intent to exert influence on them by prejudging the colonization tasks for the California of the future, Portolá exposed his views as to what an ideal land development should consist of, mostly in the spirit of enjoyment of his last days among colleagues and friends, but also, perhaps, to justify himself unconsciously for his astounding decision.

During the wide areas of conversation, Portolá mentioned that, in his opinion, the Spanish colonizing impulse was almost spent. In fact, the Spanish colonization of America was ending in failure. He asserted strongly that the practice of sending a minimum of people to colonize a maximum of territory was basically an error. It is a colonization of blood, drop by drop. The American Indian was, in the long run, an invincible race. Cortés, for instance, had accomplished the prodigious feat of subduing with one hundred men, hundreds of thousands of Indians, the most civilized on the Continent. But, from that victory, and from all the victories over the Indians that had followed since, what remained? Nothing. It had been a useless effort — gold and silver mines were then abandoned, and an ever deeper resentment by the Indians had resulted. The Spaniard always and constantly defeated the arrows and the savagery of the Indians, but they could never defeat, and would never defeat the indifference of that fatalistic and stoic race which won through passive resistance.

Considering, for example, Baja California and the northern provinces of Sonora and Sinaloa, Portolá expounded with enthusiasm. After two hundred and fifty years of toil and untold expense, they remained in the same primitive state with the same insignificant penetration as when Cortés first explored them, dreaming of establishing a base there for active navigation to the Orient. Their gold and silver mines, their pearls and other riches still continued to be forbidden to the colonizers — still with the silent population who were apparently indifferent, but hostile to the bottoms of their souls. Neither the Cross nor the Sword could make any headway in the arid field of native tenacity.

Portolá extended his talk to remarks of a more general character. The work of the *Conquistadors* and the colonizers of America was neither remunerative nor did it grant personal glory for those who had accomplished it with blood and sweat. On the contrary, for every one of them there had come a moment when jealousy and mistrust of those who had remained in Spain converted him into a delinquent or a vulgar criminal. Columbus, Cortés, Pizarro and many others ended in disgrace, in prison or prosecuted *en rebeldia*. A sort of vile espionage was maintained around every royal envoy sent to America. Nobody could escape this ordeal. With the apparently inoffensive practice of keeping diaries and making period reports to the court, it happened that the *visitador general* acted as spy and controller of the viceroy; the latter acted as spy of the governor and any heads of expeditions; the military men informed on the work and behavior of the geographers; the religious men reported against all the representatives of temporal power, giving credit only to priests and missionaries. Even at home, in the court, the clerks and chroniclers despoiled everyone from credits and merits to exalt the king.

Portolá continued saying that the system was a mere reflection of the disastrous traditional concept of colonization held by the crown. Colonies, in spite of the public rhetoric of the evangels and the implanting of the cross, were considered by Spain as simple factories for the miraculous production of gold. This idea had originated mainly at the time of ascension to the throne by Philip III in 1598. Given exclusively to pleasure and to religious retreat, the king had delegated all his power to the Duke of Lerma who commercialized the monarchy in great scale. Lerma continually sent demands to the colonies for gold and more gold.

Under Philip IV, the Count-Duke of Olivares did not limit himself to mere demands, but converted the native *peons* of Baja California and Northern Mexico into complete slaves. The results were catastrophic. On the Gulf of California, for example, a sector which once yielded twenty percent of all the gold sent to Spain, Olivares's tyranny provoked the uprising of the Indians, the massacre of a few Spaniards and the closing of the mouth of the mines, blocked and lost since then.

The climate of corruption and inefficiency of a monarchy such as the Spanish one could not produce any other results, affirmed Portolá. It would be difficult to find an other epoch so paradoxical and tragic as the Spanish historical period from 1500 to 1700. In two hundred years there had been only five kings who had full mental faculties. Charles II and Juana, who was totally demented, ruled during seventy-three years. During a lapse of sixty-seven years, under Philip III and Philip IV, the king did not pay the least bit of attention to public affairs. Under Philip II all imaginable errors were diligently planned and stubbornly executed.

Only in a madhouse could one find a similar succession of insane and depraved persons as among those who held the absolute power in Spain from Charles I to Fernando VI. Charles II did not leave the breast of his nurse until the age of six, and during the last nine days of his life, already entirely insane, did not receive any other nourishment than milk from a woman's breast. Philip II married four times, once with a fourteen-year-old princess who was betrothed to his own son. The son became insane, either due to his father's persecution or his paternal-inherited blood. The prince and the princess taken from him died almost on the same day, under circumstances that raised the rumor that the king was the assassin.

Philip III and Philip V suffered utter melancholy. The latter who ended the Austrian dynasty and began the Bourbon dynasty remained no more faithful to the inaptitude of the Hapsburg sovereigns. Under such disastrous monarchies, the population of the Peninsula declined from twelve million in 1500 to six million the "year of grace" of 1769 in which Gaspar de Portolá made those comments.

As a consequence, and as a final decision, the explorer of California made this statement: "Not even with scepter in hand and as a full king could I be convinced to remain here to colonize this territory for Spain!"

Diario del Viage que haze por tierra D.n Gaspar de Sortolá Capitan de Dragones del Regim.to de España Governador de Californias á los Puertos de San Diego y Monterrey situados en 33 y 37 grados haviendo sido nombrado Comandante en Gefe de esta expedicion por el Ill.mo Señor D.n Joseph de Galbez en virtud de las facultades Vice-Regias que le hà concedido su Excel.a Dicha expedicion se componia de 37 Soldados de Cuera con su Capitan D.n Fernando de Rivera deviendo este adelan-tarse con Veinte y siete Soldados, y el Governador con diez, y un Sargento

Horas	
6	El dia 11 de Mayo salí de Santa Maria ultima mision del Norte, escoltado de quatro Soldados en compañia del Padre Junipero Serra Presidente delas Misiones y el R. D.r Miguel Campa; en este dia se handuvo como quatro horas con poquisima agua para las Bestias, nada de pasto, por lo que Elegió á marchar por la tarde para lograrlo aunque sin agua.
5	El n. handuvimos por buen camino as co horas paramos en el parage que llaman la Posa d'agua dulce sin pasto.

The title page and first entries of Portolá's diary describing the California trek.

Chapter Twenty-Four

On July 9, 1970 Gaspar de Portolá, accompanied by Engineer Miquel Costansó, boarded the *San Antonio*, sailing from Monterey for San Blas and New Spain. Prior to this sailing, he had transferred his command to Lieutenant Fages and had placed the new colony under the protection of the Catalonian Volunteers. In the course of time these colonizers were to become the first farmers and fruit growers of fabulous California.

Before leaving Monterey, on June 15 Portolá had dispatched a group of mounted men to Mexico City to make a complete report to the viceroy of New Spain of the official act of occupation and the taking possession of the Port of Monterey and Alta California in the name of Spain. The group was composed of two Catalonian Volunteers, one regular soldier and one sailor. A short distance south of San Diego the mounted emissaries met Captain Rivera i Montcada who was returning with cattle and provisions for the San Diego encampment. He attached five of his soldiers to the group to escort them as far as Mexico City. The Portolá emissaries arrived at Mission Todos los Santos, near Cape San Lucas on August 2 and there boarded a boat to cross the Gulf.

On August 10 Viceroy Francois de Croix received the important report from Portolá. The bells of the cathedral rang to announce the sensational news, and, as though pre-arranged, all the bells of the other churches and convents joined in the triumphant peal.

The ship carrying the explorer of California passed San Diego in whose bay the *San Carlos* remained at anchor, and made headway toward San Blas. After landing, Gaspar de Portolá stayed at Tepic, in Banderas Bay, for a few days to recover from the hardships of the voyage. From there he sent additional information to the viceroy and wrote a brief personal note addressed to his beloved Elisa.

In Mexico City the accomplishments of the Portolá expedition were the general topic of conversation. The viceroy ordered an immediate printing of the message as written by the governor himself in order that it might be widely diffused throughout the Spanish possessions, Spain and the foreign countries. A triumphal welcome was prepared for the valiant captain of dragoons who suddenly had acquired the stature of a Spanish conquistador.

Friends and enemies of the brave military man commented on his deeds each in his own way. Don Oleguer de Siscar, father of Elisa and resident of the Real Audiencia in Mexico, discussed it proudly almost as though it concerned the prowess of a member of his family. Elisa was thrilled. In private in the quiet of her room she read and reread the letter sent by Gaspar. Mixed in her heartbeats was excitement and unruly emotions caused by her imagination of all these marvelous adventures and accomplishments. In public, in the streets, and at the Viceregal Court Elisa was admired and envied by the entire feminine world.

Portolá's enemies, on the other hand, bit their lips as they faced the undisputed triumph of the brand new "conquistador." Nevertheless they could not understand why the hero of the California enterprise had not remained there to gather the fruits of the conquest. They used this oddity as a new excuse to defame him, saying that Portolá was only a bubble of vanity, not allowing the most elemental sense of duty prevent him from abandoning the post in order to rush to Mexico City to gather worldly glory. They expected him to return to California as soon as the celebrations were over, assuring themselves that the pompous military man would return to Monterey to enjoy the newly-created office of governor of Alta California and to prepare to repel the Russian invasion if the country of the Czars finally overtook it.

A few days later when Portolá entered the capital of Mexico as the hero of the hour, popular acclaim was greater than had ever been seen before in New Spain. The cavalcade, led by the band of Portolá's regiment, passed through the principal thoroughfares. From his official carriage, among the stately vehicles of the highest authorities, Portolá greeted the people with his irresistible smile, and his svelte silhouette was doubly admired at this hour of triumph. The splendid cavalcade made its way to the old cathedral where a solemn *Te Deum* was to take place with the viceroy and visitador general in attendance. Later the "last Spanish conquistador in the Americas" would be feted at the Palace of the viceroy.

Portolá was anxious to find himself alone with Elisa. Interminable official conferences with Viceroy de Croix and Visitador Galvez kept him tied down all through the day so that the happy moment did not arrive until evening, shortly after the Grand Ball which had been organized in his honor. The moment Elisa entered, the impatient conquistador rushed to meet her, excited as never before in his life. A short while later, during a dance, the happy couple disappeared, unnoticed, into the semi-darkness of the terrace. There was a full moon and the air was exceptionally mild and perfumed for the high altitude of the Valley of Mexico. Leaning against the stone balustrade overlooking the garden, the two lovers enjoyed moments of supreme happiness. Words were few; Gaspar had brought out the precious medal of the Virgin of Mercy, and as a miraculous talisman, the small golden disc seemed to talk more eloquently than the most tender of speechmakers. The lips of the two lovers joined for the first time and thus fulfilled the ultimate hope of their lives.

Not many days later, the venerable president of the Real Audiencia, Don Oleguer de Siscar, announced the betrothal of his only daughter Elisa to the captain of dragoons, Gaspar de Portolá, explorer of California.

The news stirred the whole capital. The ladies of the court with envy and regret rushed to congratulate Elisa. The enemies of the popular captain now understood the reason why Gaspar De Portolá had left his promising position of *amo and señor,* lord and master of New California, so abruptly.

The person who was probably most upset by the engagement announcement was the zealous Dominican Father Alonso, who once again felt himself duty-bound to act diligently in the defense of Holy Mother Church. The marriage of a devout Catholic young lady to a proven heretic could not be tolerated. He began acting immediately to forestall the wedding.

Father Alonso, however, was forced to recognize that time and circumstances had altered, and that it was not feasible now to apply the same procedures which had been so successful in Barcelona. Right then Portolá was a popular hero, and no direct scheme against him had a chance to succeed. Furthermore, after the expulsion of the Jesuits, the rumor was that the next victims of the new policy of the crown would be the Holy Inquisition itself. Without the power of the Holy Inquisition, Father Alonso realized that any accusation of heresy would be empty of value.

In the past few months a feud had developed between the members of the Council of the Inquisition and the authority of the viceroy. This would make any campaign, direct or indirect, even more difficult to undertake. In spite of these facts, Father Alonso persisted in his purpose. He requested an audience with the Council of the Holy Inquisition and, supported by the necessary documents, formally denounced Gaspar de Portolá as a proven heretic. When the aggressive Dominican produced the transcript of Nobility of the Portolá family with its fateful H over a cross as an eloquent stigma, there was general shock. The entire council stood and remained standing in dramatic silence for a few moments.

When discussion resumed, it was done most cautiously. Some of the council argued that this was certainly not the most appropriate time to antagonize the civil authorities even more. It was dangerous to begin persecuting someone who was enjoying the immunity of a hero at that time.

The name of the *conquistador* of California, a name now famous in all the territories of the Crown, could not be smeared like that of an anonymous citizen.

Father Alonso impetuously asserted that the man who had enacted the sacrilegious expulsion of their brothers of the Company of Jesus could well and decidedly be branded as a declared enemy of the Holy Mother Church!

After a prolonged debate, the final vote went against Gaspar de Portolá, and the council declared the marriage of a heretic to a faithful daughter of the Catholic Church to be a sacrilege.

The news of Portolá's condemnation created a sensation. The crowd in the streets staged violent demonstrations. The Civil authorities considered this condemnation as a new provocation.

During these trying days a curious incident occurred. Two carriages, that of the head inquisitor and that of the president of the Real Audiencia both entered a narrow alley at the same time. The alley led to the small square which was the entrance to Plateros Street. Both coachmen, on explicit orders from the respective occupants, refused right of way to the other carriage, invoking equal rights authority in accordance with the identical rank level of each master. At the beginning, the incident provoked a verbal quarrel between the two illustrious *hildalgos*. Then the equal stubbornness of the two gentlemen produced a frowning silence, and a complete bottleneck in the public alley. The news of this startling incident spread immediately through the entire city. Men of every social rank came to that narrow thoroughfare to watch the astonishing drama of personal pride taken to its limits. It was a true duel — one without apparent solution. The contendents held equal rank in levels of authority, and the conflict must be declared an impasse.

Because of the fact that one of the carriages was occupied by a member of the Inquisition and the other by Elisa's father, people chose to see a relationship between the incident and the condemned betrothal of Siscar's young daughter and Captain Portolá. The civil authorities chose to see the whole affair as gloating on the part of the representatives of the Inquisition for having put the power of the civil authorities in jeopardy.

For seventy-two hours, the two carriages with their respective occupants and coachmen remained on the spot with neither relenting. Finally the viceroy decided to intervene. A palace attendant came to the narrow and congested alley with written orders signed by Marquis de Croix himself, directing both carriages to back up at the same time and at equal speed out of the alley exactly as they had entered. Thus neither rank of authority was violated, and a traffic problem never registered in the history of transportation was solved genially.

This coincidence contributed toward bringing the rivalry between the civil and Ecclesiastic authorities in the capital of New Spain to an extreme. Meanwhile, the rumor persisted that the viceroy had set November 3 as the date for issuance of the order for the dissolution of the Holy Office in Mexico.

On that announced day people in the streets became excited, and the viceroy had to take extraordinary measures to avoid riots. A number of troops had been stationed around the Convent of Saint Bernard where the Palace of the Inquisition was located. No doubt this act prevented the populace from taking justice into its own hands to accomplish the rumored dissolution.

The critical moment passed, and believing the caution of the viceroy to be a sign of weakness, the Council of Inquisitors became bolder. To show the authority of the Holy Office, an announcement was made that on the following Sunday the execution of the latest condemned heretic would take place at the public-burning scaffold. This culprit was an unfortunate woman accused of adultery. It was her legal defense by the Royal Audience which had caused the conflict regarding proper jurisdiction between civil and ecclesiastical authorities.

This announcement aroused the entire capital. There was great expectation and doubt as to whether the burning would actually take place or not. As announced, the following Sunday at daybreak, the public scaffold which was located at the intersection of San Diego Street and the Alemeda paseo was decorated in mourning, ready for the execution. It was guarded by the hooded agents of the Holy Office. The people began to gather early in anticipation of more than the execution itself, in expectation of violent action to prevent the execution since it constituted a challenge to the authority of the viceroy.

At the scheduled time, shortly after sunrise, the unfortunate Maria Josefa Morales, with a pale face and tearful eyes, was taken from the dark underground cell of the Inquisition palace to be brought to the public scaffold. The pitiful victim, barefooted and dressed in the defaming *sanbenito* worn by those condemned to death, walked slowly through the silent crowd with her eyes on the ground. The members of the Council stepped up to the scaffold behind her, and in the name of the Prosecutor of the Holy Office, a hooded bailiff read the sentence condemning the sinner Maria Josefa Morales to death at the stake, in public and exemplary execution.

At that very moment, however, a mounted squad of the Viceregal guard appeared at the corner of Tacuba Street. Ominously, the squad advanced to the foot of the scaffold. An officer of the Royal Audience mounted the wooden stairs and served the head of the council an edict from the viceroy declaring the procedures illegal and granting a governmental pardon to Maria Josefa Morales. The crowd shouted approval of the pardon and celebrated the victory of public justice.

The Chief Inquisitor ordered the culprit returned to her dungeon for solitary confinement, and climbing into his official carriage, ordered the coachman to rush him directly to the Viceregal Palace.

When the Grand Inquisitor stood face to face with Viceroy Marquis de Croix he learned the truth regarding the rumors that had been spreading. There did, in fact, exist a Royal Decree suppressing the Inquisition in Mexico. There was, however, a provision that the order could be implemented at any given time at the discretion of the viceroy, while waiting for the final clarification of matters of jurisdiction between the Holy Office and the Royal Audience.

Chapter Twenty-Five

S adly, the high clergymen of the Mexico cathedral watched the strife between the authority of the viceroy and that of the Inquisition. With their usual caution they had remained neutral while awaiting the final results of the conflict. With the latest incidents and the announcement of the forthcoming suppression of the Holy Office in Mexico, the venerable prelates began to be concerned. They now conceived the idea of acting as mediators, and without wasting any time, the entire ecclesiastical body left the cathedral office and crossed the Zocalo for an official visit to the viceroy at his palace.

The Marquis de Croix, either because he was actually busy or because he had already come to the end of his patience, kept the prelates waiting in the antechamber. An hour passed, and, finally, the dignity of the visitors could no longer tolerate such humiliation. The chief canon arose and said, "Let's withdraw, my lordships. Our role as mediators can be considered ended, a failure. With his lack of consideration, His Excellency, the Viceroy, had just placed us on the field of his adversaries. Let's accept the will of God."

All the dignitaries present accepted this hasty decision, although they all recognized that the church's contention with the state was already a lost cause. One of the canons commented, "Marquis de Croix after all is as much influenced by French currents as the King himself. Maybe we should continue to fight instead of keeping faithful Christian resignation, no matter how holy." None of his colleagues seemed to listen, and with the plan of going to the palace of the Inquisition to file their complaint, they departed silently.

The Council of the Inquisitors, still feeling its spiritual authority totally unimpaired, devised the new tactic of indicting the viceroy himself. He was summoned to appear at ten o'clock promptly on the morning of the first work day of the following week, to answer before the Council of the Holy Office.

Viceroy de Croix appeared punctually on the day appointed, but he did not come alone. He left his escort squad, armed with musketry and manning two field artillery pieces, at the door of the palace.

The highest authority of New Spain was kept waiting a few minutes before the door of the council hall. After a short while Viceroy de Croix took out his watch, and, addressing the usher, said, "If I am not out of this palace within ten minutes, the artillery pieces will begin shelling, and will demolish the building."

The council cleared matters with the energetic viceroy in less than a minute. The inquisitors were very nervous as they watched the marquis leave exasperatively slowly and sedately. No shelling became necessary.

During this civil-religious feud, the wedding of Gaspar de Portolá and Elisa de Siscar seemed doubtful. Judging from appearances, many reasoned that the Siscar family, being completely Catholic, would never allow their daughter to marry a so-called heretic. On the other hand, as long as the condemnation of the Holy Office remained in existence, there was no possibility whatsoever that the marriage could take place in church, and the Siscars would never allow a civil ceremony.

Among those who reasoned this way was the vindictive Lieutenant Ruiz Mendez who aspired to Elisa's hand himself. Ruiz Mendez discussed the matter with Father Alonso and expressed the fear that the Holy Office might concede to pressure.

"Leave it in my hands," Father Alonso assured him. "Remember that ever if the Holy Office should retract its condemnation, I still have the powerful weapon of the confessional. I have not yet lost my influence over the girl's mind."

Encouraged and boastful, Ruiz decided to pay a "friendly" visit to his rival, if only to exult in the precarious position in which he believed Portolá to be. With premeditated casualness, one afternoon the lieutenant dropped in at the residence of the man from Balaguer.

Vincent allowed his master's rival to enter, but reluctantly. He informed the visitor that Don Gaspar was busy at the moment in the hand of his barber since he needed a haircut and beard trimming, but he would enter anyway to announce the visitor.

Left alone, Ruiz strolled around the vast library-sitting room of the captain of dragoons, insolently prying about the furniture and decorations. When Vincent returned, he found Ruiz standing before the escutcheon with the Portolá coat of arms.

"King or Nothing?" he commented sardonically.

"Yes, my master's motto." retorted Vincent, coldly.

A few minutes later, Gaspar appeared, jovial and trim, irradiating vigor and happiness.

"Hello, Mendez!" he greeted his visitor cordially. "Sit down — What will you have? I have just received a case of *malvasia* from Sitges."

"Good! That will remind me of better times in Barcelona!" Mendez answered pointedly.

Portolá nodded to Vincent, who, taking a tray with him, withdrew for a few minutes. At the same time, Gaspar responded to Mendez' remark.

"Apparently you are not very pleased with life in Mexico."

"Well," Mendez confessed, "it is a rather provincial existence — and with so much intrigue!"

"What about love affairs? How are you faring?" Portolá asked, not without intent.

"I can't complain!" And going on, "What about your problem with Elisa?"

At this moment Vincent returned with the drinks.

Evading an answer, Portolá exclaimed, "Let's drink!" And, raising the glass to admire the clear gold color of the wine, he added, "Our wine growers in Spain are miracle workers!"

The two men toasted one another with their glasses and drank.

"Smoke?" asked Portolá, opening a box of Havana cigars.

"No thanks, I don't smoke," said Mendez.

"It's not good to give up any manly pleasure in life, no matter how small it may be!" Gaspar lit his cigar.

Mendez began to feel that he was losing ground, so, in reaction, he charged, "Gaspar, you have us all concerned with your abandonment of California. You could have been a king there!"

"There are kingdoms whose crown is worthless!"

"After so great an effort — really, luck is against you — as in the case of Elisa."

Portolá turned his head, suddenly alert and distrustful, "What do you mean, Elisa?"

As though wishing to make it seem unimportant, Mendez said, "Oh, nothing." But then he added, "After so many years of pursuing her, now the Holy Office foils all your plans!"

"Do you think my misfortune allows you to hope?"

"Oh, no. Poor me!" exclaimed Mendez in false modesty, "I know that in competition with you, I am bound to lose in feminine conquests."

"That's why you tried to take advantage of my absence while I was away in California?"

"Don't worry! Elisa wouldn't yield her heart to the first passerby."

"I am very sure of that."

"But, with the Inquisitors for enemies ..."

"I'm not worried!"

"Anyway, it would be a shame if, after abandoning California, you should also abandon the kingdom of the heart of Elisa — I was just looking at your coat of arms — your motto — "

Mendez arose, and taking a piece of chalk from the top of the table, went to the escutcheon and crossed out the first part of the motto, leaving only the word NOTHING."

Portolá, considering this a provocation, was about to get angry and throw his insolent rival out, but, at that moment Vincent opened the door to let Don Oleguer and his beautiful daughter Elisa enter the room.

"Gaspar!" cried Don Oleguer, "we bring you good news!" He began to rush toward Portolá.

Only then did the newcomer notice that his future son-in-law had a visitor.

"Oh, I am sorry! Excuse me," he said, turning to Mendez.

Gaspar, somewhat ironically, intervened.

"Lieutenant Mendez is a trusted friend."

Don Oleguer then burst out with the entire story.

"The viceroy has just declared all the sentences and condemnations of the Holy Office in Mexico null and void. So, my dear Gaspar, you are no longer a 'heretic'."

Gaspar and Elisa looked at each other triumphantly, and as Don Oleguer concluded, "So now you can get married!" the happy lovers rushed into each other's arms.

Ruiz Mendez would have liked to vanish into thin air. He had not expected such a finale.

"But that isn't all!" resumed Elisa's elated father, "the viceroy signed, before my very eyes, early this morning, two decrees which I believe will make you very happy. One promotes Don Gaspar de Portolá to the rank of major, and the other appoints him governor of Puebla, the peaceful Mexican province. Congratulations, my boy!"

Don Oleguer stepped forward to embrace Gaspar, but Portolá stopped him, "One moment," he said.

Going to the table, Gaspar took the piece of chalk used by Mendez and moved toward the coat of arms. He erased the chalk line Mendez had drawn over the word "KING" and crossed out the word "NOTHING."

Lieutenant Mendez picked up his three-cornered hat, and probably cursing the moment he had had the idea of paying a call on Portolá, left without another word.

Chapter Twenty-Six

The people of the capital of New Spain noisily celebrated the publication of the Royal Decree which suppressed the Inquisition in Mexico. The hateful power of the fanatical sector of the Catholic Church which, during more than three centuries had filled the history of Spain with horrendous crimes, had now definitely ended, at least in Mexico and in other Spanish-American colonies.

The physical application of the decree took place, dramatically, with the demolition of the public scaffold in front of the Palace of the Inquisition. The viceroy personally attended the ceremony and announced publicly that in order to erase the ignominious blemish forever, the gardens of the Alameda would be extended to cover that corner of the city, to become part of a beautiful public park.

The people acclaimed the progressive Marquis de Croix, and, for the first time, felt that the breeze of liberalism had penetrated the Spanish colonies. That night the citizens of the old viceregal city could sleep in peace without fear that some hooded agent might force them violently from their beds to throw them into the horrid dungeons, maintained by intolerance and fanaticism.

The popular joy was not to last very long, however. Only three days after the demolition of the crematory, a virulent typhus epidemic spread throughout the city. Thousands were hit, and the number of deaths was great. It was an unfortunate calamity, but, coming as it did after the celebration of the end of the Holy Office, many superstitious people as well as religious elements, said that this epidemic was a punishment from God. On the other hand, the anti-church segment began a rumor that the Inquisitors had poisoned the waters of the canals in vengeance against the people. These rumors produced a difficult situation, but the tact and good sense of the authorities prevented angry demonstrations and riots.

On the fourth day of the epidemic, Gaspar de Portolá was called urgently to the residence of Don Oleguer de Siscar. Elisa was gravely ill.

When Portolá arrived, the family doctor had just left the patient's room. His diagnosis: another victim of the general typhus epidemic.

Portolá felt his blood turn to ice. He asked to see his sweetheart. The handsome officer entered the sick room with a knot in his heart. Elisa was half asleep, consumed by a high fever. Gaspar found her more beautiful than ever; amid the fine laces and silks of her bed she appeared to be transformed into the heroine of some legend. Gaspar took Elisa's hand carefully, finding it light and warm.

Doña Amalia told Gaspar that, according to the doctor, nothing could be predicted until the high fever had lowered. The loving mother wiped a tear from her eyes, and Gaspar turned to hide his own tearful eyes. As he left the room, Don Oleguer put his hand on Gaspar's shoulder.

Gaspar sat in an armchair where he remained for a long time with his eyes fixed on nothing.

For three days and nights Elisa remained unconscious with alternate periods of delirium and spasms. The high temperature would not drop. The doctor came to see the patient at least once a day in spite of the hundreds of other calls he had to make. Gaspar did not leave the head of Elisa's bed. He spent many deeply painful hours with the first night particularly torturous and full of ominous worry. What would Gaspar become if Elisa were to die? He refused to imagine it, but how could he escape the desolation in his mind? He felt that all hope for a happy life had crumbled. Sometimes he cried bitterly; other times he seemed insensible to the blows of fate. Elisa's parents had to force him to eat or to rest.

On the fourth day Elisa became conscious.

Her return to life was preceded by the sweet smile of one awakening from a pleasant dream. Gaspar who was at the head of her bed, as usual, began to call everyone, almost delirious with joy. Don Oleguer and Doña Amalia as well as all the servants rushed into the room fearfully, but their pale faces became all smiles as though they were present at a miracle.

Gaspar left the room for a few moments, and Vincent came back with an armful of white nards which immediately perfumed the entire house. Elisa smiled more with her eyes than with her lips. Gaspar took her hand.

"Don't exert yourself, dear!" he advised, afraid that emotion might harm her.

"Gaspar!" breathed Elisa.

The entire day was like a holiday for the lovers. Outside, the sun shone brightly. Early autumn days in the high valley of Mexico are clear as a quiet, peaceful blue lake, and golden like the silken skin of a young girl.

The young couple promised each other eternal love. Portolá talked about a few days of convalescence in the high mountains, among lillies and ferns along running streams. Above them Ixtaxihualt with its snow-crowned peaks and its shape of a sleeping woman, not unlike Elisa herself, would rise. The distant sound of bells of some small village church would rise from the valley below. There would be perfect peace.

Later they would move to their governmental palace at Puebla. Within the inside patio with its beautiful arches and walls covered with

Talavera tiles and its ever-murmuring fountain, they would know romantic evenings, calm and serene. During the day, for the benefit of the people on the streets, Elisa would be "la señora Gobernadora", and when her carriage went through the streets, the awed Indians would remove their wide straw hats, and with amazed eyes would admire her dazzling robes of silk imported directly from China.

Society people would vie for the privilege of her invitations, and elegant gentlemen would kiss her hand devotedly, but cautiously, remembering that she was the wife of *"el señor Gobernador,"* the vital Don Gaspar de Portolá.

Elisa smiled somberly on hearing these humorous stories and closed her eyes tiredly. Gaspar got up quietly and tiptoed to close the lace curtains at the large window before he left the room silently.

That same evening, however, at about ten o'clock, the entire Siscar household was in turmoil. Elisa suffered excruciating abdominal pains; nothing seemed to give her relief. The doctor was sent an urgent call, and, on arrival, gave her a sedative.

Elisa slept well the rest of the night, but concern continued to stir the entire household. The doctor refused to predict anything. Gaspar was disheartened. Don Oleguer and Doña Amalia tried to remain calm and serene for his sake.

On the seventh day, Elisa's illness had not lost any of its gravity; on the contrary, at the doctor's latest call, he had shaken his head pessimistically. A few hours later Elisa became totally prostrated. Cries and tears of servants, friends and family did her no good, and she soon fell into a coma. Shortly after midnight, Elisa was dead.

For Gaspar de Portolá, the death of Elisa seemed the end of the world. He remained for long hours crying while he knelt at the head of Elisa's bed, unable to accept the reality of his great loss.

At dawn Gaspar, still with tears in eyes, went to the wide window. The sky was covered by a grey mist. He had the impression that everything outside had died too; he doubted that the sun would ever shine again.

In the small cemetery of Tacubaya, the sad silhouettes of Don Oleguer de Siscar, Gaspar de Portolá, one representative of the Royal Audiencia and two good friends of the family cut dramatic figures against the grey sky of that cold morning in early November. A recently dug grave was open before them with its humid smell of newly-stirred earth. The coffin containing the cold body of Elisa had just been lowered to the bottom of the grave. A priest at the head of the opening was whispering funeral orations. A few steps behind, two native servants stood with bent heads, hats off. The grave diggers were waiting for the priest to finish so that they could resume their task, indifferently saddened.

The burial of Elisa, reduced to extreme simplicity, reflected the tragic circumstances in which all this was happening, in the midst of an epidemic. Normally, the burial of the daughter of the Honorable President of the Royal Audiencia would have been a grand spectacle, with the viceregal authorities at the head of the mourners and with a full compliment of church dignitaries chanting the last rites. All the prominent people of colonial Mexico would have been present.

Today, however, the cemetery held only small groups, like the one attending Elisa's burial, burying with the same simplicity the bodies of loved ones. Burial facilities had proven to be completely insufficient, and grave diggers could not delay in their work if they wanted to attend to all the cases needing their services. This abnormal situation made the burials even more pathetic than usual, and the entire city presented the sad mood of implacable calamity.

As the priest finished, the grave diggers grabbed their shovels again. Each of the mourners of the dead girl kissed, respectively, a lump of earth and let it fall over the coffin before it was finally covered. The spongy, acrid-smelling earth very soon covered the simple, hastily-built coffin. The mourners stood silently until the grave had been marked with the customary elongated mound of earth. Vincent and two Mixtex servants covered the clay earth with bunches of nards.

At the last moment, Gaspar de Portolá saw, in the small promontory covered with flowers, the white body of Elisa resting as it had not long before in her bed of lace and silk. He wiped a tear from his eyes.

Don Oleguer took Gaspar by the arm, and by soft pressure indicated that it was time to leave. Gaspar removed a wreath of everlasting flowers from the mortuary hearse, and, as his final act, placed it at the head of the little mound. Without his realizing it, this last gesture might have symbolized his renunciation of any or all kingdoms he might have dreamed of. That same afternoon, the grieving Gaspar de Portolá left Mexico City and moved to the neighboring city of Puebla as its new governor.

Chapter Twenty-Seven

The early period of Gaspar de Portolá's life as governor of the city of *Nuestra Soñora de la Puebla de Los Angeles* was a time of torture and sadness and solitude. He was existing rather than living. No matter where he went in the sumptuous rooms of the palace, he seemed to detect the perfume of the invisible presence of Elisa, but he always ended by actually smelling the strong fragrance of the nards that had covered her grave the day of her funeral.

Time, however, is a wise healer of wounds and sorrow. Little by little Gaspar became accustomed once more to his bachelor life, now more lonely than ever before, and was able to hide from his subjects his deep loneliness and longing.

The grieving Governor sought various alternatives until finally he became passionately interested in fine arts. From his high position he was able to give strong impetus to the school of painting which flourished in the city during his tenure in office. Soon the magnificent churches of this southern city were enriched with masterpieces that Portolá himself acquired and donated, or that he managed to have the state acquire for the national patrimony.

This placid period of governership was characterized, not only by these intellectual activities, but also by Portolá's discreet, human and paternal rule, radiating goodness and empathy. He felt himself as a man first more than a governor first.

Portolá became so aloof from the intrigue and scandals of the Viceregal court that sometimes Puebla might be thought of as a sort of colonial oasis, having no connection at all with tumultuous Spain. Portolá seemed to rule there as an individual and autonomous sovereign, or as the representative of a colonial empire in which tyranny and absolutism had never existed.

His planned aloofness also had made Portolá forget any of the old ambitions or dreams of grandeur he might have had in the past. Old glories, victories on battle fields or on fields of romance or adventure seemed now to be strange dreams he may have had during feverish moments. His discoveries in California themselves seemed now to be some marvelous, fantastic story he might have read in a fiction book.

One day, however, he received a visitor who suddenly returned him to the passionate reality of the territory of California. Gaspar's private secretary announced the visit of the distinguished lady Doña Eulalia Callis, already known to Portolá by name. She was the wife of his old friend Pere Fages, head of the Company of Catalonian Volunteers, presently governor of California residing in Monterey, having succeeded Portolá. Monterey was the location now of the most important presidio in the territory.

The attractive and elegant lady was visibly shaken and angry. Certain that she found herself facing a genuine friend, with typical Catalonian frankness, hotly and fully outspoken, she explained the purpose of her visit — she came for advice. Without mincing words, in her sharp and picturesque way, she explained her troubles in California. Doña explained that, after many requests, she had acceded to the urging of her husband, Don Pere, to join him in Alta California. She had been distrustful of uncivilized territories, and she had not wished to come to America to colonize. At any rate, Doña Eulalia left Mexico City and traveled to the distant wilderness of California.

The trip had been horrible, and all the unpleasantness for no purpose. Her arrival in Monterey had created enormous curiosity since she was the first white lady to arrive in that remote and savage area. She had been greeted everywhere with the honor and distinction due the wife of the governor, but, at the same time, she had been looked upon as an attractive animal of some rare species.

On arriving in Monterey she had thrown herself into the arms of her sturdy husband whom she had not seen in three years. Don Pere, needless to say, the lady confessed, had showered her with flattery and attention. For a while she had lived, surrounded by comfort, and even luxury. In fact, she said, she had felt the grand lady his warm letters had repeatedly promised she would be if she went to Monterey.

"Very soon," the lady cried angrily, "I was to discover the lies of my husband! Through a confidence I learned that Pere had a mistress, and what a mistress! An Indian! My cheeks are still burning with shame!"

Somewhat calmer, Doña Eulalia then explained,

"One day I went personally to the house of 'the other' and started a proper row. Immediately after, I went to the mission to speak to Father Junípero Serra and requested that he file my case for divorce with the Tribunal of the Reta in Rome."

With a new outburst of violence, she continued, "My husband and I had frightful fights, with his denying everything. So, I ordered my carriage and returned to Mexico City."

There were some tears, and don Gaspar tried to console her.

She went on, "Now I discover that Pere loves me, loves me truly. He cannot live without me, and my outburst of jealousy had created personal difficulties for him. It seems that the fathers have been unfriendly to him for a long time, and were only waiting for some scandal or some incident to undermine him in his post of governor, and I, fool that I am, have given them the proper grounds.

"Now I know that Father Serra himself has travelled to Mexico City to request from Viceroy Bucarelli my husband's removal! That's why I came to see you, don Gaspar. I knew the real friendship between you and my husband, and I know the great influence you have at the Viceregal Court, particularly in matters regarding California. As for me, I don't know what to do. I find that I love my husband too, and understand that I pre-cipitated him into disgrace. Can't you do something for him, my dear friend?"

Even though he detected a touch of the picaresque in the entire affair, Gaspar tried to calm the distressed lady, and promised sincerely to intervene with the viceroy in favor of his friend and excellent governor Pere Fages.

On more familiar ground, Gaspar tried to explain the true back-ground of the matter to the excitable lady. He explained that he had already warned her husband about some conflict of this nature when he transferred his military command and title of governor shortly before leaving Monterey into Pere's hands. He told her that he had received reports which indicated that Don Pere had carried out an extraordinary task in California. He had organized new explorations, making important discoveries. He had, in fact, initiated the material colonization of the territory with most commendable practical sense.

Portolá continued explaining that the ideas of colonization of the fathers usually did not go along with the concepts of the military and of the civilians. On the other hand, the angelic missionaries should not forget that they, at the same time, are also mortal, and naturally, resentful of other authority, particularly military, which might obstruct their tem-poral ambitions.

The drama of the Spanish colonies had always been this dispute for temporal power between the various authorities and between these and other institutions charged with handling the spiritual power. The Fran-ciscans were no different from the Jesuits, the Dominicans or the Inquisitors of the Holy Office.

After a short pause in which Doña Eulalia seemed lost in a sea of remorse, Don Gaspar resumed.

"Regarding the petty unfaithfulness of husbands who have lived alone in the wilderness for over three years, far from beloved wives, one must be human enough to understand that it is of very minor importance."

Doña Eulalia was about to jump like a wounded panther, but she bit her lip and decided, instead, to smile kindly. She got up gracefully, and offered her hand to Gaspar to be kissed. Portolá promised sincerely again that he would approach the viceroy on the matter, and to help his old friend Fages, one of his colleagues in the exploration of California.

For a while the visit of the general lady compatriot awoke some nostalgia in the governor's mind. He wondered whether it would have been better for him to have remained in Monterey to enjoy his self-created kingdom, no matter how empty or imaginary it might have been. As he reconsidered, he concluded that the difficulties encountered by his successor indicated that even in that remote station there was no freedom from envy and intrigue, and that he himself would probably have had the same problems as Pere Fages, if not greater ones.

After this brief moment of regret, Portolá once again immersed himself in the sedentary existence of the governship of Puebla.

The year 1783 was coming to an end. Portolá no longer felt young. This was proven by the fact that life in Puebla no longer had any incentive for him. He had exhausted all emotional and sensory avenues. Portolá found himself looking to the past. As at long length happens to all expatriates, the illustrious Balaguerian felt homesick. The image of Catalonia projected itself in his mind like the image of a beloved awaiting him in the distance. He considered the possibility of a return to his native country.

In 1775 Gaspar had made a short visit to Barcelona and had returned again to New Spain. On April 22 of that year he had been promoted to the rank of lieutenant colonel and had made a short stay in Balaguer, his beloved home town. He had visited there to take care of family matters.

During his absence of almost fifteen years many things had changed in the paternal mansion. In 1743 at the death of Don Francesc de Portolá i Subira, Gaspar's father, the main rights of inheritance had passed to in-laws due to the disappearance of Gaspar's two elder brothers and his two sisters. Don Gaspar had to straighten out some of these matters.

In 1776 Portolá, who had been provisionally attached to the Quartermaster Offices in Barcelona, was promoted to full colonel, and he returned to Puebla. Soon he began to feel homesick again. He thought deeply about the fact that his mission in America seemed at last fully ended. His native land might be a better sinecure for his spent and tired heart, mainly injured by the loss of his beloved Elisa.

Gaspar traced a mental balance sheet of his disturbed life, and he did not feel much regret. His main purpose had been accomplished. *He had lived!* This was the really important fact in his life. If now, in his old age, he found that he had not amassed a fortune, he found too that he had no need for one. He did not feel any humiliation at the fact that he had found it necessary to appeal to the viceroy to advance him the money necessary for his long passage home. He had never worried about money matters. He has discovered that one's generosity is always corresponded to and compensated for by the generosity of others.

Now there was the matter of non-material things — his motto, for example, "King or Nothing!". He did not regret having adopted it. He did not blame himself in any way. "King or Nothing!" — Actually, he could not say that he had accomplished it one way or the other. If he were not "king," neither was he "nothing." Alternately, as often occurs, he had been both things at the same time. Figuratively and temporarily he had been "King" in California; temporarily he had also been "King" in Elisa's heart.

Later having abandoned the California kingdom he had conquered, and having been face to face with death because of Elisa, he had been "nothing."

All in all, however, Gaspar de Portolá was sure of one thing; he had been "King" within himself — king of a kingdom no one could take from him. In this sense he had been faithful to his motto. In things of honor and dignity, in matters of conscience, he had been faithful to himself, and that made him a true Portolá, worthy of all his noble ancestry.

As a result of this mental and spiritual balance, Portolá requested his transfer to Catalonia. His military record was impressive enough for him to assume that no authority would dare refuse this normal request of the brave colonel and distinguished governor of Puebla.

The request granted, Portolá undertook the return trip. He landed in Barcelona, but he did not delay his first visit to the scene of his childhood. With deep reverence, he entered his ancient manorial home, the stones of which talked to him of nobility kept immaculate through the centuries. He visited the old stables where he could still feel the presence of Tomás, the loyal stableman. He went to the attic where he had played so many days, discovering every day mysterious and unexplored places full of darkness and adventure.

He came back down to the main halls and walked into the unforget-table studio where the kind preceptor Don Claudi Monclus tried so hard to give him a princely education. He felt emotional on discovering the demolished swallow's nest on the back porch which had been tolerated each year for his sake in spite of all clean-household rules. The big bed with its solomonic wooden columns where his father and many other ancestors had died inspired reverence in him.

Later Gaspar went roaming in Balaguer's surrounding areas. He climbed to the almost-demolished Castle of the Counts of Urgell, in which every stone might contain many pages of history. He strolled by the river, the never-forgotten Segre in which he had swum many summer afternoons despite parental prohibitions. The weeded banks of the river was the region where many hours had been spent in secret treks which Don Claudi had denounced as escapades of a "barefoot prince."

Gaspar went riding to the grounds of the old monastery *Les Franqueses* near the picturesque inn where his first love, the naive Aneta, had lived. In similar spirit he had visited the Monastery of Pedralbes on the outskirts of Barcelona a few days before. It was here that he had met the unfortunate, always-mourned Elisa. Gaspar had reached emotional saturation, and decided to terminate his romantic pilgrimage.

Gaspar de Portolá's return to the peninsula awakened vivid interest in Barcelonan authorities, and they became anxious to pay adequate homage to the heroic explorer and conquerer of California. In spite of his avowal that he was returning home for rest and peace, the municipality and other regional institutions organized several festivities in honor of the illustrious citizen. The military authorities, in turn, could not allow the glorious return of the gallant colonel and former governor to pass without notice. The captain general of Catalonia sent a request to Madrid, and a few days later Don Gaspar de Portolá i Rivera was appointed lieutenant of the king, a privileged rank equal to that of brigadier or brigade general.

By mid-May 1784, Gaspar was installed in his new position in the city of Lleida, in western Catalonia. There was no higher authority above him than the governor of the province. In the governor's absence Gaspar assumed his functions and was his representative.

As the king's lieutenant, Portolá presided over the meetings of the municipal corporation of Lleida, with the privilege of breaking tie votes, if any. He fulfilled these functions until August 21, 1784. After this date, the corporation minutes record Portolá's absence due to illness. He was not actually ill, but rather at the end of his strength. At five o'clock in the afternoon of October 10 of that year, the illustrious discoverer and conqueror of Alta California passed away, serenely, quietly and elegantly, just as he had lived.

Shortly before his death, the elderly Balaguerian military man had dictated his last will and testament, appointing as executors of his legacy "His Most Illustrious Bishop of the Diocese, His Excellency, the Governor of Lleida, Field Marshal Lluis Blondel de Drouhet and Don Drancesc Pines, Lieutenant Auditor for the Army." As further proof of Portolá's deep sense of humanity and of his democratic spirit, in his testament he bequeathed all his earthly possessions (all his share in the vast family estate) to public welfare institutions. With part of his liquid assets the magnificent House of Mercy, popularly known as the Hospice, was built.

This valuable artistic building later became the Palace of Deputation. For his family Gaspar left only an annual pension to his brother Joseph, the Benjamin of the family, at that time lieutenant in the Infantry Regiment of Guadalajara.

The death of the notable lieutenant of the king was deeply felt by the citizenry of Lleida, and his funeral constituted a stately demonstration of their sorrow. The Municipal Council presided over the funeral procession; six officers of the local garrison were pallbearers; and a squad of Walloon Guards escorted the bier and fired military volleys as a last honor. A large crowd of people accompanied the hero to the ceremony and gave tribute in final homage to their illustrious compatriot.

Gaspar de Portolá, nine feet underground, would have been proud of such popular tribute. Glory followed him until the grave. Even so, if he had been able, posthumously, to express his philosophy, no doubt, with Voltaire's sharpness he would have stated that, in fact, he had fulfilled his motto "King or Nothing!" Now, finally and definitely, he was "nothing."